Praise for The Myth of No Big Deal…

"This comprehensive study not only highlights the profound impact of later-life divorce on its adult children and their parents, it also underscores the particular life stage each generation is traversing and the interactive influence each has upon the other throughout an evolving divorce process. Kudos to Wendy House for offering thoughtful recommendations for successful adaptations to an often unforeseen family rupture and for unveiling a neglected but ever-increasing population of adult children and their later-life divorcing parents. This work will benefit all participating members of the later-life divorce family as well as those who teach them, those who listen to them, those who counsel them, those who love them. Clinicians and the general public will be enriched and enlightened by this timely investigation. Read it and pass it on to a friend."

–Barbara S. Cain
Author of *Autism, The Invisible Cord, A Sibling's Diary,*
Silver Medal Winner, Mom's Choice Award

"With compassion, evidence, and understanding, Wendy House travels the landscape of later-life parental divorce, leaving no emotional, financial, or relational stone unturned as she eloquently shatters the common belief that it is "no big deal." For most of the parents who split up, at any age, and for their adult children, of any age, it is a very big deal indeed—though often one that is unexpected and whose consequences may not reveal themselves for years. House combines her sensitivity and skills as a psychotherapist with her training as a social psychologist, allowing her to move easily between individual stories and the larger societal framework. For adult children and their divorcing parents, this book will be revelatory and immensely helpful."

–Carol Tavris, Ph.D.
Social Psychologist and Author, *Mistakes were Made (but Not by Me):
Why We Justify Foolish Beliefs, Bad Decisions, and Hurtful Acts*
and *Anger: The Misunderstood Emotion*

"Wendy House's approach, caring tone, and desire to help readers build supportive, if revised, family relationships during and after later-life divorce makes an important contribution. *The Myth of No Big Deal* presents a thoughtful consideration of the issues faced by adult children at different stages of development when their parents divorce after a long marriage. It incorporates many rich case examples which help to connect readers to the real challenges facing adult children, providing clear evidence that the later life divorce of parents clearly is a "Big Deal." Drawing on her years of clinical practice, House argues that no matter one's stage of adulthood, parental divorce needs to be acknowledged and integrated into one's own sense of identity, the meaning of family ties, hopes about current and/or future relationships, and a changing relationship with one's parents. This book will undoubtedly touch the lives of all the generations involved in later life divorce—parents, adult children, their close friends and partners, and the adult children's own children. Bringing a hopeful voice to this significant change in family ties, House encourages parents and children to find new ways to define and enact the sense of family. *The Myth of No Big Deal* is a major contribution to the field of family science, uncovering the many, nuanced ways that later-life divorce of parents impacts their adult children and the family system."

—Barbara M. Newman, Ph.D.
Developmental Psychologist &
—Philip R. Newman, Ph.D.
Social and Community Psychologist
Co-Authors, *Development through Life: A psychosocial approach* and
Theories of Human Development.

THE MYTH
OF
NO BIG DEAL

Healing from the Overlooked Impact of Later-Life Divorce on Adult Children and Families

Wendy Fisher House, PhD

Flint Hills Publishing

Flint Hills Publishing
Topeka, Kansas
Tucson, Arizona
www.flinthillspublishing.com

Printed in the U.S.A.

Paperback Book ISBN: 978-1-966323-52-5
Electronic Book ISBN: 978-1-966323-53-2

Library of Congress Control Number 2025924225

I dedicate this book to my mother, Ferne Forman Fisher,
who modeled care and respect for all human beings.

And to my father, David Fisher, whose family story parallels those
in the pages which follow.

CONTENTS

Prologue

We have all known families who had young children when the parents divorced. We knew there would be disruption and heartache. We knew it would be hard going for a while. We hoped that, over time and with favorable circumstances, family members would move past the pain and find new ways to be happy and feel connected.

But how many of us know people who were already adults when their parents divorced? Probably a lot of us. We just aren't aware of it because adult children of divorce don't talk about it much. Even when they identify themselves, we likely assume they had it easier and were less impacted because they were already adults when it happened. Right? Wrong!

This book sets out to correct that damaging misperception. First, being an adult does not insulate anyone from the effects of parental divorce. Along with younger children, adult children generally experience sadness, anger, confusion, disruption, and a profound sense of loss. Additionally, their adult status increases the likelihood that they will be pulled to take sides, be used inappropriately as confidantes, and may even have to assume the burden of responsibility for a troubled parent.

Second, while this group, children of later-life divorce, has mostly been under the public radar, it is a burgeoning number. U.S. divorce rates have been going down steadily for 40 years except for people over 50, where they have *doubled*, and for people over 65, where they have *tripled*. Every year around half a million adults from age 18 to their late 40s or beyond enter into the ranks of "Adult Children of Divorce." While the entrance itself may be quiet, the effects reverberate throughout their lives.

For Adult Children

Perhaps you are one of them. Maybe you just graduated from high school. Perhaps you have gone on to, or even graduated from, college. Started a job. Entered professional or graduate school. Married. Started a family. Maybe you were already the parents of teenagers when you heard that your parents were splitting up. This book is for you.

And it is for you even if you passed these milestones long ago and are only now ready to look back at how your parents' divorce has affected you. Your experience has been ignored and invalidated far too long. Fortunately, there is still a chance to gain understanding, self-compassion, and deep healing

For Parents

As the parent of an adult child, this book is for you, too, no matter where you are in the divorce process. Even if you are currently in the midst of your own divorce challenges and pain, you can still be a parent who wants to know what your adult children are going through and how you might make it a little easier for them. This is no small feat, and it will likely make an enormous difference for your lifelong relationship with them.

If your divorce occurred years ago, it is possible that you were unaware of how it impacted your adult children. Looking back on it with the wisdom and perspective you now have can open up important lines of communication between you and your children which can still promote healing even years later. **It is never too late to experience and share compassion and understanding.**

The fact that you have picked up this book speaks volumes about your commitment to being a positive influence in their lives. After all you have both been through, you are still their *parent* and they are still your *children* no matter how grown-up they are in years. And you are still a *family*.

For All

For both adult children and parents, your family will never be the same following a later-life divorce. But that doesn't mean you *don't have* a family. You have the opportunity to forge a new sense of your family and your place in it. This book encourages both parents and adult children to be aware and respectful of your own and each other's needs and struggles during this turbulent time while still maintaining healthy and appropriate parent-child boundaries.

There are many losses associated with divorce. To hold onto a solid, healthy parent-child relationship prevents yet another loss. To improve or even mend a troubled relationship may not be out of reach. While it may not seem likely at this moment, being part of a healthy (albeit newly-constructed) family is still possible. **And even when our families are far from perfect, they remain an important influence in our lives.**

In this book, we will try to keep in mind what is happening on both sides of the generational divide when there is a later-life divorce. In addition to the challenges posed by divorce itself, parents are facing their own developmental challenges—everything from mid-life crises to end of life fears and regrets. Coping with these compelling and absorbing challenges can be all-consuming. It can drain parents' energy from thinking about what may be going on with their children. Many are in denial that their adult children will be affected by their divorce. Some may have waited until their children were out of the home, thinking this would lessen the impact.

But adult children also face their own developmental challenges when they get hit with the news that their parents are divorcing. They are taking steps toward independence from their families of origin. They are finishing their education, selecting occupations and careers, choosing partners, and starting families. Quite simply, they are at various stages of trying to forge their own adult lives just as their parents' lives are coming apart.

Anyone who has ever had the experience of diving into the water knows how important it is to push off from a firm surface. Whether from a riverbank, a low diving board, or a high platform, if the surface is steady the dive may be relatively smooth, even if not always graceful. If the platform itself is shaking and unpredictable, the diver may well do a belly flop!

Expanding this metaphor, what if the adult children are further along when their parents divorce? What if they are already in the water, so to speak, when this happens? Contrary to the myth that divorce at this stage poses "no big deal" for adult children, there will likely be profound ripple effects which, at times, could feel like a tsunami.

In the following chapters we will lay out the reasons for the growing number of later-life divorces. We will then illustrate the impact of parental divorce on adult children at three different life stages. And, at the end, there will be separate chapters for parents and for children which summarize these points and provide recommendations for negotiating constructive pathways throughout the divorce process—pathways which maximize the possibility of healthy outcomes for both generations.

Some of you may have picked up this book out of desperation for just such recommendations. You may want to turn there immediately. While that is understandable, I hope you will go back and read the earlier chapters. Like it or not, the topic of later-life divorce is as complicated as it is important. Putting it in the context of everything else that is going on in the lives of both parents and adult children will greatly increase your understanding of, as well as your compassion for, each other's challenges and struggles.

PART I

Overview and Context

-1-
The Phenomenon of Later-Life Divorce

Divorce rates rose through the 1960s and 70s, peaking around 1980. Since then, the number of divorces has steadily fallen with one notable exception. Divorce rates are on the rise for older couples, spawning the term "gray divorce." While their unique needs are being recognized, those of their children (who may already be adults) have mainly been overlooked. This tendency to downplay or ignore the impact of divorce on adult children results in the "myth of no big deal" and stands in the way of deeper healing for both generations.

The Parents

Sophia and Ted

Sophia, a pediatric nurse practitioner, felt she might have made a mistake to marry Ted, a chemical engineer, when he went missing half-way through their wedding reception, bored with it all and wanting a nap. Still, she kept pushing through more than 25 years of a loveless marriage, the best part of which was their two children now in college and beyond. She'd been brought up to think divorce was not an option and her mother's mantra, "You've made your bed, now lie in it," rang in her ears all those many years.

The turning point came when she was diagnosed with ovarian cancer. Ted dropped her off for a hysterectomy, and he only returned when she was due to be discharged from the hospital. Given a clean bill of health, her children grown up, and having a solid professional career to support herself, Sophia decided she would be better off on her own. She expected her children would not be surprised. After years of witnessing their parents' marriage on life support, she thought they might even encourage her decision. To her surprise, they did not!

Martin and Jillian

Martin and Jillian, both successful college professors, were seen on campus as the perfect couple. By the end of a busy summer, they had thrown a lavish wedding for their daughter, sent their older son off for his junior year in Peru, and delivered their younger son to begin his freshman year at a nearby college. Everything seemed to be going according to plan. They were finally going to be empty nesters.

Jillian received a prestigious fellowship for a year's sabbatical in France. Martin needed to stay on campus for the first semester to launch a program he'd worked hard to get funded, but he would be joining her after the Christmas break. A devoted dad, he was relieved to be staying home in case one of their children—all in the midst of big changes in their own lives—hit a snag and needed someone nearby.

Halfway through the fall semester, Jillian came home for her brother's funeral and announced she had fallen in love with a woman she'd met and no longer wanted to be married. Martin was shocked, furious, and heartbroken. Each parent pled their case to their three children, hoping to receive their whole-hearted support—Martin because he felt he was the injured party and Jillian feeling her liberally-raised children were now adults and should take it in stride.

Amanda and Harry

For years, Amanda had been embarrassed by her housepainter husband Harry's drinking, mishandling of money, and lying to his customers. Her own strong work ethic (her husband labeled her a "relentless penny-pincher") kept the family afloat, although barely. To put her kids through school (community college for her son and a paralegal degree for her daughter), Amanda unbegrudgingly took on a second job. These qualities plus her deep religious faith held the marriage together, and Amanda took great satisfaction in seeing the children settle into their careers and marriages.

Once the grandchildren started coming, Amanda put her focus on them and less on the dissatisfactions in her marriage. She seemed to be cruising into the final stages of her life until she started noticing both an escalation in Harry's drinking as well as calls from his creditors and customers who felt they'd been "stiffed." The final straw came when Amanda confronted him about his behavior, and he attacked her physically. Now, fearing for her safety as well as for her own good name in their small community, she felt she had no choice but to leave.

Larry and Emily

Larry and Emily had recently celebrated their 25th anniversary alongside their blended family of four adult children and seven grandchildren. With their children (ages 24 to 37) off on their own, they were actively planning their retirement dream of a world cruise. As Larry put it, "This was going to be us."

Instead, he was blind-sided when his world as well as his future dreams fell apart one night. During their ritual cocktail hour, Emily simply announced she wanted a divorce. Up till then, this seemingly happily remarried couple was considered by many to be the poster child for blended families. Soon their children and grandchildren would be reeling from the shock and wondering if anything can last if "Mimi and Pops" couldn't make it.

These and other stories accumulated in my psychotherapy office where I met with clients for over four decades. Women and men coming to a decision to end marriages of 20, 30, even 40 or more years. While their reasons for leaving (lovelessness, affairs, incompatibility, mental illness, domestic and substance abuse, or just growing apart), were varied, there was a common thread—the hope that their children who were launched or launching into adulthood would largely be spared the deleterious effects they knew divorce could have on younger children.

The Adult Children

On another day, at another hour, I would be meeting with a young adult whose parents were divorcing, or an older adult whose parents had divorced when they were striking out on their own, now years ago. Frequently, they did not connect the issues they were currently grappling with—relationship problems, career decisions, loneliness and anxiety, estrangement from or enmeshment in their families—to their parents' divorce. Many of these clients seem to have bought into the same misguided thinking as many parents: adult children should not be negatively affected if their parents divorce when they are "all grown up." While this mindset might provide false comfort to divorcing parents, it is harmful to their children.

Heather

For example, Heather, a college student, had been aware that her parents weren't getting along all that well. They had seemed to be going off more in separate directions ever since she went away to school. She didn't talk about it much, but it was in the background. Sometimes she wondered if, as an only child, she shouldn't have gone so far away to school.

She was in therapy with me because of her tendency toward perfectionism and her fear that her grades might not be good enough to get into medical school. Over time, Heather was starting to lighten up and enjoy her time with her group of friends. She had begun a relationship with a fellow premed student who made her laugh more and worry less, and they had lined up summer jobs together at a national park. With the academic year wrapping up, she felt ready to take a break from therapy and enjoy her summer plans.

When she arrived for our final session, Heather immediately began sobbing. Her parents had scheduled a Zoom call the night before to inform her they were separating. Quickly pulling herself together, she kept apologizing to me, saying she shouldn't be so upset since she was 20 years old and no longer lived at home. Her roommate had apparently chastised her for making such a big deal of the news, saying her own parents had divorced when she was in middle school and that had been much harder. But, for Heather, the bottom had fallen out of her world. Barely able to concentrate, she did poorly on her finals, canceled her summer plans, and flew home hoping she could change her parents' minds.

Brian

Brian, the youngest in a large family, had been taking his time getting his adult life together. Now in his early 30s, it was finally happening. He had kicked an addiction to video games, was steadily employed, and living on his own. Always a bit shy and awkward around women, he had started seeing someone he met online. To his surprise, it was developing into a serious relationship, and they were talking about her moving into his apartment in a few months.

That's when he learned his parents were divorcing. His father's health had deteriorated in recent years to the point he was unable to work. Overweight and suffering from COPD and diabetes, he couldn't get around much, and he became angry and depressed. Medical bills piled up from his doctors' appointments and prescriptions. Brian's mother was 10 years younger than her husband and decided she had had enough.

Brian's older siblings had long since moved away and were too busy with work and their own families to get involved. They were mad at their mom for abandoning their dad but also angry at him for not having taken better care of himself and his marriage. This left Brian the last one standing between their father's demise and his rescue.

Brian's apartment had a tiny second bedroom that would accommodate his father's medical equipment, so Brian felt he had no choice but to have his father move in with him. Taking on this responsibility left little time or energy for anything else but work, so Brian put his plans with his girlfriend on hold. After hearing Brian's story, I said sympathetically, "Your parents' divorce can really change your life even as an adult." He looked at me sadly and said, "What life?"

Austin

Away at college, Austin worried a lot about how things were going at home for his mother Dana and younger sister Katie. In the past couple of years, Austin's father, once bright and affable, had become someone he hardly knew. He'd lost one high level professional job after another because of erratic behavior, and he seemed angry all the time. When he was home for the summer, Austin noticed his father's anger escalating into fits of rage. He had witnessed his father strike his mother and throw a lamp at his little sister. His mother was a strong and competent woman who'd once been deeply in love with her husband, but Austin recognized that her tolerance was being pushed to the limit. A resourceful woman, Dana had made all the right moves to get help for her husband, including mental health support, but his condition baffled several mental health professionals, and he refused to follow the recommendations of others.

When Dana decided she and her daughter were no longer safe, she asked her husband to leave. Austin was not shocked. In fact, he was relieved. He was also surprised by how sad and confused he felt that his once happy family could not be resuscitated even by his mother's heroic feats. When did things cease to be okay at home? What had been real? And now, were his mother and sister safe? What would his father do? Would his violent behavior escalate? While Austin's feet were on his college campus, his heart and thoughts were often back at home.

The Myth of "No Big Deal"

In meeting with clients on both sides of a later-life divorce, I found myself wishing I had a book to hand to them. To the parents, a book that says: "You have a right to end a long marriage, but don't assume your children won't be affected by that decision." To the adult children: "Just because you are legally an adult, it doesn't mean that your parents' divorce won't break your heart, interrupt your plans, and create doubts about the past and the future." I wanted to be able to share a book that validated the legitimate issues and concerns of *both* parents and adult children. A book that could help them communicate and heal *together* as they moved through this critical transition.

I hope this will be that book for you, the reader, wherever you are in the divorce process.

Unfortunately, researchers as well as mental health professionals have paid little attention to the impact of later-life divorce on adult children. This perpetuates the myth that it is "no big deal." It allows parents to feel less guilty about breaking up the family. It also allows them to focus primarily on their own substantial challenges of divorce without having to think about how their children will handle it. This neglect can harm their relationship with their children.

Equally harmful, this myth causes adult children to second guess the legitimacy of their feelings and reactions. If it is true that, as adults, they shouldn't be much impacted by their parent's divorce, they may be ashamed to admit that they are struggling. They may downplay their reactions, push them aside, or even deny them outright. Their silence only further perpetuates the myth and leaves them feeling confused and alone as they navigate this upheaval in their lives.

Over the long haul, ignoring or invalidating the experiences—both emotional and logistical—of adult children causes harm to them and their families. This is true for the families they grew up in and the ones they have started or will start on their own. Not only are parent-child as well as sibling relationships at risk, future generations can be affected by this ignorance and lack of compassion.

The Phenomenon of Later-Life Divorce

Addressing this harmful myth would be important even if only a small number of adult children were involved, but that is far from the case. Even though divorce rates in the U.S. are at a 40-year low, divorces have steadily declined for all groups *except* adults 50 years and older, where they are on the rise. According to the National Center for Family and Marriage Research at Bowling Green University, from 1990-2019 the rate of divorce *doubled* for people over 50 and *tripled* for people over 65.[1]

This striking and continuing phenomenon has been called by different names: the Gray Divorce Revolution, Empty Nest Divorce, and Silver Splitters. More than 300,000 older couples divorce every year. Conservatively, if each couple has one to two children, there could be half a million adults each year who become children of later-life divorce. Researchers, attorneys, and financial advisors have recognized the gray divorcees' needs for legal, financial, and mental health services. Unfortunately, their offspring have not received the same attention.

Research and Earlier Books

We now have a few studies which focus on how parental divorce impacts adult children. While most of these are small studies with non-representative samples, their findings are consistent with each other, as well as with clinical impressions of mental health professionals. From pioneering studies nearly four decades ago, to recent reports, we learn that adult children are generally shocked by the news that their parents are divorcing and feel as if their world has turned upside down. They tend to doubt their own judgment, wonder if anything about their childhood was real, and question whether any relationship can last.

However, even with consistent findings, the impact of later-life parental divorce on adult children has received little attention from either researchers or the media. As a result, the general public as well as many mental health professionals remain oblivious to its effects. We continue to be taken by surprise not only by the growing phenomenon of divorce at this life stage, but also its profound impact on adult children. Every decade or so, the media briefly brings this into focus when a famous long-married couple separates: the Gores, Maria Schriver and Arnold Schwarzenegger, the Gateses, the Bezos, Nicole Kidman and Keith Urban. Then it is quickly forgotten, and the pain of the thousands of not-so-famous older divorcing families festers unacknowledged.

Let's take a quick look at several of these pioneering contributions. Far ahead of her time, Barbara S. Cain, a clinician and researcher at the University of Michigan, noticed students in the 1980s struggling when their parents divorced while they were away at college. This spurred her to conduct one of the first studies of this population. Cain interviewed 50 students on two college campuses. Her surprising findings, published in the *New York Times Sunday Magazine*, demonstrated that young adults are actually strongly affected when their parents divorce![2]

The same pattern of results appeared in the first book to address the unique challenges of adult children of divorce. Fintushel and Hillard's *A Grief Out of Season* was based on results from a questionnaire study of over 100 subjects. Although this included a broader age span (18-42 years), the findings were remarkably similar to Cain's—shock, doubt about their own perceptions, worry about relationships with parents and siblings, and distrust of romantic involvement. Research was beginning to show that adult children, like their younger counterparts, still feel abandoned and unsupported when their parents divorce.[3]

In spite of small research studies in the 1980s and 1990s, it wasn't until 2006 that a book was written specifically for adult children dealing with their parents' later-life divorce. Brooke Lea Foster's *The Way They Were* was based on her personal experience as well as interviews with more than 75 fellow adult children. Foster was determined to fill the information void for young adults like herself. She poignantly addressed the myth that adult children are unfazed when their parents divorce, as well as the harm done when their experiences are not validated:

Nothing tested me more in my adult life than my parents' split. I can say that now without feeling embarrassed or weak. For a long time, that's all I felt. I was twenty-six years old at the time. I had moved out of my childhood home to attend college several years before. I was in a long-term relationship. I had a great job and a small circle of close friends. My parents weren't sick or dying. I had all of the things that should make you feel rooted. Yet, when my parents announced they were separating, I felt as if the world had collapsed in on me.

My age made everyone assume I'd be fine. Even I decided I was overreacting. I figured, I'm an adult. I should be able to handle this. So I felt guilty hurting so much, as if my grief were out of place or unwarranted…

I envy young children going through a divorce. Everyone worries about them. They're sent to psychologists. Thousands of studies analyze their development through life. Dozens of books square off on how divorce impacts them. Parents go out of their way to ensure that a young child's transition is smooth. They're expected to hurt.[4]

Fast forward to 2020 and Hughes and Fredenburg's book, *Home Will Never Be the Same Again.* Even though it had now been decades since the challenges of adults dealing with parental divorce were first identified, these authors concluded that the needs of adult children continue to be ignored or dismissed. Their extensive search for relevant studies on this population had turned up little and prompted them to write their book as a comprehensive guide. Featuring stories of adults from 19 to 50 years old, they focused more than previous writers on the varied reactions of adult children who are at different life stages when their parents divorce. Still missing, however, was serious attention to the reasons for divorce, specifically, whether or not trauma or abuse were involved.[5]

Why This Book?

Like the writers mentioned above, I hope to expand awareness and understanding of the growing phenomenon of later-life divorce. In the process, I hope to debunk the myth that parental divorce at this stage is "no big deal" for their adult children. Additionally, this approach makes five unique contributions.

First, we will take a family systems perspective, addressing what is occurring on both sides of the generational divide when there is a later-life divorce. We will look back and forth between the challenges parents face during and following divorce and the impact divorce has on their adult children. This family systems lens enables us to see how changes in one party can have ripple effects on others within the family.

Our goal is to focus with empathy and compassion on the needs and challenges of all parties—the divorcing parents, but even more on their adult children who have received much less attention. With so much going on for each generation during divorce, it is easy to understand that they could be oblivious of, yet affected by, each other's experience and reactions. When we consider the needs of both parents and their adult children, we are better able to support *families* as they move through the divorce process and redefine themselves in new, hopefully healthy, formations.

Second, we will frequently differentiate later-life divorces that are the result of deleterious circumstances like emotional abuse, substance abuse, domestic violence, and mental illness from those that are the result of couples "growing apart" or "moving on." Adult children are less likely to be surprised when their parents' marriage ends because of anger, dysfunction, and/or abuse. They may even be relieved. Yet these adult children may be less likely to have two relatively healthy and functional parents prior to, during, and after the divorce. On the other hand, when seemingly happy-enough couples divorce, their adult children may be shaken to the core and question whether anything they believed about their childhood was real. Just as they are moving out into the world, they may fundamentally distrust their own judgment.

Third, roughly utilizing Erik Erikson's Eight Life Stages,[6] we will take into account the developmental stages of both parents and adult children at the time the parents divorce. Are the parents still young enough to feel they have sufficient time to start a new chapter of their lives or are they facing old age? Where are their children in forging their adult identities and forming what they hope will be lasting relationships? We will devote separate chapters to the unique experiences and needs of:

Launchers, the youngest adult children who are late adolescents to their early 20s. They have not yet established lives outside the parental home.

Emerging Adults in their mid-20s to mid-30s or so. They are further along in establishing themselves in careers, their own residences and relationships.

Middle-Aged Adult Children in their 30s, 40s and beyond. They likely have families, and some may have experienced their own divorces.

Fourth, throughout this book we will emphasize that divorce is a process and not an event. We will try to remain mindful of a longitudinal perspective. What are the pathways out of the inevitable throes of later-life divorce for both parents and adult children? Do the pathways differ depending on why the marriage ended? When we validate the challenges and pain they (especially adult children) face, are they more likely to grieve their losses, heal, and move on with their lives? What resources and supports do all parties need in order to eventually thrive both individually and as a family?

Fifth, it will become clear along the way that maintaining firm and appropriate parent-child boundaries is central to successfully navigating the inevitable upheavals inherent in the divorce process. Healthy boundaries provide the opportunity for everyone to take care of themselves, to grieve and to heal. They also greatly increase the chances that both generations will eventually arrive at a compassionate understanding of each other's experience, and thus, avoid estrangement and further loss.

In Summary

This book highlights the weighty challenges of later-life divorce for both parents and their adult children. Unfortunately, it still *is* a big deal when parents divorce after their children are adults. Denying this thwarts the healing process for all family members. You can't deal with a problem if you don't acknowledge that it exists.

But this book also gives hope. What is needed is sufficient opportunity and time to grieve along with appropriate resources and support. When these are present, there will be healing and growth. Families in their new formations can once again experience optimism, reconciliation, belongingness, and even joy.

Whether you are the parent or the adult child of a later-life divorce, I hope this book will validate your experience and provide support and useful recommendations. I hope it will also deepen your understanding of each other's experience while maintaining appropriate parent-child boundaries. With favorable conditions and the passage of time, I hope your new post-divorce family—whether headed by single or re-partnered parents—might even be healthier and more growth-promoting than your original family.

All endings are also beginnings.
We are just not aware of it at the time.

Mitch Albom, author and journalist

Chapter One Notes—*The Phenomenon of Later life Parental Divorce and Its Impact on Adult Children: An Overview*

1. Susan L. Brown and I-Fen Lin, 2012. "The Gray Divorce Revolution: Rising Divorce Among Middle-Aged and Older Adults," 1990-2010. *Journals of Gerontology Series B: Psychological Sciences and Social Sciences.* See also numerous articles by Brown and Lin published by the National Center for Family and Marriage Research at Bowling Green University. More recently (April 28, 2025) the *Toledo Free Press* did a feature on Brown and Lin's research indicating that in 1990 people 50 or older accounted for only 8.7% of divorces. By 2019, that figure had grown to 36%.

2. Barbara S. Cain, "The Price They Pay: Older Children and Divorce," *New York Times Magazine*, February 18, 1990.

3. Noelle Fintushel and Nancy Hillard, *A Grief Out of Season: When Your Parents Divorce in Your Adult Years*, 1991, Little Brown & Co.

4. Brooke Lea Foster, *The Way They Were: Dealing with Your Parents' Divorce After a Lifetime of Marriage*, 2006, pps. 3-4, Three Rivers Press.

5. Carol R. Hughes and Bruce R. Fredenburg, *Home Will Never Be the Same Again: A Guide for Adult Children of Gray Divorce,* 2020, Rowman & Littlefield Publishers.

6. Erik H. Erikson, *Childhood and Society,* Second Edition, 1963, W.W. Norton & Company. In the following chapter we will discuss the application of Erikson's life stages to our understanding of the challenges of later-life divorce for both parents and adult children.

Developmental Life Stages and Divorce

Everything occurs in a context—including divorce. When it happens, parents may also be facing the challenges, responsibilities, and crises of mid-life or, for some, late life. Their adult children are facing the challenges of forming identities, forging careers, and establishing or maintaining lasting relationships. Each generation may have little appreciation for what the other is going through. Parents may have forgotten their youthful struggles and adult children have not yet experienced the stage of life their parents are in.

Divorce—the whole *process* not just the *event*—is a significant experience for both parents and their children no matter when it occurs in the life cycle of a family. It is accompanied by very strong feelings and the necessity to make major changes and adjustments. But divorce is not the only challenge that parents and children are facing when it occurs. Both generations are also mired in the demands of the life stages they are in, and the impact of divorce is different for family members at each developmental stage. In short, the *context* in which divorce occurs matters!

As you read this chapter, locate where you are (or were) in the life cycle when divorce occurred in your family. Then, parents, be aware of where your children are (or were) and try to recall the challenges you faced when you were at that age. Adult children, while it will probably be easy to locate yourself on this developmental continuum, it will be harder for you to identify with your parents' challenges. You have not yet confronted the inevitable issues of their stage of life.

Context Always Matters

Every person's life is a unique story with an almost infinite variety of twists and turns. No matter how well we may know people, we cannot easily predict how their lives will unfold. That is because, in addition to their personal characteristics, their behavior is influenced by the social contexts in which they live as well as by the distinctive life events and experiences they encounter along the way.

I received my Ph.D. in social psychology, an area of psychology which simultaneously considers what is going on inside an individual (emotions, attitudes, personal characteristics, experiences, etc.) as well as that individual's social context (family, work environment, and social networks). When I subsequently trained as a clinical psychologist, I naturally looked at my clients as unique individuals existing in a larger social context.

Sometimes, in order to better understand a particular client, it was helpful to use a zoom lens, focusing in-depth on what was going on inside. At other times, broadening the focus like a panoramic lens led to greater understanding. I always viewed clients in their interpersonal context. They grew up in a family of some sort and currently had a network of relationships from healthy and strong to dysfunctional and scattered.

Erikson's Eight Ages of Man

I also viewed each client somewhere on the continuum of psychosocial development. They were progressing through an age-related set of stages or stuck/arrested at an earlier stage because of obstacles or deficits encountered along the way. Erik H. Erikson's *Eight Ages of Man*[1] influenced my thinking here.

In this 1963 classic, Erikson laid out eight stages of psychosocial development from birth to old age. Other writers have tweaked or expanded upon Erikson's stages, but I think they continue to provide a useful framework for understanding the challenges of human development in general. And, for our purposes, they can help us understand the challenges of later-life divorce in particular. Divorcing parents and their adult children are grappling with their own developmental tasks when their family structure changes dramatically.

Along with Erikson, I believe that the level of mastery of a previous stage (from only partial to mostly complete) influences a person's chances of successfully mastering the next stage. If major obstacles or disruptions occur during a stage, a person may arrive at the next stage without the necessary resources and robustness needed for success. Later-life divorce potentially creates just such a major disruption for parents and adult children alike.

We will not be focusing on Erikson's first four stages since they occur prior to adolescence and adulthood. That is not to diminish their importance. In fact, successful completion of the tasks associated with these early stages are the critical building blocks for the stages we will be looking at: establishing basic trust in the world and one's caretakers and developing autonomy, initiative, and industry. How well these important tasks were mastered in childhood creates the foundation and skill set for entering into adolescence and adulthood, whether or not parental divorce is in the future.

The Adult Children

Erikson's Stages 5 and 6 cover most of the adult children we will be considering.[2] It will be helpful to have these two stages roughly in mind when we examine the impact of parental divorce on the youngest and Emerging Adult Children in Chapters 4 and 5. I say "roughly" because these days there is considerable fluidity in early adulthood.

Compared to the 1960s when Erikson was writing, young people now are generally taking longer to achieve full adulthood. They are marrying later (if they marry) and are remaining longer in, or even returning to, the parental home. They are taking longer to start or finish school and to make career choices. Nevertheless, somewhere in the rough age span from 18 to the late 20s and early 30s, young adults must enter, and hopefully master, the following two developmental stages in order to move on and experience fulfillment in the final two stages of life.

Stage 5: Identity vs. Role-Confusion

Developing a robust sense of self, or what Erikson called "ego identity," is the core successful outcome of Stage 5. During adolescence and into young adulthood, the fundamental question is: "Who am I?" Answering this with confidence and conviction enables individuals to move on throughout life with a sturdy sense of knowing themselves and a strong sense of their meaning and value to others. They enter adulthood with a sense of independence, control, and personal style. Sixty years ago, Erikson thought this stage was completed by age 18, but today we would expand it well into the mid-20s.

Moving from childhood to adulthood often involves considerable disequilibrium and insecurity. Early on in adolescence, behavior may appear unpredictable and chaotic. Youth lacking a strong sense of identity (due to inability to settle on an occupation or confusion over their gender or sexual orientation, for example) may experience profound self-doubt and loneliness.

Ideally, young adults need ample opportunity to experiment with different roles and identities in order to figure out who they are and where they belong. This requires what Erikson called a *moratorium*,[3] a safe time set aside to try out different identities and find the right fit. Such ideal conditions are more likely to exist when one's family provides a stable and supportive backdrop. Without the chance to experiment with different roles and identities before having to settle down, young people may emerge into adulthood riddled with confusion about who they are, what they want in life, and even what they believe. They may flounder from job to job and from relationship to relationship, unsure where they fit into the world.

As we will see in Chapters 4 and 5, young adults whose families are disrupted by divorce during this critical time will feel the impact. For the youngest adult children, childhood may end abruptly. They may be thrust into independence and adult responsibilities before they are ready. Some may literally become homeless. Others may prematurely latch onto relationships or careers they may later regret. Still others could become the belly floppers who flounder for years, never fully able to assume adult responsibilities.

Parents who divorce when their children are still establishing their core identities need to recognize the additional stress divorce adds at an already critical time in their children's development. The challenges of their divorce could rob their children of the chance to experience a moratorium or abruptly cut it short. Their children may have still been benefiting from the opportunity to try out different roles in order to form a strong sense of self with which to navigate the rest of their lives. In spite of their own pain and preoccupation during the divorce process, parents need to do their best to remain in their roles as Mom and Dad and support their children's healthy experimentation with future roles.

We saw how news of her parents' divorce affected Heather in Chapter 1. As a young college student, she was making good use of the moratorium that college can provide. She was exploring premed courses to see if they were a fit for her. She had started a romantic relationship and was heading off for an interesting summer job. When she learned that her parents were divorcing, she dropped all of her plans and rushed home to focus on them. Her moratorium had ended.

Stage 6: Intimacy vs. Isolation

When young adults enter Stage 6 with a strong core sense of self, they will be ready for healthy intimacy. This involves the capacity to commit to partnerships and affiliations, and the ethical strength to make the necessary sacrifices and compromises to abide by these commitments. Erikson felt that this would result in forming deep relationships and a reliable social network.

An individual with a solid set of intimate relationships feels connected, valued, and loved. Central to this is often the commitment to a romantic/sexual partner, but intimacy is broader than that. Fulfilling intimate relationships include close, enduring friendships as well as honest, loving relationships with family members. These significant relationships are characterized by the give and take of support and loyalty.

Emerging from Stage 5 without a strong core identity leaves people feeling vulnerable and wary of losing themselves in romantic partnerships and close affiliations. To protect a fragile sense of self, a person may put up walls to keep others from getting too close. This may feel like the safer option but isolating from other people physically and emotionally only cuts one off further from positive connections and support.

Although they are watching their peers fall in love, marry, and start families, young adults lacking a strong core self may gravitate toward shallow intimacy with their partners or avoid forming partnerships at all. Isolated and distanced, they may become lonely and depressed. All of these qualities are associated with negative health outcomes including substance abuse and suicide.

And how is the challenge of developing intimate relationships impacted by parental divorce at this stage? Many adult children view their parents' marriage as the prototype of what they can expect from a committed partnership. If this has been negative or even abusive, they may be reluctant to engage in intimate relationships of their own. Or they could resort to an idealized vision of marriage, quite the mirror image of the one they observed, which would leave them ill-equipped to deal with the realities and vicissitudes of actual relationships.

Keeping in mind, however, that divorce is a process and not an event, over time there may well be positive outcomes for adult children who observe a parent ending rather than tolerating an unhealthy marriage. They may now have a powerful example that it is possible as well as legitimate to leave an untenable situation. Nevertheless, it will likely still be disruptive in the shorter run.

For adult children who thought their parents' marriage was positive and expected it to endure, the shock of hearing about their divorce can cast doubt on their perceptions of the reality they thought they knew. What did they miss? When did things go wrong? Was any of it real? It can also affect their expectations for enduring intimacy. Just as they are confronting the challenges of finding and committing to partners, they begin to doubt whether anything lasts. Is there no such thing as "happily ever after?"

Whether or not their parents' divorce catches them by surprise or they welcome the end of their parents' unhappy marriage, adult children in Erikson's Stage 6 will be full of feelings and concerns. If the world signals that these feelings are not legitimate (by dismissing or ignoring them), they may experience shame and further self-doubt. They may isolate or retreat from family members and close friendships, feeling confused and embarrassed. It is not surprising that some young adults begin to question their own intimate relationships. Some who are already married may wonder if they are doomed to fail.

Brian, in Chapter 1, had taken a while to figure out who he was and wanted to be, but he was finally getting there. Now in his mid-30s, he had a good job, his own place, and was about to ask his girlfriend to move in with him. That's when his mother left his father who was in poor health. Brian felt he had no choice but to put his relationship on hold and have his father move in with him. He also felt jaundiced about marriage since the vow about "in sickness and in health" seemed to carry no weight.

Hopefully, consideration of the important challenges for young adults in Erikson's Stages 5 and 6 underscores that this is a very busy and critical time all on its own. It is a time when many adult children still turn to their parents for support and encouragement. When parental divorce is added to the picture, their challenges are likely to increase at the same time that resources for addressing them may decrease. Lucky indeed are those adult children whose functional-enough families remain relatively steady and unchanged, giving them firmer platforms from which to launch their adult lives.

The Parents

Divorcing parents are facing their own important developmental tasks in Erikson's Stages 7 and 8. As with their adult children, viewing parents in the developmental context of their life stages reminds us of the challenges they are confronting during these years apart from the decision to divorce. With so much to master for both generations, no wonder most have limited capacity to feel compassion for each other's struggles. Each generation is trying to stay afloat. Parents and adult children are managing their own developmental tasks as best they can when the upheaval of divorce is added to the mix.

In Chapter 3 we will explore *general trends* which explain the rise in divorce rates for persons in their 50s and beyond as well as *specific reasons* for leaving a marriage after 20+ years. Looking at the issues parents are facing in Erikson's final two life stages adds further understanding. We will see how the challenges inherent in these stages can influence, and sometimes even cause, the divorce decision. Likewise, divorce at these later life stages can greatly impact the quality and quantity of the other challenges older parents face. Not surprisingly, when divorce occurs at these final two stages, parents of adult children are often in sufficient personal crisis that they are unable—at least temporarily—to focus on the needs of their children.

Stage 7: Generativity vs. Stagnation

Generativity vs. stagnation coincides with a broad span of middle adulthood, roughly between ages 40 and 65. Much of the focus for adults during these years is on establishing and guiding the next generation, but it is not just about parenting one's own children. It is also about productivity and creativity more generally. Adults in Stage 7 are striving to find meaning in their lives by doing things that contribute to the larger society or to future generations. They are hoping to accomplish something which will outlast them and leave a mark at least on their small corner of the world.

If they feel they have succeeded, they will have a sense of satisfaction and purpose. They can stand back and see their roles as workers and/or family members as consequential. Watching their children grow into adulthood or taking pride in a lasting and loving relationship with a life partner may be as fulfilling as success in the workplace or through volunteer activities. And because they are not yet in the *final* life stage, they may feel they still have time for additional accomplishments.

On the other hand, failure to successfully engage in productive pursuits during these years can result in a sense of stagnation and failure. Not finding meaning in work, family, or other pursuits can lead to feelings of regret, defeat, or bitterness. Some may blame themselves for the sense of failure. Some may blame other people or groups or simply feel that what happens in their lives is out of their control.

These years are ripe for a mid-life crisis. Looking back as well as ahead, people may feel their lives are on the wrong trajectory. They may regret missed opportunities in their work or personal lives. If they feel there is still enough time remaining that they might find greater fulfillment, they might consider alternatives. Those who anticipate having decades ahead of them may make major changes in their work lives or personal lives like Sophia, whom we met in Chapter 1. With a clean bill of health after a cancer scare, she was ready to leave a loveless marriage and had hopes for a better life.

People in Erikson's 7th Stage are no longer as intensely engaged in parenting if their children are launched or launching. They are freer to focus their energy on work and relationships. If these have not been rewarding or meaningful, they may feel an urgency to make changes while there is still time. In the realm of work, they may feel freer now to switch careers or to begin a career if they have been a stay-at-home parent or part-time worker. And if their marriages have been unfulfilling, they may consider leaving. Perhaps they have been waiting to divorce until their children are out of the home.

It is easy to see how the challenges of Generativity vs. Stagnation could be a catalyst for divorce. They can also be a consequence. One partner in a marriage may have derived a sense of fulfillment from raising children in the context of a supposedly happy-enough family unit, but the other spouse, experiencing stagnation, wants a divorce. The rejected spouse, feeling failure and fear for the future, may invest in work for a compensatory sense of accomplishment as well as financial survival. Both spouses could feel a sense of urgency to validate their worth by finding a new partner while there is still time to experience romance and good health.

Stage 8: Ego Integrity vs. Despair

Fast forward to the final stage of life (approximately age 65 until death) where, surprisingly, we see the highest rise in divorce in the rate of divorce. Erikson considered this old age and a time for reflection and review. Today with life expectancy greater than when Erikson was writing, adults at the younger end of this range are often in good health. They may feel there is more time for change than Erikson believed. At the higher end of this age range, there will be much less opportunity to make changes.

With less time remaining than in Stage 7, there is more poignancy when looking back over the events in one's life. For Erikson, elderly people who could look back with a sense of satisfaction in having taken care of important things and people would have ego integrity. They would accept that their one and only life cycle was "something that had to be." As they take stock of their lives, these fortunate individuals feel a sense of order and satisfaction which eases the anticipation of death.[4]

By contrast, arriving at this final life stage riddled with a sense of regret and failure results in despair. These people are fearful that their lives will come to an end without accomplishing the important things they had hoped to do, without becoming the people they had hoped to be. They feel that time is now short—perhaps too short—to make a fresh start and put together a more meaningful life. Sadly, as they anticipate death, they may feel that their lives were wasted.

As with people in Erikson's Stage 7, we can imagine how the challenges of this final stage can be both cause and consequence of the experience of divorce. When people don't feel at peace with how their lives have unfolded, they might be willing to end a long marriage even if it feels risky. We saw this with Amanda in Chapter 1. She preferred to approach the end of life alone rather than continue in an unhappy and abusive relationship.

But long-term marital partners who feel abandoned at this final life stage might well be thrown into despair no matter the quality of their pre-divorce lives. This could be especially true for older women whose work life outside the home (if there even was one) was valued far less than their role as homemaker. For them, divorce could feel like the invalidation of their entire lives.[5] With precious little, if any, time left to build something new, they may feel they have lost their reason for being. Clearly, older men can also experience this level of despair as we saw with Larry in Chapter 1 whose retirement dreams were shattered when his wife left him.

While the sense of time urgency is likely greater for the oldest (Stage 8) vs. middle-aged (Stage 7) adults, both are actively striving to find meaning and purpose. They want to feel their lives mattered somehow so that they can leave behind a legacy of accomplishment. Some will opt for divorce, hoping, perhaps urgently, to ward off stagnation or despair. Others will be devastated by a divorce they didn't want.

We know that divorce at any age sends the parties into crisis, at least temporarily. At earlier life stages, people have more time and resources to recover and rebuild their lives. Parents divorcing in these later-life stages are in crisis not only because their marriages failed and major adjustments must be made, but also because they may be fighting against time to still find meaning and fulfillment in their lives. Self-absorption, a focus on one's own needs and even survival, is likely to take over at least for a while, leaving these older parents unlikely to appreciate the impact of their divorce on their adult children.

In Summary

Individuals need to be viewed in a social context and so does divorce. In this chapter, we have seen that divorce impacts people differently depending on their developmental life stage. Adult children are trying to establish their identities and foster solid relationships. Their parents are trying to establish legacies that will outlive them and to be able to look back on their lives without regret.

These formidable tasks require and deserve considerable energy and focus. So does responding and adjusting to divorce! Taken together, we can see why both generations—parents and their adult children—can become overwhelmed when divorce is added to the already challenging tasks of their developmental stage. Hopefully, being more aware of what is happening for each generation can lead to greater compassion *across* generations—compassion that respects parent-child roles and boundaries. Whether you are the parent or the adult child reading this chapter, I hope you have come away with greater empathy for each other as well as for yourself.

We are now ready to take a closer look at the parents who are divorcing in later life (Chapter 3) and their children at three different stages of adulthood. (Chapters 4, 5, and 6)

Chapter Two Notes—*Developmental Life Stages and Divorce*

1. See Erik H. Erikson, *Childhood and Society,* Second Edition, 1963, W.W. Norton & Company, for fuller discussion. Briefly, Erikson's first four stages (and their positive outcomes) are:

> *Trust vs. Mistrust* (Infancy: 0 to 1 ½ years). Infant's basic needs are met resulting in a sense of trust.
> *Autonomy vs. Shame and Doubt* (Toddlerhood: 1 ½ to 3 years). Child asserts independence and control of their body and environment.
> *Initiative vs. Guilt* (Preschool: 3 to 5 years). Child develops a sense of purpose, explores new situations, and activities.
> *Industry vs. Inferiority* (School Age: 6 to 12 years). Child develops competence and skills, building confidence.

2. Erikson's Stages 5 (Identity) and 6 (Intimacy) cover most of the adult children we consider in Chapters 4 (Launchers) and 5 (Emerging Adults). The oldest children we consider in Chapter 6 (Middle-Aged Adults) are from their mid-30s and well beyond, possibly into their 50s and 60s. Whether successful or not, most have already dealt with the challenges of Identity and Intimacy faced by Launchers and Emerging Adults. In fact, the older ones in this group are facing the same mid-life challenges as are younger parents in Erikson's 7th stage (Generativity). Likely their own parents are in Erikson's final Stage 8 (Ego Integrity).

3. Erikson's concept of a moratorium provides the opportunity for a young adult to explore a variety of roles that will help form their identity or sense of self. It is also provides the opportunity to explore relationships before settling on a life partner. A moratorium gives a young adult the time and freedom for self-discovery before taking on full adult responsibilities. Once they enter adulthood and have people depending on them at home or at work, it is hard to go back. We will see in the following chapters that parental divorce can greatly foreshorten or even eliminate a young adult's opportunity for a moratorium.

4. The life of Anna Mary Robertson Moses ("Grandma Moses") exemplifies ego integrity vs. despair. She started painting in earnest at age 78 and became a popular folk artist in the 1950s. She is quoted as saying: "I look back on my life like a good day's work, it was done, and I am satisfied with it. I was happy and contented. I knew nothing better and made the best out of what life offered."

5. In 1982, Barbara Cain reported on the women she had spoken with who were

in a "Divorce Over 60" support group. (Barbara S. Cain, "The Plight of the Gray Divorcee," *New York Times Magazine*, December 19, 1982.) Most of them had devoted their lives to their husbands and families and were ill-prepared for any role other than homemaker. In their cohort, most believed marriage was forever and divorce meant failure. Fortunately, women over 60 facing divorce today are likely to have a greater life expectancy than in the 1980s. In addition, they have likely been in the workforce themselves and no longer derive their identities solely from their marriages. In fact, they are often the ones initiating divorce.

PART II

The Parents

-3-
The Parents: Why are They Divorcing?

There are many reasons why marriages no longer work for one or both partners. Some couples may simply grin and bear it. Some may seek and find solutions other than divorce. For others, divorce may be the only answer. And although spouses may divorce, parents are forever parents even if their children are adults.

We saw in Chapter 1 that divorce rates in the U.S. have been declining for forty years except for adults over 50 where they have doubled and over 65 where they have tripled. Here we will look more closely at explanations for this surprising trend. No explanation can eliminate or neutralize the pain and disequilibrium felt by parents or their adult children when this happens. However, it can be empowering to have a better understanding of the motivation and momentum behind this uptake in later-life divorce.

As a divorcing/divorced parent reading this chapter, you are likely to find explanations and examples matching your own experience. They may stir up strong feelings. If so, I hope you will reach out for support but it should be from someone other than your adult children. Your children need a general understanding of what is happening and why you are divorcing or have divorced. Beyond that, be mindful of what is and isn't appropriate to share with them. They do not need details that make either of you uncomfortable even if they press for them. You are the parent, and they are your children, even though they are now adults. It is your responsibility to maintain healthy parent-child boundaries, an issue we will explore at length in Chapter 7.

If you are an adult child reading this chapter, you may feel like skipping it in order to get to the next three chapters which deal with *your* needs and issues, not those of your parents. You may be thinking there's already been enough focus on them and their divorce. That's understandable. You don't need to read these chapters in any particular order.

However, I hope you will return here eventually. Gaining a general understanding of the reasons for the increase in later-life divorces will likely help you place your family's experience in context. Looking at specific case examples, you will probably realize that you are not alone in what you have been experiencing. Your feelings and reactions are perfectly normal. And while you probably want to know why your parents decided to divorce, you don't want the kind of information that violates appropriate parent-child boundaries. With healthy boundaries, you will be able to see divorce from your parents' perspective as well as your own and have compassion for what *all* of you have been going through and may experience in the future.

GENERAL EXPLANATIONS

Age and Life Expectancy

In 1950, the average life expectancy in the US was around 68 years. By 1980, it had risen to around 74 years; and by 2020, nearly 80 years. With a shorter life expectancy, earlier cohorts of parents may have seen their lives as winding down and moving toward a conclusion once their children were launched. Now, in the 21st century, Americans expect to live many more years after raising their children, even though they are marrying later and their children are taking longer to grow up and leave home.

Depending on how young they are when their last child is out of the house, they can still see 10, 20, 30 or more years ahead of them. If they have experienced their marriages as unhappy or unfulfilling, they can imagine there is still time to start a new life. They may remain single, or they may re-partner or remarry but, unless they are already very elderly when this happens, they can reasonably hope to have ample time to create a more satisfying existence.

We saw this with Sophia, the pediatric nurse practitioner. She filed for divorce from her emotionally unavailable husband after she got a clean bill of health following cancer surgery. She was still in her late 50s and eventually (and cautiously) found her way to online dating sites. After a few unpleasant experiences, she met Gary who was recovering from divorce after the end of his own unfulfilling marriage. The two fell in love, married, and slowly and respectfully blended their adult children into a warm but loosely-knit stepfamily. They had plenty of time ahead of them to expect a long and rewarding experience of traveling and grandparenting together.

Deirdre Bair presents a particularly poignant illustration of this for octogenarians in her book *Calling It Quits*.[1] In their mid-80s, Caroline and Ted had been married "53 placid years" when her kidneys failed and she got a transplant. After she recovered from a harrowing near-death experience, Caroline told her husband she didn't know how many more years she might have, but she knew she didn't want to spend them with him! Being in Erikson's final life stage, this decision resulted in significant disruption for both Caroline and Ted who had limited time left to make necessary adjustments. It disrupted the lives of their middle-aged children as well.

It is not only health crises that alert people to life-expectancy issues. Anticipating retirement, celebrating a milestone birthday, and watching one's peers set off on new beginnings or new relationships also make people aware that there may still be time left to make changes and move on. Most people are aware that they are generally in better health and feel "younger" than their parents did at their age.

Financial Independence of Women

Over this same time span, women have been entering the workforce in record numbers.[2] In the 1950s the average woman was not employed outside the home and had no independent source of income. By the 1970s it was increasingly common for women—even women with young children—to be in the workplace. With increasing education and career ambitions, married women entered the workforce where single mothers were already well-established. Today many women have their own careers and know they will be able to support themselves.

Men, too, are now aware that their wives are more able to support themselves. They can think about ending a marriage with less of a financial burden (i.e., costly spousal maintenance) than was the case in earlier years. Their wives might even earn as much or more than they do. In addition to not having to anticipate years and years of maintenance, if the children are already over eighteen, they would not have to pay child support.

Lessening Stigma of Divorce

In the 1950s, there was a significant social stigma attached to being divorced. This was especially true for women when it was widely thought they needed to be in a relationship to be valued. Being divorced meant that a woman had failed to keep her marriage intact. In the 1960s and 70s, as more and more women gained the financial independence to leave unhappy marriages, divorce became much more common. Nearly everyone had experienced divorce somewhere in their extended family or friendship network, and the familiarity seemed to lessen the negativity associated with it. Although there may still be remnants of shame and failure associated with divorce, the stigma has greatly lessened, making the decision to divorce more palatable.

It also became easier as divorce laws themselves became more liberal. California was the first state to pass a no-fault divorce law in 1970, and by the 1990s all 50 states had some form of no-fault divorce. For the most part, people no longer had to report or invent negative reasons such as adultery, abandonment, or cruelty to get a divorce. Couples could claim irreconcilable differences or irreparable breakdown of the marriage. They could move on without public disparagement of themselves or their partners.

Empty Nest Syndrome

Unlike the trend today, many of the older couples divorcing after 25 years or more were quite young when they married. Many of these marriages occurred when the partners were in their late teens and early 20's—right out of high school or college. This was a time when birth control was less available and premarital sex (let alone living together) was less acceptable. Many of these young people did not know each other well before marriage. Many didn't know *themselves* all that well either. They often still had school ahead of them and had not established themselves in careers. Viewed from the perspective of Erikson's life stages, many had not yet formed a strong identity or sense of self prior to committing to a life partner.

If they had children right away, there was little time to develop interests as a couple apart from parenting. Divisions of household labor that made sense early on when there were young children may have ceased to fit as the children grew up and/or the women became more involved in the workplace. Stresses may have arisen, and resentments may have deepened, that were never addressed during intense childrearing years.

When their children began to leave home for work, school, or marriage, parents who had not been nurturing their own relationship could find it empty. With more years looming ahead without children as their main focus, some feared a lonely and bleak future if they remained married. Some couples used this as a wake-up call and a chance to strengthen their marriages, but others felt it was too late.

Anita's Story

Illustrative of this is Anita, a devout Catholic who had been in a lonely, distant marriage for years before she realized it. She was deeply in love with Stan when she dropped out of college to get married. Twelve years and four children later, she was preoccupied with being a mom. And Stan, a plumber, worked extra hours to make ends meet. If he had free time, he coached his kids' softball games or went bowling with his brother-in-law.

Over the years, Anita got enormous pleasure from watching her children grow up. She had high expectations for them and fostered their achievement aspirations. As they became more independent, she got in touch with her own aspirations and went back to school for her teaching degree. Her maturity and life experience, coupled with her leadership skills, led her to move quickly out of the classroom and into high level administrative positions.

Anita was in her early 50s when her youngest child walked out the door for college and she felt there was no life left in their home. At work, she got respect bordering on adulation for her competence and compassion. In her marriage, she felt unappreciated and almost invisible. Stan's work life had become rather lackluster, and he missed having the kids around for diversion. He was shocked and furious when Anita told him they needed to get counseling or she was thinking about divorce.

When he refused to go, and divorce was inevitable, Anita contacted me. Although Stan remarried rather quickly, he remained bitter. He refused to speak to Anita or even be in the same room with her. This created a continuously stressful string of situations for their young adult children who were in the throes of graduations, weddings, and having babies. Listening to Anita's accounts of these unnecessarily painful occasions was, in fact, one of the reasons why I decided to write this book.

Growing Apart

Despite some overlap with the empty nest explanation, growing apart merits its own consideration. People now have higher expectations for marriage than they did in the 1950s and 1960s. It is not enough to have a partner with whom to weather life's stages. People now expect marriage to provide companionship, friendship, romance, and sexual compatibility. They are looking to their marriages for happiness and fulfillment. Furthermore, a couple's expectations may have changed and even diverged over the course of a long marriage, as they have for the public in general.

Susan Brown of the National Center for Marriage and Family Research (NCMFR) at Bowling Green State University found that most later-life divorces are not the result of severe discord but rather of couples simply growing apart.[3] This trend was heightened during the COVID-19 pandemic since empty-nesters or recent retirees had little to distract them from noticing an unfulfilling relationship. Brown also felt that the pandemic made people aware of their own mortality. They had more time to think about their life goals and what they were willing to accept in their marriages even if they were not conflictual. If their marriages felt like empty shells, they might decide to leave.

Growing apart is the explanation often given when famous couples divorce after a long marriage. In 2010, the world was shocked when Al and Tipper Gore announced they were divorcing after a 40-year marriage. The American news media was flooded with articles about the famous split and briefly paid lip service to the rise in divorces among older couples generally. Newspapers and magazines in the U.S. and abroad saw the Gores as the quintessential American couple. They had weathered so much—Al's tour in Vietnam, the near-death of their son, Tipper's depression, and losing the 2000 presidential election. Now, in their early 60s, it seemed they were in the home stretch. If they couldn't make it to the finish line after all they had been through, what hope was there for the institution of marriage?

Fast forward a decade and the world was again forced to think about trends in gray divorce with the splits of two more famous couples. Jeff and MacKenzie Bezos announced their divorce on Twitter in 2019 after a 25-year marriage. In 2021, Bill and Melinda Gates ended a 27-year marriage. Both couples insisted at the time that the divorces were amicable and that they would continue to support one another and work together to co-parent their children. The Gates' public statement to the media simply said they no longer felt they could grow together as a couple in the next phase of their lives. While other factors may have played a part, it was well-known that Bill and Melinda Gates had developed different interests within their foundation and had been living powerful but parallel lives for some time.

Examples from my own practice illustrate the impact of both the empty nest and growing apart on the lives of couples outside of the limelight. Observers may look for a precipitating event that might explain the ending of a long marriage, but there may not be one. Many marriages may end more with a fizzle than a bang. They may have been losing vitality for years as one or both of the partners began to move off in new directions that undermined the couple's original connection. Instead of the marital balloon suddenly popping, it may have been slowly deflating until all the air is gone.

Sharon's Story

Sharon was often on her own raising their five children while her husband Dave, a commercial pilot who flew mainly international flights, was away. She considered his life glamorous and her own mundane, but he earned good money and she became self-sufficient by necessity. Over time, as she became quite adept in managing the house and the children all on her own, Sharon came to relish her independence and felt enormous satisfaction that she was able to function so well by herself.

When Dave came home, she found herself experiencing him as an intruder who cramped her style and wanted her full attention. Sharon and the children had developed their own routines and ways of doing things, and sometimes Dave felt left out. Each time they would try to work on this as a family, but then Dave would be off again, and the cycle would repeat itself.

Eventually, with their final child about to leave home, things came to a head. Dave was thinking about retirement and hoped Sharon would jump at the chance to spend all their time together, joining him in some new interests he'd discovered while traveling. She felt she hardly knew him anymore, felt unappreciated, and almost suffocated.

Living alone after they divorced, Sharon said she hardly noticed a difference. For Dave, however, the difference was huge. He scrambled to create a home that would entice their five young adult children to visit. Too late, he began to recognize what his wife had been managing all these years and how he had ignored her attempts to get his attention.

Zeke's Story

For years, Zeke, a busy and highly intellectual academic, had been happy to let his wife run their home and manage their children. Once they were off to college and beyond, he found his wife boring and unstimulating. With his career successfully established, he was ready to coast a bit at work and turn attention to his personal life where he wanted to have new adventures and explore his sexuality.

The couple tried for a while to find common interests and to revive their sexual relationship, but this only further convinced Zeke how far apart they had grown. His wife felt they had a "good enough life," but he felt young enough and determined enough to see if he could find something better. Their adult children were confused and angry.

It was primarily his concern about his adult children that motivated Zeke to contact me. He was recently single and feeling liberated from his unfulfilling marriage. He felt his new-found enjoyment in life was palpable and was puzzled that his children weren't happy for him. Like many who choose to divorce at this stage, he had considered ending his marriage when his children were younger but decided against it. He didn't want to miss any part of those important parenting years, and he knew that young kids are affected by divorce.

What Zeke hadn't anticipated was how much his children would still be affected by divorce once they were adults. At first, he resisted the idea that his decision impacted their lives in part because it put a damper on his delight in being single and having new romantic pursuits. But Zeke was invested in being a good dad, so he followed up on my recommendation that he start conversations with his children and be open to really hearing what they were feeling.

Two very important outcomes resulted from this. Responding to the healthy boundaries his children set, Zeke vowed not to share information about his dating experiences which they had found uncomfortable. He also heard that his ex-wife was struggling with depression over the divorce, and his children felt the need to rally around her. This made it impossible for them to share his happiness over being single. Zeke made sure not to speak negatively about his ex and to respect and support his children's loyalty to her as their mother.

These conversations with his young adult children nudged Zeke out of his self-absorption with his new-found freedom and back to the realization that the divorce had complicated their lives too. He kept his romantic pursuits to himself and set aside regular times when he invited his children individually and altogether for a home-cooked meal. He surprised them with his new culinary skills and invited them to join him in preparing new recipes. Slowly but surely Zeke and his children began to feel like a family again, and he rekindled his interest in the important events in their young adult lives.

So far, the explanations we have considered (from life expectancy to growing apart) are essentially benign even if their consequence—divorce—can feel devastating to all parties. With enough time left to make positive changes, and sufficient resources for a fresh start, one or both parents may decide to leave an unfulfilling marriage. When the last child is launched or launching, parents may feel that the active parenting years are behind them. They can put their energy into trying something new—a new career, a new relationship, a new adventure.

In the absence of obvious problems or open discord, their children, like Zeke's, may not have seen this coming. They were likely busy working at their own developmental milestones—with their parents' lives as a predictable backdrop. These are the adult children most likely to experience shock and to question their own perceptions. They are the ones who look back on their childhood memories and wonder what, if any of it, was *real.* If theirs was the "All American Family," if theirs were the parents who remained married when their friends' parents had divorced at a younger age, then *why now* would things come apart? Can any relationship be expected to last?

TOXIC SCENARIOS OF SUBSTANCE ABUSE, DOMESTIC ABUSE, AND MENTAL ILLNESS

Quite a different scenario exists for adult children who grew up in a toxic home environment. This can run the gamut from frequent episodes of parental anger and fighting to abuse and trauma. Even when parents try to shelter their children from the full impact, they probably are still aware that something is amiss.

We will look separately at substance abuse, domestic abuse, and mental illness. All involve overt behaviors which children may well have witnessed and found frightening. They may have wished for years that their parents would divorce and put an end to their toxic experiences. They may side with the parent they see as the victim of the other parent's destructive behavior, but they may also be confused as to who is at fault. Both parents may have been preoccupied by the negative behavior and unable to give their children the attention they needed.

If the long-suffering parent is able to successfully exit the abusive situation, what happens to the troubled parent? Divorce allows a spouse to detach from a troubled, abusive, or mentally ill partner and their problematic behavior. Minor children might be cushioned from the worst effects, but adult children may be expected to assume some responsibility. There are *ex*-husbands and *ex*-wives, but not *ex*-dads or *ex*-moms. Depending on their resources and life stage, adult children might feel obligated to step in when their other parent steps out.

So, children of a traumatic divorce situation are much less likely to be caught by surprise. They may even be relieved. Yet they are less likely than children in the more benign scenarios to have two healthy, well-functioning parents prior to, during, and following a later-life divorce. Let's look now at some scenarios of abuse and trauma.

Substance Abuse

It is no surprise that substance abuse and other addictions can wreak havoc in a marriage. What may start as an occasional problem with alcohol, drugs, or gambling can, over time, spin out of control. Behaviors that were tolerable at one point may accumulate and reach a breaking point so that a spouse may—reluctantly or emphatically—decide to end the marriage. This may happen after years of encouraging and even seeking treatment, or it could happen after a particularly upsetting event.

Caroline's Story

Caroline put up with her husband Frank's drug and alcohol abuse for years. She loved him deeply and considered him her savior because he steadfastly defended her against her emotionally abusive family. More than once his excessive drinking led her to ask him to leave when their twin boys were young, but she took him back once he promised to go to AA. Things got better for a while, but he only briefly attended AA and started drinking and using again.

Because Frank was excelling at work and getting raises and promotions, Caroline told herself his substance abuse couldn't be that bad. However, his moods became more erratic, and he often seemed either frantic or exhausted. The final straw came after their twins went to college and drug dealers started showing up at their home in an upper middle-class gated community. When she could no longer deny that her own safety was at risk, Caroline made Frank move out, but she held onto hope that they might reconcile in the future.

Caroline and Frank never totally stopped loving each other. It took years of therapy before she decided she needed to file for divorce and get on with her life. Even after that she often hoped things might change so they could remarry. They never did.

Caroline was eventually able to move forward. She remained thankful for ways that Frank had been a positive presence in the early years of their marriage, and she cared deeply about him as a troubled person. Still, she had come to see that she deserved a life not defined by the roller coaster of addiction.

At the time her divorce was final, Caroline was an attractive woman in her late 50s. She kept busy with her wide circle of family and friends, and she did a little dating. Eventually she met Bill, a happy, healthy man whose marriage had also ended because of substance abuse. They discovered their mutual love of dancing, traveling, and spending time with grandchildren. Neither had ever dreamed they could feel so comfortable and content.

Caroline's sons were greatly relieved to see their mother so happy. However, the earlier years of their parents prolonged separation and post-divorce hope of reconciliation had been confusing for them just as they were launching their young adult lives from this shaky platform. They worried about their distraught mother and often felt responsible for their troubled father. We will look at this from their perspective in Chapter 9.

Chad's Story

Chad was well aware that his mother's drinking was out of control. Her drunkenness in social situations was a source of embarrassment for his father's professional career in their small community. When Chad came home from college, he could feel the tension between his parents whenever his mother announced it was time for "happy hour." He was both troubled and reassured knowing his father was committed to the marriage "till death do us part." Unpleasant as it was, at least it was a predictable situation, allowing Chad to prioritize his own life when he wasn't at home.

It came as a surprise, then, when his mother announced that she wanted a divorce. She was tired of her husband constantly nagging her to control her drinking. Chad felt caught in the middle, feeling concern for and loyalty to both parents. Eager to escape this heavy sense of responsibility, Chad embraced the opportunity to take a job out of the country when he finished college, but he also felt guilty for running away. His younger sister Lily felt he had abandoned her, and she found her own way to "leave" by smoking marijuana on a daily basis.

I met Chad when he moved back home several years later. His father had remarried a woman who required his full attention, so he didn't have much time for his son or his daughter. Chad found himself trying to manage his mother's escalating drinking problem all on his own. He had little time for anything outside of this and his job as middle school teacher. We will pick back up with Chad in Chapters 8 and 11.

Judy's Story

Judy's story is surprisingly similar except that she was 82 when her marriage ended after more than 60 years. She and Steve had been a couple since high school. By the time I met her, Judy had been tolerating Steve's lifelong pattern as a functional alcoholic. Over time she developed strategies to avoid awkward social situations by having them arrive late and leave early. She chose to sleep in a separate bedroom on a separate level in their home, and she made excuses for Steve's behavior when their daughters and grandchildren visited.

Although both Judy and Steve were often miserable, it was another seemingly stable and predictable situation. Surprisingly, it was Steve who announced on his 85th birthday that he wanted a divorce. Judy's initial shock and hurt quickly gave way to a sense of liberation. She only wished *she* had initiated this years ago. However, divorce at this final life stage affected three generations. Judy and Steve's middle-aged children and young adult grandchildren were stunned and worried about them both. In Chapter 6, we will look more closely at grandchildren's reactions when their grandparents divorce.

Joe's Story

Joe's story sadly illustrates the long-term negative effects of addiction before, during, and following a later-life divorce. Joe's drinking and bankruptcy eventually led his wife to divorce him once their children were no longer living at home. He had been unhappy and felt unappreciated in a basically platonic marriage for years. He would have ended it earlier but didn't want to miss watching his children grow up. Looking back, his version was that his wife's constant desire for a bigger house, private school for their kids, fancy car, etc. is what drove him to overwork and turn to alcohol.

Ironically, once the bankruptcy concluded, neither had a house. His wife had to get a job for the first time in her life and could only afford a small apartment. Joe, once a brilliant man with a promising career, was essentially homeless for several years as his drinking escalated and he lost a series of jobs. For a while, he moved in with his elderly and emotionally abusive mother. After she died, he hit an even lower bottom including a near-fatal suicide attempt.

Fortunately, Joe eventually stumbled his way out of denial and into sobriety and was able to reignite his earlier entrepreneurial career. Despite this success, his adult children remained estranged from him. He had been missing-in-action for much of their young adult lives, and they continued to see their mother as the victim. Alcoholics Anonymous as well as our psychotherapy sessions taught Joe that he needed to give them time to trust him again so he remained cautiously optimistic that they might someday reconnect.

Domestic Abuse

Likewise, it is no surprise that marriages can end because of domestic violence and emotional abuse. Family members, including adult children, may have been wishing for years that their abused parent would get out of the marriage before something tragic happened. Often, they are angry at the perpetrator and side with the victim/survivor, although that is not always the case. Sometimes the children themselves have been abused and have safety concerns of their own even after the divorce.

Tillie's Story

Tillie's situation involved both substance abuse and domestic violence. For years she felt neglected and lonely while her husband was out drinking with his friends after work on the assembly line at an automotive plant. Eventually, when her children were older, she went back to school. After they were no longer living at home, she started her own successful pet-sitting business. Tillie now had her feet solidly on the ground, and her husband became increasingly jealous and insecure. When he came home drunk and threatened to kill her, she knew it was time to leave, and called the police.

This resulted in a front-page news story involving a dramatic stand off with the police and Tillie being held hostage overnight. Nevertheless, despite all the negative publicity, as well as criminal charges against their father, two of their four children sided with him. They had not witnessed his violent behavior, and they saw him as the parent less able to manage on his own. This was especially true of their oldest child who held her mom responsible when her dad showed up on her doorstep with nowhere to live when she was newly married. Their second and third children were stuck in the middle trying to make peace between two warring parents. The youngest child, already sliding into the early stages of alcoholism, estranged himself from the whole family.

Dana's Story

We briefly met Dana, Austin's mother, in Chapter 1. Always bright and destined for success, she went on to medical school where she met Terrance. They put off marriage until they both got their M.D.s and felt certain their future aspirations were compatible. They supported each other's career advances, and they functioned as buffers for each other in dealing with their complicated families of origin. Once they felt secure that they could succeed as a two-career couple, they began to start a family.

Dana was at times surprised at how happy she was and felt lucky to still experience Terrance as "the love of my life." They became even closer during a difficult pregnancy and functioned well while managing health challenges of one of their children. Then Terrance's moods and behavior began to change. He was often depressed, and he started running into problems at work. Determined to overcome what was shattering her dream, Dana sought therapy for them as a couple, but things did not improve.

With Austin, their older child, off at college and their daughter, Katie, still in high school, Terrance's depression deepened and he became violent. He frightened Dana and Katie when he flew into a rage and began destroying property. Dana recalled that her decision boiled down to this: "He got depressed, and I stayed with him. He got angry, and I still stayed with him. Then he got dangerous, and it was over, but it was still hard on the kids."

After the divorce, Dana and her children lived in terror for months while Terrance threatened to burn down their home. Eventually, neither child wanted any contact with their father.

Marie's Story

Like Dana, Marie had also launched one child off to college, and the last was a senior in high school when she finally knew she had to leave her abusive husband, Mitch. The worst of the abuse, including marital rape, occurred when they were alone. So Mitch thought no one would believe Marie if she told them how bad things had gotten. Once he threatened to push her into a partially-frozen pond, insisting later that he was just teasing, and he frequently told her she had gotten so fat no other man would want her.

Many years before, when he tried to choke her, Marie had attempted to call the police but Mitch ripped the phone out of the wall just as Marie had dialed. The police showed up anyway, but even with the phone on the floor and bruises beginning to appear, Mitch charmed them and no report was filed. Marie felt there was nothing she could do. Mitch sensed her resignation and began to belittle her and hit her in front of their children.

With the empty nest looming large, Marie cautiously volunteered in the high school library. She almost immediately began to receive compliments about her competence and friendly manner with students. When she shared this with Mitch, he became enraged and choked her into unconsciousness. This time, when she recovered, she decided things couldn't go on like this. She confided in a teacher she'd gotten to know who found her an attorney and referred her to me.

We immediately began working on a safety plan for leaving. Neither of her children wanted to hear details of why she filed for divorce. They even questioned Marie's reports of violence despite having witnessed such behavior directed at her and at themselves. It took years before they admitted that they were trying to "stay neutral" out of fear that their increasingly violent father would turn his full wrath onto them.

Emotional Abuse

Apart from physical violence, years of emotional abuse can also accumulate and lead to a later-life divorce. Emotional abuse in a marriage involves non-physical behaviors intended to control, humiliate, isolate, and/or frighten one's partner. Being harder to see, this form of abuse can be under the radar of even an adult child.

An emotionally abused spouse may need to leave in order to preserve their mental health and well-being. Yet, without visible scars, their children may be even less sympathetic than Marie's who had actually witnessed their father's abuse. In order to justify the decision to divorce, an abused parent may feel compelled to plead their case by providing details of emotional abuse which may have accumulated over many years. However, hearing intimate examples of these intangible forms of abuse can feel like a parent is crossing the line into inappropriate sharing that a child does not want to hear.

Hannah's Story

Hannah had endured emotional abuse beginning on her wedding night. A virgin when she married, she shyly emerged from the bathroom in the prettiest nightgown she and her sister had been able to find at Walmart. Her new husband informed her that she looked like "white trash." This belittlement went on for decades leaving Hannah's self-esteem depleted.

Almost miraculously, once their three children were launched, she got up the nerve to say she wanted a divorce. Hannah's husband initially responded by removing the battery from her car so she couldn't leave. Eventually, she found her way into an attorney's office as well as mine.

These events caught her children by surprise since the worst of the emotional abuse had occurred in private. When Hannah attempted to share details defending her decision to divorce, her children were clearly uncomfortable, so she didn't persist. However, their father didn't hold back from trying to convince them that their mother was mentally unstable and had ruined his life.

For the first few years after her divorce, Hannah was quite lonely. Her self-esteem as a woman and mother was very low, but eventually she agreed to venture out into a women's group where she was welcomed and appreciated for her kindness and courage. She made connections there that got her back in touch with her musical talents and into a small country music band. She never spoke negatively about her ex-husband, but her adult children, watching her blossom into a stronger, happier person, began to see beyond their father's accounts.

Mental Illness (Neurotic, Psychotic, and Personality Disordered)

With advances in therapy and medication, many mental illnesses can be managed successfully—especially in the context of a supportive marriage and family. However, sometimes even with reasonably effective treatment, it is more than a spouse may have bargained for or is capable of handling. Untreated, mental illness can weigh heavily on a family and a marriage. This can be especially true if the person denies there is a problem or refuses treatment. Severe untreated depression, as we saw above with Dana's abusive husband Terrance, can lead to traumatic experiences for family members.

Charles' Story

For years, mild-mannered Charles endured his wife's rage attacks. A frustrated actress whose career was sidetracked after their children started arriving, Miriam became more and more unhappy and unstable. Charles had a demanding career in public administration and worked long hours, coming home to an often-enraged wife who had gone to bed early. He rolled up his sleeves, made dinner for the family, and helped the children with their homework.

Over the years, he mostly tolerated Miriam's behavior since the outbursts were mainly directed at him. Many times, he tried to get her to go to couples therapy and admitted that his work schedule could be partly to blame. Miriam would have none of it, screaming that Charles' character flaws were the problem and that she played no role in their marital troubles.

He waited until their children were out of the home as he didn't trust Miriam to parent younger children on her own in a shared parenting arrangement. At that point he felt he could walk away from this burden, but their young adult children were not so lucky. Now they had an increasingly unstable mom to worry about in addition to college and jobs. In Chapter 8 we will revisit Charles and his adult children in family therapy.

Andrea's Story

Some mental conditions are less extreme and don't entail danger like Miriam's severe personality disorder or Terrance's severe depression. Nevertheless, they may still be intolerable. For example, Andrea's life became increasingly restricted as her husband (a severely obsessive-compulsive dentist) became more and more controlling. Although she was always tidy in the ways she kept house and managed her appearance, her husband began criticizing her for not doing enough to combat germs. His fear of flying evolved into a fear of trains and even long car trips which meant they rarely visited family.

He refused to get help, insisting that his progressively limited world was reality. With their children through college and doing well enough, Andrea left and found a laid-back and adventurous new partner who loved to travel. Her children generally supported her decision. They were sad that their father made little effort to visit them. When they visited him out of loyalty as well as concern, he made them feel like messy intruders.

Enrico and Emma's Story

Enrico and Emma were a newly married couple when Enrico's father left his mentally ill wife. It was unclear, especially to this young couple, what exactly was wrong with her, but she had been difficult to be around for most of Enrico's life. His father said she had become increasingly paranoid, and he thought she was showing signs of early dementia. Still, he never pushed her to seek help and get a diagnosis. After Enrico and his sister were both married, he just said he'd, "had enough." He seemed eager to get out and perhaps find a happier situation. In his late 50s, he quickly found a new partner whom Enrico and Emma enjoyed spending time with.

Enrico experienced a sense of easy normality around them, which he hadn't known growing up. He also experienced guilt as well as a strong sense of responsibility for his mother as she became progressively erratic around finances and self-care. Out from under the burden of his ex-wife's mental struggles, Enrico's father was clearly thriving. However, ill-equipped by their youth and meager financial resources, Enrico and Emma started having serious strain in their own marriage as Enrico increasingly took on the role of caretaker for his needy mother.

That was what brought them to my office. They eagerly accepted my assessment that the strain they were experiencing appeared to have less to do with any incompatibility in their marriage and more to do with the heavy responsibility thrust upon them for Enrico's mother. This young couple was eager to learn how to set firm limits on what they could and couldn't do for her, and they convinced Enrico's sister to get more involved and share some of the load.

Perhaps most important, they asked Enrico's father for help. To their surprise, he was remarkably willing to arrange for (and finance) care for his ex-wife. This clearly made the young couple's life much easier. It also alleviated some of his own guilt around the divorce and paved the way for Enrico and Emma to once again truly enjoy spending time with him and his new wife.

OTHER SCENARIOS RESULTING IN DIVORCE

Infidelity

Where does infidelity fit?[4] Certainly, it can be traumatic for a spouse to discover a partner's unfaithfulness. However, current research supports clinical wisdom that affairs (sexual or not) do not always spell the end of a marriage. They can be both the cause as well as the consequence of estrangement between partners. For some couples, discovering a spouse's affair is a wake-up call to seek help and revive the relationship. For others, it can be a final straw, a ticket out, or even a wound that never heals as we will see below.

But for adult children of a couple where an affair is a part of the divorce, there can be very strong feelings. Almost by definition, affairs are secret, so adult children are likely to be shocked when they hear of them. Shocked because one or both parents violated the vows of monogamy, but perhaps even more shocked to realize that sex can still play such a major role in one's parent's life. This can result in questions and revelations that children, even as adults, don't want to think or know about. And if the clandestine partner eventually becomes a step-parent, the cloud of infidelity can hover over the relationship.

Justin's Story

Jan was crushed when she discovered her husband Justin's on-going affair with a colleague at his workplace. Despite his offering deep-seated apologies, making amends, years of individual and couple's therapy, and a subsequent 5-year period of monogamy which both of them validated, Jan continued to withhold affection (and often, sex). Her impervious sense of injury would not allow her to re-engage in the marriage. Both were miserable, and after their children were out of the house, Justin had done enough work in individual and marital therapy to feel he didn't deserve Jan's continued rejection.

Their children had a sense that their parents hadn't been happy for years, but they didn't find out about the infidelity till Justin filed for divorce. Even though Jan found the marriage joyless, she was determined to stay in it. Justin feared she would do her best to alienate their three adult children from him.

Sadly, he was right. When the children learned about their dad's affair five years earlier, they sided with their mother as the injured party and for years maintained only minimal contact with Justin while he continued to pay for college tuition and weddings. We will check back in with Justin and his adult children in Chapter 7.

Fran's Story

Fran's husband Carl also said he could never again trust her after she confessed to having had a one-night stand when she went alone to her 30th high school reunion. Although bright and witty, she was less educated than her husband who had several advanced degrees. Throughout their long marriage Carl had often made Fran feel she wasn't smart enough or attractive enough and blamed her for his frequent bouts of impotence. He'd never been interested in getting to know her high school friends and had no interest in going with her to her reunion despite her urging. So, Fran had gone alone.

Back with her high school classmates, she felt a renewed sense of being valued as a person. For a brief moment, and with a little too much to drink, she enjoyed feeling desired again by her old high school flame. Riddled with guilt when she got home, she told Carl what had happened.

For both, the affair signaled that the marriage was in trouble but only Fran was willing to seek help. This is when I met her and supported her through a very difficult divorce process. Carl used the affair as grounds for divorce, leaving Fran feeling immense shame as well as betrayal. He managed to leverage a better financial settlement by promising not to tell their adult children about her affair. This left their children bewildered about why their parents were divorcing and, sensing some sort of secret, they were angry at them both.

Eventually, after both parents had found more compatible new partners, their children felt relief and moved on as well. The story of Fran and her new husband's blended family is a remarkable and unanticipated success. We will revisit it in Chapter 8 and feature it in Chapter 11 as a reminder that healing from divorce happens and new family formations may be healthier than the original ones.

Other Types of Dishonesty

Sometimes one partner feels compelled to end a long marriage because of their partner's illegal or dishonorable actions. In Chapter 1 we met Amanda whose housepainter husband's lies and indiscretions finally exceeded her tolerance level. Calls had accumulated from creditors as well as from customers who felt they had been "stiffed." Her husband's explanation for these never added up, and she feared her own good name in their community was being tarnished. Despite a strong religious commitment to stay in a marriage "for better or for worse," she felt she had no choice but to leave.

Barbara and Paul's Story

Barbara and Paul provide a much more affluent example. Both were brilliant, only children and the first in their families to go to college. They met in law school when they were on the law review, fell in love, and went on to successful careers in different prestigious law firms on the West Coast. They enlisted an *au pair* to help in the raising of their two gifted children.

It seemed like they were living out a dream until Paul, a tax attorney, tried to outsmart the IRS. He kept assuring Barbara that everything was on the up-and-up and he was going to win their years-long audit. By that time, they were living in a heavily mortgaged McMansion and their children were off at private colleges.

Barbara was caught totally off guard when she discovered, almost by accident, that Paul had lost his case and declared bankruptcy. Days later, on New Year's Eve, they were evicted from their home. Barbara initially filed for divorce thinking she could protect some of their assets and possibly remarry down the road, but the dream as well as the marriage had been shattered. In Chapter 5 we will see how this totally disrupted the lives of their young adult children.

Sexual Orientation and Gender Identity

The over-50 cohort contains people who may or may not have fully known/embraced their sexual orientation when they married. Coming out as gay, lesbian, or transgender was rare for these generations. Some married thinking they could be happy in a conventional heterosexual relationship. Later, as the world became more accepting of a variety of lifestyles, some were willing to leave long marriages in the hopes of finding greater fulfillment. Sometimes they had the support and understanding of their spouses, sometimes not. When a long-term marriage ends for these reasons, their adult children will face two major challenges: dealing with their parents' divorce as well as adjusting to changes in one parent's gender/sexual orientation.[5,6]

In Chapter 1, we met Martin and Jillian the university professors who appeared to be the "perfect couple" until Jillian fell in love with a woman she met when she was on sabbatical. It turned out that their liberally-raised millennial children handled their mom's emerging sexual orientation more easily than the parental divorce. They claimed to be okay with their mom being lesbian but were furious that their parents divorced, even though neither wanted to remain married.

Other adult children supportive of LGBTQ+ issues may be sympathetic to a parent's decision to divorce when this is the reason. That was true for the grown children of a woman, Darcy, who started to write children's books when her children left home and fell in love with her female editor. Similarly, Luis, a psychologist, fell in love with a male colleague whom his children already knew and considered part of the family. And when another man, George, told his wife he was gay after their youngest child left for the Peace Corps, no one was surprised or upset. Interestingly, the adult children in these three scenarios seemed to have greater compassion for the parent leaving a long marriage to express their sexual orientation than for the parent left behind who felt confused, rejected, and heart-broken—but that is not always the case.

Jody's Story

Jody was in her 50s when she told me about her parents' divorce when she was a freshman in college, now more than 30 years ago. Her father, a Methodist minister, had informed his wife before marriage that he was attracted to men. She married him anyway, looking forward to being a minister's wife and harboring her own secret—an abortion she had as a teen.

They managed to create a close-knit family for many years. However, once their children were out of the home, neither parent wanted to continue living with their sexual incompatibility, and Jody's father wanted to come out as gay. Jody had no inkling that her parents were not happy together so news of the divorce as well as her father's sexual orientation came as a shock.

It was also more shocking 30 years ago than if it were to happen today. For a number of years, Jody's parents' lives were upended. Her mother focused in earnest on her maternal role, seldom dating and totally investing in her grown children's lives.

Her father experienced both shame and liberation. Unfortunately, he also viewed his children as peers. More than once, he showed up at Jody's college dorm and tried to get himself invited to fraternity parties. In later years he wanted to share stories of his failed romantic liaisons with Jody and her brothers.

Neither parent remarried, so Jody and her older siblings have been dealing for more than 30 years with two single parents now well into their 80s and requiring care in separate states. Jody is sad that neither parent ever found a compatible partner. She also wishes she knew a whole lot less about their sexual relationship and activities!

WHEN LATER-LIFE DIVORCE INVOLVES STEPPARENTS

Not all couples who divorce later in life were in first marriages. Some were in second, or even third and beyond, each marriage of varying lengths. How adult children of these couples respond to parental divorce likely depends on both the duration of the marriage and their perceptions of its viability. Surely, children, including adult children, who see a parent couple and uncouple many times are affected by this instability. They may have low expectations about lasting relationships both for that parent and for themselves. Their issues are important and compelling but go beyond our current focus.

However, some second marriages are of sufficiently long duration that the couple's adult children and stepchildren may have many of the same reactions as the children of an original marriage. If the marriage had appeared to be a long-term committed partnership spanning 20 or more years, their adult children will also be shocked, saddened, and angry. In some cases, it is not uncommon for an adult child to have formed as close (or closer) a relationship with a stepmother or stepfather as with their original parent. This is especially true when an original parent had less or little contact while their children were growing up.

Amy's Story

For example, Amy's parents divorced when she was a toddler. Her father moved away, and she saw him very infrequently until he relocated to a nearby state when she was a teenager. She adored her stepfather who had been a reliable and loving presence in her life since she was five. He was the one she always imagined would be walking her down the aisle when she married. Now in her mid-20s, when Amy learned that he and her mother were getting a divorce, she wondered if that would still be possible.

Claire's and Peter's Story

Peter's wife Claire had formed a strong bond with Peter's stepmother Anne around the young couple's fertility struggles. Now Claire was understandably crushed to hear that Anne and Peter's father were divorcing. Claire had just found out she was pregnant and wondered if Anne would ever see the baby. Peter also felt deep sadness as Anne had been a steady and loving figure in his life for 23 years.

Larry and Emily's Story

We briefly considered Larry and Emily's situation in Chapter 1. However, it merits a longer story because it illustrates a range of complexities for both parents and adult children when older re-married couples end long marriages. Some of these complexities occur for original families as well, but some are unique to stepfamilies.

When their marriage ended, Larry and Emily were in Erikson's final life stage and their children were mostly middle-aged with families of their own. Both had been married before and brought young children with them into their relationship, now more than 25 years ago.

Larry, an anesthesiologist, had married when he was in medical school. Twin girls were born soon after. By the time he was done with his residency and the twins were seven, he and his wife felt like roommates and agreed to divorce. Fortunately for their children, they easily agreed on shared custody and remained good friends. They celebrated holidays and birthdays as a family even after they both remarried.

Emily's story was different. Ten years younger than Larry, she separated from her husband when her son Mason was only two months old. She was an attractive up-and-coming star in the hospital's Human Relations Department when she met Larry. Mason was four when they married. Larry adopted him shortly thereafter and was the only father Mason remembers.

It wasn't long before Amelia was born, and Larry and Emily's family grew from "yours" and "mine" to "ours." Mason grew up having a little sister. Larry's twins lived nearby and, until they left for college, often babysat for Mason and Amelia. Friends and relatives considered them the poster child of blended families.

With all four children now adults and several with families of their own, Larry was ready to retire. He and Emily were already planning to take an around-the-world cruise once Emily was ready to stop working. Until then, their Saturday night ritual was to have a cocktail, go to dinner, then end up in their hot tub. He'd thought everything was fine between them when they celebrated their 25th anniversary in Hawaii with their children and seven grandchildren.

Then, one night during their cocktail hour, Emily announced, "I want a divorce." Larry felt his world was falling apart and sought counseling, but Emily wasn't interested. To this day, Larry isn't really sure what went wrong, but Emily started acting strange, spending all her time with her women friends, accusing Larry of infidelity, and purchasing an expensive sports car for herself. Just weeks before their divorce was to be final, Emily's lawyer notified the judge that a psychiatric evaluation had found her incompetent and she was involuntarily committed for serious depression, something her late mother had struggled with.

Despite Larry's obvious concern for Emily's well-being and willingness to take care of her, she wanted nothing to do with him. Her mental health did not greatly improve, but the divorce was eventually finalized. Every day, Larry felt lonely and especially hated eating alone. He filled his spare time with volunteer activities and pickle ball with friends. He didn't think he'd marry again but he hoped to meet someone and find companionship in his retirement years.

Their blended family—adult children as well as grandchildren—also experienced major disruptions. When Emily announced her desire to divorce, Mason abruptly stopped speaking to Larry and didn't allow his children to connect with their grandfather even though they had always been close. When Larry ran into Mason and his family in town, he was devastated when Mason greeted him as "Larry" instead of "Dad."

After we started meeting, Larry cautiously reached out to Mason. He had recently found out that Emily would be discharged to Mason's care following the latest round of ECT treatments. Knowing how stressful this would be for Mason and his young family, Larry offered to help him sort through issues of guardianship as well as residence since Emily was unable to live on her own.

Mason gradually let Larry back into his life. He desperately needed parental support and realized that it was his mom, not Larry, who was responsible for the divorce. Hopefully, this meant one less loss for both Larry and Mason, but Larry was amazed at the way divorce magnifies or recreates fissures in stepfamilies.

For Olivia, one of Larry's twin daughters, and her family, the divorce had its own set of consequences. At first, Olivia's kids were upset and confused that "Mimi and Pops" weren't a unit anymore. Later, they had to grieve that they might never see Grandma Mimi again and they felt like she didn't care about them anymore. They were also worried that Pops seemed so unhappy and cried easily.

Olivia tried to reach out to her stepbrother Mason, but he didn't take her calls in the early months. More recently, they made a plan to get the cousins together for an afternoon. When Olivia made a visit to the hospital, Emily refused to see her. This was hard for Olivia as Emily had been her role model and strong supporter for years. She missed the many ways Emily had been a devoted grandmother to her children.

Amelia, the youngest and single, felt adrift. She had been living successfully on her own for several years half a continent away, and while she never thought of moving back home, she always assumed that home would be there if she needed it. She was in no position to assume her mother's care and was thankful that it looked like Mason would step up. Although she didn't live nearby, she called her father almost daily to check on his well-being. She was often puzzled and irritated that he didn't have more information about her mother. Mason, preoccupied with his over-burdened life, rarely thought to keep her updated.

Despite the unique undercurrent of mental illness running through Larry and Emily's story, it nevertheless demonstrates the multi-generational ramifications of later-life divorce for blended stepfamilies. When a long, seemingly well-functioning second marriage ends, the lives of the couple's young to Middle-Aged Adult Children, as well as their grandchildren, are thrown into disarray in many of the same ways we see with families from an original marriage. In addition, there is an even greater risk of losing highly valued relationships if latent schisms emerge.

In Summary

In this chapter we looked at explanations for ending a long marriage—from general to specific and from benign to traumatic. Some couples experience these same circumstances but do not divorce. Some of them hunker down, tolerate an unhappy situation, and might have been better off divorcing.

Others take action and find their way to resources to improve their marriages. These more fortunate ones see where things are heading before it is too late. They know they want something better, and they seek help. That help can come in the form of couples therapy, pastoral counseling, talking to a wise friend or family member, reading a book, or simply learning to communicate honestly.

If successful, they have spared themselves and their adult children the pain and disruption of a later-life divorce. If not successful, at least they know they tried. Hopefully, along the way they became aware that their decision to divorce would affect both their own and their children's lives and sense of being a family.

For you adult children who have read this chapter about parents, we hope there is a valuable takeaway. Your parents are still your *parents* but they are also *people* hoping for meaning and fulfillment in their lives. If they choose to end an unhappy or unhealthy marriage in the hopes that they might still find love, or joy, or safety in the later stages of their lives, perhaps you will feel greater compassion for them as they arrive at this point. But, as we will see in the next three chapters which consider adult children's needs at different ages, we also hope your parents will feel greater compassion for how their divorce impacts you as you are negotiating your own important life stages.

And, as a repeated reminder, this greater understanding and compassion between the generations needs to occur within appropriate parent-child boundaries. Parents and children can never truly be peers. You will have greater empathy for each other's situation with appropriate boundaries firmly in place.

Chapter Three Notes—*The Parents: Why Are They Divorcing?*

1. Renowned non-fiction writer, Deirdre Bair, divorced after a forty-three-year marriage. She kept hearing stories of other couples divorcing late in life and decided to conduct her own informal survey, mostly by telephone. Bair ended up interviewing more than 300 men and women and compiled their stories into her 2007 book *Calling It Quits: Late-Life Divorce and Starting Over*, 2007, Random House.

2. Gail Collins, *When Everything Changed: The Amazing Journey of American Women from 1960 to Present*, 2009, p. 272, Little, Brown and Company. Collins reports that in 1960 62 percent of households in the U.S. had a bread-winner dad and a stay-at-home mom with one or more children. A mere 25 years later, only ten percent of the families fit this "Ozzie and Harriet" mold. From 1970 to 1976 the number of women with preschool-aged children working outside the home went from less than a third to 43 percent. That number rose to 50 percent in the next decade.

3. Susan L. Brown, co-director of the National Center for Marriage and Family Research, interview with *The Wall Street Journal*, "Bill and Melinda Gates Divorce Highlights Rise of Older-Age Splits," May 5, 2021.

4. For a fuller discussion of the effect of affairs on marital outcomes see Esther Perel, *The State of Affairs: Rethinking Infidelity,* 2018, Harper Paperbacks and Tammy Nelson, *Open Monogamy, A Guide to Co-Creating Your Ideal Relationship Agreement*, 2021, Sounds True.

5. There are now accounts of how gender transitioning impacts a long marriage. Some couples choose to remain married while others may divorce before, during, or after a transition. For example, see Jennifer Finney Boylan, *She's Not There: A Life in Two Genders,* 2003, Crown.

6. In Jane Isay's book *Walking on Eggshells*: *Navigating the Delicate Relationship Between Adult Children and Parents*, 2008, Vintage, she writes with warmth and wisdom about navigating the delicate relationship between adult children and their parents. In the epilogue, Isay shares that ten years prior to her divorce, her husband told her he was gay and found a new partner. The couple made the decision to remain married thinking it was the best thing for their family. With both of their sons out of the house, in the summer of her 50th birthday and 25th anniversary, Jane decided she needed to end the marriage and "try for a fuller

life." Years later, she apologized to her younger son who had been a junior in college at the time of the divorce. His response surprised her. He told her he felt he had lost her, along with the sense of being a family, long before the divorce. Sadly, this couple's decision to remain married in order not to disrupt their children's lives did not have the desired effect. The energy required to keep such an important secret had sucked the vitality out of their family.

PART III

The Adult Children

-4-
The Youngest Adult Children of Divorce: The Launchers

An astronaut is preparing to launch into space. What is the margin for error? Is the launching pad sturdy? What are the weather conditions? Will the takeoff be smooth? A swimmer is preparing to dive into the river. How firm is the surface on which he stands? How deep is the water below? Will the dive be graceful? Excitement mingles with danger, and preparation butts heads with the unknown. Much depends on the steadiness and predictability of the platform from which they both take off.

The youngest adult children—those from eighteen to their very early 20s—experience the greatest disruption in their daily lives when their parents divorce. Barely adults beyond the legal definition, they are the most vulnerable to the negative effects of divorce because they are often still dependent on their parents for many of their basic needs. They are the Launchers, the ones most affected by the firmness of the family platform as they are making their way out into the world.

If they are still living at home, they are likely to be exposed to their parents' deteriorating relationship. In addition to witnessing painful arguments and stand-offs, they may observe one or both parents' acting out behaviors, such as staying away for periods of time without informing their children of their whereabouts. Their distraught parents may be preoccupied and self-absorbed. They may seem less invested in their roles as Mom and Dad. For their young adult children, the family home likely feels confusing, chaotic, and unpredictable—a far cry from a steady launching pad!

Much of the accumulated literature on young children and divorce still fits these late adolescents who are only nominally adults. Without their own residences, they, like younger children including their younger siblings, will be concerned with the fundamentals of where and with whom they are going to live. Where will they sleep? Will there be a place to store their accumulated belongings? Will both parents welcome them in their new households? Will they lose contact with one of their parents? Since they are nearing the age of independence, parents may be unaware of the extent to which these children feel displaced.

While this chapter may be relevant for many late adolescents still living at home, it focuses more on the very young adults who have taken (or are in the process of taking) the first small steps toward leaving home. They are dangling a foot out the door toward post-high school involvements—college, trade school, an entry-level job. All are still working on forming a sense of self or identity, Erikson's Stage 5, and a few may be in the very early phases of forming intimate relationships, Erikson's Stage 6. Developmentally, they are at a stage where they would greatly benefit from having a *moratorium,* that is a safe time and place to experiment before having to fully assume adult roles and responsibilities. Unfortunately, their parents' divorce at this time may cut short that crucial opportunity.

Let us consider the stories of four very young adults who are still early in the process of launching from their families of origin. These illustrate how this experience differs when the parental platform is stable versus coming apart. Two are off to college as freshmen, and two are trying out options of living on their own while in the work force at least part-time.

If you are reading this chapter as a Launcher yourself, see which of these scenarios speaks to you and what you are facing. Or perhaps you are older now but were in this group of youngest adult children when your parents divorced and are just now recognizing the effects their divorce had on your life. Either way, since divorce is a process and not an event, it is important to keep in mind that many of the negative experiences of a vulnerable Launcher can heal over time.

As a parent reading this and the following two chapters, I hope you will come away with increased understanding and compassion for how your divorce has affected/will affect your adult children. Whether Launchers, Emerging Adults, or even Middle-Aged at the time of the divorce, they definitely feel/felt the impact. And that impact was likely most profound for this youngest group, as we will see below.

Ashley's Positive Empty-Nest Scenario

Ashley's parents, who have been happily married for more than 25 years, are delivering her to college. She is their youngest child, and they have done this routine before with her siblings. They help her set up her dorm room, meet her roommates, and take her out for a final meal together before they head home. When they hug goodbye, eyes welling up with tears, they talk about the next time they will see her—parents weekend, Thanksgiving, or sooner. All are aware that Ashley's starting college represents a major change, but they are also reassured that most things at home will remain in place until they are together again.

Mom and Dad will have some adjustments to make when they return home, but these are tempered by the sense that they have begun the process of successfully launching their "baby." Now they will have more time for themselves and each other on a daily basis. They can have dinner together, eating what they want and when they want. They no longer have to factor in Ashley's sports practices, school activities, and latest dietary fads. Hopefully, over the years they made time for each other as partners not solely as parents. If so, they anticipate the empty nest not as strangers but as couple, looking forward to the possibilities of this next stage of their lives.

Meanwhile, back at college, Ashley is making her own adjustments. She is learning to live on her own and making increasingly more important decisions independent of her parents. However, if she experiences rough patches such as running out of money, coming down with mono, having trouble with roommates, or struggling with organic chemistry, she knows she can turn to her parents for support and advice. When she does go home for Thanksgiving, her familiar room awaits her, and everyone is eager to hear about her experiences at college. *She* is the major change agent. Her new life, adventures, and opinions are the focus. Her parents and family serve as a stable backdrop against which her evolving life stands out. This fortunate young adult is diving off a sturdy platform.

Jaden's Shattered Nest Scenario

In stark contrast to Ashley's nearly idyllic scenario is Jaden's story. An athlete and honors student throughout high school, Jaden was accepted into every college he applied to. His parents drove him halfway across the country to his prestigious first choice school. Like Ashley's parents, they helped him unpack and set up his dorm room, said goodbye, and headed to their hotel room as they needed to be off early the next morning.

As soon as they got to their room, Jaden's dad informed his wife that he wanted a divorce. He had purchased an airline ticket for her to return home, and he would be driving somewhere he chose not to disclose.

Jaden's mom was in a state of shock and felt her world had collapsed. After an emotional and sleepless night, she flew back home not knowing much about her husband's whereabouts or future plans.

Jaden's dad had only minimal and surreptitious contact with his son for weeks. His mom did her best to keep the marital disruption secret for some time, but Jaden knew something was wrong. His mother didn't sound like herself and asked surprisingly little about school. Eventually, Jaden's dad told him he had filed for divorce and was seeing a new woman. At first, Jaden was stunned. Then he was furious. Had he totally missed what was going on in his family? Was anything he thought he knew about his parents real?

With the rug yanked out from under him, Jaden could not concentrate at school. He felt extreme bouts of homesickness, fluctuating between wanting to run home to see what was going on and wanting to distance himself from both parents. His mom seemed too needy, and his dad seemed like someone he no longer knew. Conversations with each parent contained negative information about the other—things he didn't want or need to know.

When it was time to make plans for Thanksgiving vacation, Jaden decided to stay at school. He turned down invitations to go home with new friends because he was embarrassed to say what was going on with his own family. His dad had plans with his new girlfriend and her kids. His mom said she wasn't up to cooking this year and there was nothing to celebrate anyway. It sounded like she was preparing to put the family home on the market.

Jaden started to worry not only about where he'd be living in the summer but also about whether there would be enough money for him to stay in school. His grades were uncharacteristically mediocre. Clearly, this second college freshman was standing on a very different, very shaky platform. His highly anticipated launching was not going according to plan.

These two scenarios are almost mirror images of one another. Both involve young college-bound adults from seemingly intact families which implies a certain amount of stability and affluence. But there the stories diverge. Ashley is the one whose life is changing while her family situation generally remains stable and provides a safety net. Just as Jaden is preparing to launch, his safety net is disappearing. He is not sure whether anything he thought was "real" about his family might have just been a sham. When did his parents' marriage begin to unravel? Should he have seen it coming? Should he not have gone so far away to school? Can he trust his own judgment? Thinking about his dad's involvement with a new woman seemed so bizarre that he had no interest in pursuing any romantic relationships at school.

Just as important are the versions of this story for non-college-bound young adults right out of high school:

Mike's Safety Net

Mike was a solid B-/C+ student in high school but hadn't found his calling by the time of graduation. He was seen as a good kid but young for his age. His dad, a welder, encouraged Mike to follow in his footsteps, but Mike wasn't ready to commit. He thought he might want to do something more exciting—like being a fire fighter or an EMT. Extended family and friends gave him enough money for graduation so that he could think about venturing out on his own. Mike decided to take up the offer to live in an apartment the next town over with his cousin and a couple of friends.

He got a job bussing tables at a fast food restaurant and occasionally worked for a local moving company when they needed extra help. His mother gave Mike and his roommates some old dishes and pots and pans for their kitchen as well as odd pieces of furniture she no longer needed. Mike was embarrassed by her putting her imprint on his new "digs" but his roommates were very appreciative. When he went home occasionally to do his laundry and have a home-cooked meal, he was reassured to see that his old room was much the same as when he had left it.

Things were often in a state of flux with his roommates. One left to live with his girlfriend; one partied too much and left the place a mess. Another couldn't keep a job and had to move out leaving the rest to cover his portion of the rent. When the novelty of his foray into independence wore off, Mike started thinking about going to community college to get the credits he might need to be a fire fighter or something else.

His parents were supportive of this exploration just as they had supported his initial move to the apartment. He increased his hours at work and moved home so he could save money for classes in the fall. He had taken a step into the world outside the family home and realized he wasn't quite ready to be on his own. Mike had seen his older siblings come and go for a few years, so this was a familiar and acceptable pattern. He noticed that his parents were going out more and even took off for a weekend now and then. For their part, Mike's parents were noticing his increasing maturity and confidence and were relaxed about leaving him in charge of himself as well as the house.

Talia's Scramble for Survival

Not so fortunate was Talia, although she was eager to leave town right after high school. Mid-way through her senior year, her parents had told her they would be getting a divorce, and her dad would be moving out in the summer. After that, the atmosphere at home fluctuated between tense and barren. Distracted by their own looming changes, her parents no longer asked where she was going or checked on her when she got in at night.

Nor did they ask more than cursory questions about her plans after high school. She wasn't even sure both her parents would attend her graduation, and her two sets of grandparents and aunts and uncles had taken sides about the divorce and weren't speaking to each other. Without structure and supervision, Talia felt lost, discarded, and out of control. Her graduation—her launching into young adulthood—once seen as a highly-anticipated rite of passage, now seemed an afterthought.

She and her best friend, Jenna, made plans to move to the nearby city as soon as school was out. Jenna's parents helped them strategize how to find jobs and a place to live. Following a lead from Jenna's father, they both secured entry level jobs at an ad agency. Although scared and unprepared, Talia was still excited to be getting away from her family. Neither of her parents seemed very interested in her plans, beyond telling her to be careful. They emphasized how expensive it could be to live in the city and that they would not be able to help.

The two young women found a place they could afford and started enjoying the freedom of "big city life." They were meeting many interesting people and learning how to navigate the dating scene although it was often confusing. Jenna seemed to have more confidence both at work and socially, and she talked to her parents several times a week. Talia's parents were often not available when she called and rarely initiated a call. Generally, she was distrustful of the young men she was meeting. However, at other times, she engaged in risky dating behaviors which worried her roommate. All in all, they were doing okay and felt they were learning a lot about the options open to them outside their small hometown.

Then the ad agency hit hard times and had to lay off a third of their work force. Since Talia and Jenna were relatively new hires, they lost their jobs and suddenly life in the city wasn't looking promising. When Jenna decided to move back home with her parents, Talia felt utterly alone. Her childhood home had been sold, and both of her parents had moved to smaller places. She didn't know if there would be room for her to move in or whether she would even be welcome as she'd learned that they had both started dating.

Both Mike and Talia were experiencing the moratorium Erikson felt was crucial for forming a strong core sense of self. Neither knew exactly what they wanted to do with their lives. They were trying out different possibilities, seeing what fit and what didn't before having to make a commitment. For Mike, when things didn't quite work out, he could move back home for a while and leave again when he was ready. Talia lost that option and felt she no longer had a home base. Jenna was afraid Talia would panic and move in with a young man she met recently. Almost like the old game of "musical chairs," absent a safety net when the music stops, you grab hold of your nearest option, thankful to have one.

KEY ISSUES FOR THE LAUNCHERS

These four stories illustrate the key issues the youngest adult children face. As late adolescents to very early 20 year-olds, they are legally "adults" but most are far from being fully independent of their families.

Residence

Without established homes of their own, the most fundamental concern is, "Where will I live?" Parents are not legally required to provide a home once their children are 18 although many are happy to do so for a while longer. But sometimes divorcing parents themselves are struggling with housing issues. They may need to move to a one-bedroom apartment and may no longer have space for a child to live with them. And sometimes one or both parents move in with a new partner, and it is not clear that young adult children would be, or feel, welcome. Even when one parent remains in the family home, the family system will have noticeably changed.

In short, with the family home itself coming apart, there is no guarantee that a late adolescent or young adult child will feel like they have a home base. That was Talia's experience. It is not an exaggeration to say that some Launchers will literally find themselves homeless.

Finances

"Am I on my own financially?" is another big question for Launchers. Once a child turns 18, parents are not legally required to provide financial support. In most states, child support payments end at that time. As with housing, many parents may choose to continue to offer full or partial financial support to their children well past adolescence. But what if they don't? Or can't?

Far from being fully launched, these youngest adult children often experience financial hardships. Even in fairly affluent families, there will likely be less money following divorce. Each parent now incurs separate costs for housing, utilities, etc. So, who, if anyone, will help these youngest adult children cover their cell phone bills, let alone get a car, pay for school, or co-sign on an apartment or loan? And one or both parents may enter relationships with new partners who don't support helping stepchildren with these young adult expenses.

Possessions

While at first glance it may seem trivial, there is also the question of, "Where will I keep my stuff?" These youngest adult children's rooms may still be filled with childhood memorabilia—posters, music, clothes, games, and even stuffed animals. Absent a divorce, parents may be resigned to hold onto these things until their children have their own homes or until they themselves need to downsize. But, if parents divorce when their children are still late adolescents or very young adults, these belongings may forever be lost in the shuffle along with the nostalgia, security, and functionality attached to them. These young adults may be forced to relinquish these symbols of childhood well before they are ready. Or these possessions may simply be discarded without their knowledge.

Family Relationships

The youngest adult children, the Launchers, are closely tied to their parents for more than just residence and financial support. Many still rely on them for advice, guidance, and emotional support. In short, in a great many ways these young people still need to be "parented," but divorce could put this at risk.

Launchers like Ashley, Jaden, Mike, and Talia still benefit from parental input to help them make choices or problem solve when their young adult lives hit inevitable snags. But both Jaden and Talia's parents were too preoccupied with their own challenges to pay attention to their children's lives. At least temporarily, these two Launchers were left to their own devices without so much as a parental sounding board.

Relationships with parents can change drastically following divorce at any age. Research involving adult children indicates that it is the relationship with fathers that suffers most primarily due to less frequent contact, especially if they remarry.[1] Yet, as noted, this youngest group of adult children still benefits from parental contact and support. If children feel pulled to take sides in a divorce, they could end up alienated from one or both parents and the potential emotional and financial support they could provide.

And what happens if one or both parents re-partner or remarry? The younger the parents are when they end a long marriage, the more time they have to find new partners. This especially impacts their youngest adult children since they are the ones still most dependent on and involved with their families of origin. It goes without saying that the effort it takes to date and re-partner can divert significant attention from parenting, especially if parents think their young adult children no longer need this from them.

There is a lot more to say about the youngest adult children's feelings and reactions to their parents dating and re-partnering. They are likely to have intimate exposure to new partners and stepparents who may bring their own children into the family mix. Chapters 9 and 10 address this at length from the viewpoints of both parents and children. There we will see that it is very important how and when a parent chooses to involve their children in meeting new people.

Relationships with extended family members are also affected by divorce. Not infrequently, grandparents may take sides following divorce—sometimes aligning with their own child, sometimes with the in-law depending on the circumstances. The same can happen with aunts, uncles, and cousins. This can force very young adult children to walk a precarious tight rope of family loyalty just at the time they need the grounding of a strong circle of unconditional support and non-judgmental guidance.

Sibling relationships are often overlooked in considering the fallout from divorce at this stage. Even without divorce in the picture, young adults may for a while lose contact with their siblings as they leave home and start lives apart from their families of origin. Often it is the parents who keep the sibling bonds intact. They serve as the information hub keeping brothers and sisters informed on each other's whereabouts and activities during years when siblings may be too busy to stay in touch. Returning to the family home for holidays may be the main way the siblings spend time together and renew their bonds.

All this changes when Mom and Dad no longer share a home. Choices are made, sides may be taken, and extended family rituals may wane. There may no longer be space in either parent's home for everyone to gather. If siblings have taken sides with different parents, their losses may be compounded—losing each other as well as a parent. These disruptions and losses of family relationships will be further explored in Chapter 8, "Lost and Found."

This fallout from divorce can happen for children at any age, but there is a further complication once they have turned 18. Prior to the age of legal adulthood, visitation and holiday arrangements generally support children spending time with both parents, and they may specify contact with maternal and paternal grandparents as well. These arrangements may become more casual as the children move into adolescence. If at any point a child refuses to have contact with a parent, there might be a referral to therapy to attempt to mend the relationship. Furthermore, it is typical for the siblings to move as a group for visitation and holidays.

All this changes when a child turns 18 and there is no formal structure of visitation and holiday arrangements. No one can legally require an adult child to maintain contact with a parent (nor a parent with an adult child). Siblings may be scattered geographically with no one to bring them back into contact. Ruptured relationships between parent and child or between siblings might still be helped by a referral to therapy, but an adult child cannot be forced to go.

Relationships with Peers

Similar disruptions occur for these youngest adults in their peer relationships. It is likely that most of their peers' families are not reeling from divorce at this time, so peers may have little understanding of what their young adult friends are going through. Because their divorce-related challenges are not widely acknowledged, these young adults themselves may not know that intense feelings of anger, confusion, worry, and sadness are normal. Denying them or keeping them inside leaves them feeling different.

Their friends likely don't share their level of concern about living arrangements and finances. This further adds to their sense of being alone and different. As a consequence, these young adults may distance themselves from peers at the very time they could most benefit from the comfort and continuity of long friendships.

And this can be true for romantic relationships as well. With so much on their minds, these young adults may avoid or even break off close romantic ties as too risky or too much work. Others may latch onto a romantic partner to fill a void left by disrupted family relationships at a time when they don't yet know themselves. Some may be attracted to a romantic partner because of the partner's family where they may be welcomed and given the structure and stability lacking in their own family during the upheaval of divorce.

Aborted Moratorium

Will the period of a moratorium be cut short? We recall that Erikson insisted late adolescents need a safe space/time for experimenting with different roles and identities in order to develop a strong, healthy sense of self. For Erikson, this stage coincides with late adolescence, but we know now that for many young people it lasts well into their 20s. Dealing with parental divorce at this point in one's life definitely impacts the safety and security these young people are experiencing. Their freedom to experiment may be drastically curtailed because of reduced family resources, the pull to take care of a distraught parent, or their own emotional upheaval. If these young people find themselves suddenly on their own without a home or financial backing, childhood will end abruptly, likely before a healthy sense of self has fully formed.

Boundaries

Regardless of age, children are loath to hear a barrage of negative accounts of their parents. However, compared to young children, the risk of being exposed to "too much information" increases for late adolescents and young adults. They may be cast into the role of confidante by one or both parents, a risk that we will see only increases for the older adult children we consider in the following two chapters. Still, since 18-year-olds are legally adults, a divorcing parent may quite mistakenly view them as peers. If so, a mistaken parent may reason, *Aren't they old enough to be privy to the 'adult' issues that led to the split?* This is not to say that inappropriate sharing doesn't happen when parents of very young children divorce, but inhibitions may be lifted further when children are seen as adults.

Frequently, what is shared are very unappealing personal accounts or even sexual information, neither of which a child of any age wants or needs to hear. They do not want to hear that Dad was impotent or an inconsiderate sexual partner or that Mom was promiscuous before marriage or frigid since the last child was born. Nor do they want details of a parent's infidelity. These unwelcome details are too often shared simply in the course of "venting." They may also be shared more strategically to gain sympathy and support in a parent's effort to win the child over to their side.

Summing up so far, we see that the youngest adult children, the Launchers, are the most vulnerable to the negative consequences of parental divorce. Launching or barely launched, most are not fully prepared to make it on their own. Since they are legally adults, their parents may not realize that they share many basic concerns with younger children. They still need parental support and guidance. Nevertheless, they may be forced to prematurely take on adult responsibilities and worries. As a result, they may be robbed of their much-needed safe place, or moratorium, long before they have developed a strong sense of identity.

Fortunate Launchers have parents who recognize their vulnerability and limited set of adult skills. These are the parents who, despite their own divorce and life stage challenges, are able to remain in their parental roles and do not mistake these youngest adults as peers. Greatly to the benefit of their children, they maintain a healthy parent-child boundary and continue to function in their roles as Mom and Dad.

That was the case for Kelsey and her mom Meg whose story we will look at in more detail in Chapter 8. There we will see that, like Jaden, Kelsey was a college freshmen when she learned that her parents were going to divorce. Although, like Jaden's mother, Meg did not want the divorce and was struggling to control her own considerable grief, she recognized that she had to be able to function as Kelsey's parent. She quickly reached out for help for herself so she was able to offer the emotional support and reassurance her daughter needed.

Chris's Story: A Longitudinal Perspective

I want to end this chapter with the story of Chris, a woman now in her early 70s. She was 19 when her parents divorced. Her story is valuable because it illustrates a number of the issues and challenges parental divorce poses for young adults in their late teens and very early 20s. It also provides a longitudinal or long-range perspective, underscoring that divorce is a process and not an event.

Since much of this chapter highlights the immediate negative impact of parental divorce on the lives of very young adult children, it is important to see that that can change. With time and a modicum of good fortune, there is reason for optimism. Even Launchers who appear to be floundering when their parents divorce can end up leading healthy and productive lives.

Some of you reading this chapter were Launchers when your parents divorced many years ago. All these years you and nearly everyone else probably thought it shouldn't have had a big impact because you were already an adult. Chris's story points out the benefits and healing that can come years later when you view your younger self from a wiser, more compassionate perspective.

Chris reconstructed this critical period in her young life from a vantage point more than a half-century later. Only when she began sharing her story with me did she begin to connect the dots between her early struggles and her parents' divorce. Until we began to talk, she too, had bought into the myth that parental divorce should be "no big deal" for adult children.

Chris grew up in a medium-sized town in a western state not far from the capital city. Her father worked for the local newspaper and also served in the state legislature. This required that he spend weekdays in the capital and return home to his family on weekends. In the summer between her high school graduation and leaving for college, Chris ran into an acquaintance who, somewhat tauntingly, said she'd seen Chris's dad in the nearby city holding hands with a woman. Chris recalled she "swept this under the rug" although it triggered memories of her parents arguing years earlier about "another woman."

She reassured herself by thinking about her family's Sunday ritual. They would go to church in the morning and spend idyllic afternoons together listening to music, reading, and playing games. Thus, Chris headed off to college feeling loved and valued by both parents and oblivious to any serious problems at home.

When she returned home for Thanksgiving, her one-year younger sister told her there was "bad stuff brewing" (words Chris remembered with a shudder when we talked more than 50 years later). After Thanksgiving dinner, her parents sat the children down and announced that they were separating and her father would be moving to the capital city. Chris had little memory of her reaction to this beyond being glad to get back to school and avoid what could be a scandal in town as her parents were seen as pillars of the community.

When she came home for Christmas, much had changed. Her father had moved in with his new partner and her children. Her mother was distraught and leaning heavily on Chris's younger sister for support, as well as filling her with negative information about their father. Chris chose to distance herself emotionally from them both.

She returned to college, but her heart wasn't in it, and she decided to drop out at the end of her first year. She lived briefly with her father, his new partner, and her children, but she didn't feel she fit into this household. Despite being welcomed by all, the only space available to her was carved out in a corner of the basement. She moved back to her mother's house where the atmosphere was heavy with loss and her mother's grief.

Her solution was to escape to Europe with a friend where they got jobs as hotel maids in between bouts of hitchhiking. By the time the mail from home caught up with her, she learned that her father had married in the fall but neither she nor her sister had been invited to the wedding. And she also learned that her mother was going to sell the family home and marry Chris's high school principal. She recalled screaming, "Oh, my God!" as she disliked this man and couldn't imagine living in his house. As she reconstructed this timeline, Chris now seemed taken aback at how quickly her once stable young world had turned upside down.

When she returned from Europe the next summer, Dan, a high school friend and somewhat of a romantic interest, met her in New York and drove her home across the county before he went back to college. After six weeks of being miserable in her mother's new home, Chris took off again for the Pacific Northwest with another boyfriend but quickly decided Dan was "the love of my life." With no place that felt like home, she moved into Dan's college dorm room!

Chris's and Dan's families knew each other and approved of the relationship if not its timing. Chris was drawn to Dan's solid family—five kids all doing well and parents in a long and loving marriage. They welcomed Chris but were distressed when Dan dropped out of college to marry her and take off to explore South America in a VW bus, something that was not all that unusual in the late 1960s.

Interestingly, Chris and Dan got married at her mother and stepfather's home. Her mother allowed Chris's father to walk her down the aisle so long as his wife did not attend the wedding. Chris didn't challenge her mother's restrictions as she was only 20 years old.

Fast forward through a number of very fortunate decades. Chris and

Dan returned from their South American adventure, graduated from college, and eventually got distinguished advanced degrees which opened doors to two successful professional careers. As students, when they went home for vacations and holidays, Chris was relieved that they stayed with Dan's parents where she always felt she belonged. Eventually, Chris and Dan put down their own roots half a continent away and had a family of their own. Still, they visited their hometown often and maintained healthy relationships with all three sets of parents as well as siblings and stepsiblings.

Both of Chris's parents went on to have happy second marriages of 25 plus years to partners with whom they were more compatible. However, Chris's mother remained hostile to her ex-husband until he died nearly 30 years after their divorce. Chris and her sister couldn't convince her to attend his funeral with them, but she seemed to soften afterwards and began attending events involving Chris's stepmother and her children. Evidence of long-term healing was apparent at Chris's daughter's wedding where these two grandmothers sat together, chatting warmly, as Chris's stepfather, now in a second career as a minister, conducted the service.

I asked Chris what advice she wished someone had given her parents. Looking back, she focused on how much easier it would have been for her and her sister if their parents had "just been able to get along."

Although things improved slowly over time, the early years of Chris and Dan's marriage were fraught with minefields to navigate around holidays and milestone events where the extended family was in attendance. What a relief it was that by the time these milestones arrived for Chris's own children, the grandparent generation had mostly buried their hatchets.

As she told her story, Chris began to recognize, as if for the first time, the significant challenges her parents' divorce had posed when she was just venturing out on her own. She had simply taken it as a given and figured she should be able to handle it. She never gave it any weight since no one else did.

What struck her most as we talked was her abrupt loss of a sense of home. With both parents remarrying quickly and moving into their new spouse's homes, Chris felt pushed out. She felt there was no room for her in either parent's new house. In a visibly "aha moment," she made the connection to her fervent desire over the years to "always have a house large enough for everyone." She remarked that even with her own children grown and settled in their own homes, she and Dan recently bought a "huge house so no one has to stay in a cold basement."

What allowed for Chris's remarkable recovery from a very shaky launching into adulthood? Definitely a lot of good luck! But Chris was also a very bright, adventurous, resilient young woman. By escaping to school and then to Europe, Chris managed to maintain her boundaries and avoid being drawn into the marital drama. And despite her parents' inability to build a civil relationship after their divorce, Chris had a strong sense of being loved and valued by both of them. Both parents said she could stay with them even though she was not comfortable with their new living arrangements.

That solid foundation of feeling loved plus Chris's own very positive attributes left her more resilient than many less fortunate young people weathering divorce at this stage. It also influenced her choice of a healthy partner from a sturdy, loving family. Dan's family became an important source of support and a reliable (if intermittent) home base, allowing for the return to a moratorium as well as a place from which to launch successfully.

Resources were never a serious issue for Chris. While neither of her parents provided a home where she felt comfortable, they did at least offer a place to land when it was needed. They were able to provide financial support, and their new spouses did not stand in the way. Chris also was fortunate to maintain a close tie to her biological sibling since any early sides taken did not create lasting rifts. Welcomed into her stepmother's family from the beginning, she eventually became close to her and to her children. Indeed, today she is as close to them as to her biological sibling. So, instead of *losses* of relationships, over time, Chris actually *gained* important ones.

This again reminds us that divorce is a process and not just an event. Early on, we might have feared that Chris was destined for a "belly flop" launching. In fact, her outcome was far from that. In part this resulted from the availability of resources (both internal and external) at critical points. In addition, the passage of time itself can contribute to healing as it did for Chris's parents and for Chris herself. And, as we saw here, sometimes it takes *a lot* of time!

Chris did not have the benefit of having her struggles, as well as her grief, validated at the time. No one seemed to be aware of what she was going through, and she dismissed it as well. Still, revisiting her story half a century later in a compassionate context brought some healing.

After sharing her story with me, Chris decided to contact her siblings (biological and step) with questions and memories about the early divorce years. To her surprise, they were eager to talk about their own experiences and feelings, some of which they had never before voiced. This quite belated sharing provided not only validation and new insights, but also a deeper sense of connection among them.

That long-in-coming healing could happen for you too. If for you, like Chris, your parents' divorce happened many years ago when you were a very young adult, it is not too late to recognize and have compassion for what you went through when you were younger. Better yet, if you are a Launcher reading this today, don't keep your experience and feelings to yourself. Reach out for the support you deserve and start the healing process now!

Chapter Four Note—*The Youngest Adult Children of Divorce: The Launchers*

1. I-Fen Lin, Susan L. Brown, Kagan A. Mellencamp, 2021, "The Roles of Gray Divorce and Subsequent Repartnering for Parent-Adult Child Relationships," *Journals of Gerontology Series B Psychological Sciences and Social Sciences.* This article summarizes the authors' own research findings as well as those of Amato and Aquilino, showing that later-life parental divorce has a more negative effect on fathers' relationships with their adult children than for mothers' relationships. This shows up as a reduction in contact which further increases if fathers re-partner or remarry.

Taking Off from Base Camp:
Emerging Adults in Their 20s & 30s

Ready to strike out on their own adventure, whether heading off on a risky expedition or merely testing new waters closer to home, the explorers may feel excitement as well as trepidation. However, consciously or unconsciously, they are comforted by knowing that base camp will be there if and when they need to return. What happens, then, when news catches up with them that their base camp has been dismantled?

The transition from adolescence to adulthood was once short and sweet. It was also clearly demarcated and scripted. Around the time Erikson was writing, most male high school graduates took off for college, for training in skilled trades, or for the military. Female graduates might do these things, too, or they might see marriage as their more immediate goal. By their mid-twenties, it was expected they would all be married, starting families, and buying houses.

But, as we noted in Chapter 2, there is now considerable fluidity in early adulthood. Young people are generally taking longer to fully launch out of the parental home. With the lifting of many traditional expectations, they have considerably more options regarding careers and relationships and are arriving more gradually at full adulthood. They are completing school later, gaining full-time employment later, and marrying and starting families later, if at all. More and more it seems wiser to view the transition from adolescence to adulthood as a *continuum* rather than a set of discrete steps.

Faced with many more options, the process of becoming an adult has become more gradual. Full-time college students on residential campuses are largely insulated from the "real world" and relatively unencumbered by adult responsibilities and roles. For a number of years, they may have the kind of moratorium Erikson said young adults thrive in. They can experiment with a series of academic majors and romantic relationships. Nonstudents, although less insulated, are busy trying out different work situations as well as varied relationship commitments. All are living in a life stage between adolescence and adulthood which has been called *emerging adulthood* by Jeffrey Arnett and others.[1]

The Emerging Adult Children considered in this chapter have taken some concrete steps toward establishing lives apart from their families of origin. As such, they are further along the continuum than the Launchers in Chapter Four. However, they are less secure in their adult roles than the oldest adult children we will consider in Chapter Six.

In a variety of ways—a small apartment, grad school, a steady job, a dog or a cat, a regular friendship network, a romantic partner—most young adults from their mid-20s into their early to mid-30s are progressing toward establishing some semblance of a life and "home" apart from their parents. Unless something interrupts like job loss, health changes, or a crisis such as a pandemic, they are not likely to return home to live with Mom and Dad. They are probably out on their own if and when they get word that their parents are divorcing.

As with Chapter 4, if you are an Emerging Adult reading this chapter, you will likely identify with many of the issues and examples that follow. Hopefully, they will reinforce and validate that your experience, however painful, is normal when your parents' divorce at this important time in your life. Hopefully, you will come away with greater compassion for yourself and all that you have been going through.

If you are a divorcing or divorced parent reading this chapter, I hope that you, too, will come away with compassion for how divorce affects your Emerging Adult Children. This is a critical time in establishing their lives just as your marriage, an important component of their foundation, is coming apart. On top of all you are already dealing with regarding your divorce, I still hope you will find a way to keep in mind the needs of your children as they are emerging into full adulthood.

WHY DOES PARENTAL DIVORCE PROFOUNDLY IMPACT EMERGING ADULT CHILDREN?

Two lenses provide a compelling view into how later-life divorce affects Emerging Adult Children. Both perspectives—"developmental stage" and "milestones"—converge to demonstrate why this group is uniquely impacted by their parents' divorce. Viewed together, it becomes clear that it is a serious mistake to ignore or trivialize the extent to which the lives of Emerging Adults are altered when their parents divorce.

Developmental Stage Perspective

Emerging from adolescence into adulthood brings unique vulnerabilities. Many can be explained by the developmental life stages Emerging Adults are in. Because it now takes longer to achieve full adulthood, these young people are still in the throes of figuring out who they are and what adult roles they will play (Erikson's Stage 5, Identity), and they are preoccupied with forming and solidifying intimate relationships (Erikson's Stage 6, Intimacy).

In the more than fifty years since Erikson's book, the age ranges have expanded for these developmental stages. Not only is the transition to adulthood more fluid and takes longer, life paths themselves now follow less rigid gender-stereotyped roles. Although further along on the path to full adulthood than the Launchers, Emerging Adults still greatly benefit from having a moratorium which provides the energy and focus to explore and make major life decisions. With "time out" before fully assuming adult roles, they can concentrate on finding paths that best fit their strengths and interests.

This process could be seriously undermined when Emerging Adult Children hear that their parents are divorcing. Their moratorium could disappear overnight when they are forced to deal with the upheaval of parental divorce on top of the challenges of identity and intimacy. They may find themselves exhausted from worrying about losing parental support—emotional and financial. They may feel they need to put their own lives on hold to take care of a troubled parent. It is very difficult for adult children of divorce to move forward when their foundations are shaking. And yet moving forward and making life-altering decisions are precisely the developmental tasks facing Emerging Adults.

Milestones and Events

When we shift the focus from the vulnerabilities inherent in the developmental challenges facing Emerging Adults, we see that there is also a more concrete explanation for why parental divorce uniquely affects this age group. They are the ones experiencing a host of significant milestones in their lives, many of which traditionally involve the participation of parents and families. These events include important rites of passage into adulthood such as graduations, marriages, and births.

What happens when Emerging Adults are approaching or experiencing these events at the same time that their parents are divorcing or have recently divorced? If they are following paths similar to those chosen by their parents, are they now questioning them? Are their parents in a position (emotionally and financially) to make a positive contribution to these important events? Does acrimony from the divorce, be it overt or subtle, hover like a dark cloud over these supposedly celebratory occasions? Have stepparents entered the picture?

In short, will the Emerging Adults who are reaching these milestones be on center stage? If their parents' divorce was particularly contentious, there may still be palpable animosity and rifts throughout the extended families. Will a supposedly happy occasion be overcast with anxiety and apprehension? Instead of the graduate, the bride and groom, or the newborn grandchild being the center of attention, it could, unfortunately, be the warring exes.

The extent to which later-life divorce can significantly impact these milestone events definitely merits further consideration. We will return to these important occasions later in this chapter and illustrate them with stories. But first, we need to note the ways that Emerging Adults share many fundamental concerns with the youngest cohort of adult children of divorce.

ISSUES IN COMMON WITH THE YOUNGEST ADULT CHILDREN

Despite being further along on the developmental continuum, Emerging Adult Children still share some concerns with their younger counterparts. However, since they are a little older and closer to full adulthood, these concerns take on a somewhat different twist. Here we will look at the impact of divorce on a number of major issues facing this age group, illustrating them with some examples from my clinical practice.

Home

For this middle group, the Emerging Adults, the parental home has become/is becoming more of base camp than a primary residence. Yet when their parents divorce, their sense of home, whether or not it is completely dismantled, is likely to change forever. If the house is sold, if both parents move out of the family condo or apartment, the physical presence of home is gone as well as whatever comfort and security it may have represented. There is no more returning home for the summer or the holidays. Instead, it will be going to Mom's or Dad's new place, provided they have the space and the inclination to be a gathering spot for their adult children.

Even if one parent *remains in* the home, the sense of the "family home" has changed. The parent who has left took his or her personal belongings to a new place. Familiar pieces of furniture may be gone as well, and remaining furnishings will be in different arrangements. The absent parent's place at the table will be unoccupied or may be taken by a guest or newcomer.

Many of the students in Barbara Cain's college sample, discussed in Chapter 1, experienced a profound sense of loss of home when learning of their parents' divorce. Some felt abruptly thrust into adulthood, pushed out on their own, and even abandoned. This was true even though they had been away at school for several years and did not see their parents' home as their primary residence.

From my own clinical practice, Molly was in the middle of college when her parents separated. In her words:

> "I didn't have anywhere to go home to. My mother was still in the house but, when I went back, she was a shell of her former self. I hated going to that old house. It used to have a feeling of comfort but now it was the antithesis. It had disappeared. Everything I knew was gone. The nest wasn't there."

It is surprising how deeply felt this sense of displacement can be for

Emerging Adult Children who have been living on their own for a while and even have their own home address. Twenty-four year old Luke had just gotten a master's degree in public policy and would be heading off to law school in two months when his mother called to say she and his father were separating. He'd never even seen them argue. Now, looking back, he realized that it was unusual that they'd come to his recent graduation on separate flights although, once there, things had seemed all right. What else had he missed that weekend? What had he missed for 24 years! Luke told me that after he hung up the phone he shook uncontrollably for an hour. In his words:

"All I can remember is feeling totally out of control…powerless. Like the floor had collapsed out from under me. I hadn't lived in my parents' house for years and really didn't even think of it as "home" anymore. Now I was about to move even further away from them to begin a whole new chapter of my life, but I felt somehow like I'd just become a homeless person. That's crazy, I know, but I guess in the back of my mind I always thought that if something happened I could move back home."

Luke was only minimally reassured when his father called a few hours later, all business, offering to help with his upcoming move. All this very promising young adult could think about was that his default option no longer existed. Not the best frame of mind to be in as he took his next steps toward a challenging career!

Finances

Many Emerging Adult Children still depend on their parents for help in meeting at least some of their financial obligations. This is especially true if parents are currently involved in paying for college or training programs or helping with student loans. Whether in school or just getting started in a first job, they may still be on a family cell phone plan. Their parents may be helping with car payments or co-signing on rental contracts. In a myriad of ways, Emerging Adults are often not yet financially viable on their own when they learn that their parents are divorcing.

They have good reason to worry about whether their parents can or will continue to offer financial support. As their parents divide assets and establish separate residences, their own financial viability is a primary concern. Often at least one parent experiences a drop in their standard of living. A parent who had not previously been in the labor force may need to get a job.

Understandably, many parents are unable to be as generous with their children as they had previously been. They may ask their children to take over their own cell phone expenses and car insurance. They may ask them to get their own health care coverage. They may not be able to fly them home for the holidays or even help with gas money to make the trip.

Matthew's Story

Matthew's story illustrates how parental divorce can affect Emerging Adults both financially as well as residentially. When Matthew (the older son of once affluent attorneys Barbara and Paul in Chapter 3) left California for college at an Ivy League school, he never expected to live at home again. He loved school, made close friends easily, and spent his first two college summers working on Cape Cod. He was excelling as a junior at Yale when the bottom fell out of what he'd believed was his "perfect" family. The IRS caught up with his father's tax evasion schemes and their once affluent family literally became bankrupt almost overnight.

Financial strain, deception, and public humiliation irreparably damaged his parents' marriage. Worried about both of his parents, and lacking the money to pay the next semester's tuition, Matthew landed back home mid-year, now in the tiny house his mother was able to rent on a month-to-month basis. He scrambled to find odd jobs and hoped to accumulate enough money to return to school, but this did not look likely. His younger brother, a college freshman at an only slightly less expensive school, had his tuition already paid for the year. He would be moving home in the summer, facing a similar future, and even tighter living quarters for them all.

The financial impact of parental divorce on Emerging Adult Children is not always as extreme as it was for Matthew, but it is a common concern for college students. And it is a major concern for many non-student adult children who are not yet steadily or fully employed. Even for those who have entered careers or jobs with benefits, many are still hoping their parents can help them buy a car, co-sign on a loan, kick in on wedding expenses, or make a down payment on a starter home. Parents once willing to help with these expenses may no longer be able to do so.

Since Emerging Adults may be experiencing financial insecurity, a parent might try to use money to leverage a favorable relationship with them. For example, the father of my client Jamie was better off financially than his mother after their divorce. He offered to pay for Jamie to come home for Christmas but then expected Jamie to spend the majority of the holiday with him rather than with Jamie's mother who lived in the same town. This put a strain on Jamie as he tried to navigate between two households.

The father of another emerging adult, Jessica, was even less subtle in the strings he attached to financial support. When she initially balked about meeting his new partner, he reminded her that he had paid for her college. In return, he expected her to be supportive of his new relationship.

Changing Relationships with Parents

Divorce affects Emerging Adults' relationships with their parents in a variety of ways beyond financial. Some of these overlap changes noted for the Launchers, but they can play out differently with older adult children. The changes described below are primarily experienced as negative by adult children of divorce. They are highlighted here to alert both parents and children to unfortunate situations to avoid if possible or to remedy if necessary.

Of course, taking a longer time perspective, divorce can also produce positive changes in the relationship between adult children and their parents. Parents leaving an unhappy or abusive marriage may be better able to play a positive role in their adult children's lives. We will focus on these potential benefits in later chapters, but here we will focus on the immediate challenges which divorce may create.

Closeness to Mothers vs. Fathers

Studies have found that adult children tend to be closer to their mothers following a later-life divorce. They spend more time with them and feel more emotionally connected to them. Their relationships with fathers suffer more and become more distant. This is especially true if and when their fathers remarry.[2]

Interestingly, studies also show that fathers contribute more financially than mothers to their young adult children. This may be an effort to gain favor (as we saw with Jamie and Jessica) and/or it may be because they tend to be better off financially. This is somewhat surprising since fathers tend to resent paying child support for minor children and, once their children are adults, they are not required to contribute. However, with adult children, the money now goes directly to the child and not to the ex-spouse.

Boundaries

Another way that parent-child relationships can change during and following divorce involves boundaries, an issue sufficiently important to merit its own chapter (Chapter 7). The older the adult children are, the more likely their parents will mistakenly see them as peers. No surprise then that Emerging Adult Children mention boundary violations as one of the most negative ways their relationships with parents change during the divorce process. Boundary violations likely occur more for them than for the youngest adult children and perhaps less than for the oldest, but whenever they occur they are problematic.

Overwrought divorcing parents may share inappropriate information and seek out inappropriate relationships with their Emerging Adult Children. For example, Molly remembers that her mother showed up at her small apartment within hours of her decision to separate from Molly's dad.

"I was freaked out when she started banging on my door and I knew all my neighbors heard her. I had no choice but to let her in. She was sobbing and wanted me to hold her for support. She was always an 'over-sharer who kept no secrets' but this was worse. Now I heard things about my parents' relationship that were none of my business. Here she was venting about my dad with no concern for my feelings. I just stuffed them down inside because I had to be the Mom."

Similarly, Amy struggled to set limits with her mother. She was sick of her mother talking badly about her father but couldn't get her to stop.

"When I ask her to stop because it hurts me, she tells me I'm the only one of her children she feels she can talk to. I want her to be able to talk to me, but I need her to understand that the split hurt me and my brothers just as much as it hurt her and Dad."

Another emerging adult, Kevin, had always had a close relationship with his father and was fearful of losing it once his parents separated. He knew his mother had asked his father to leave because of his problems with alcohol, so when his father wanted them to hang out as "drinking buddies," he was highly ambivalent. He told me sadly:

"I took what I could get. It was always about him. But this was the only way he wanted to get together so I didn't think I had a choice. He confided in me about their marriage like I was one of his friends. I cringed inside but acted like I was listening."

Similarly, when Claudia's mother started dating, she pushed to double-date with Claudia and her fiancée. Unlike Kevin, Claudia was able to resist. She shored up her boundaries and told her: "You're my mother, not my girlfriend!"

If infidelity is part of the reason to divorce, learning about it can be very painful for adult children. This is especially true when there is also inappropriate sharing. When a parent discovers a spouse's affair, they likely feel wronged and betrayed. They may want to tell their children not only to explain why their marriage is in trouble but also to shame the unfaithful parent and gain support for themselves as the injured party. It may be necessary to share the *fact* of an affair but even Emerging Adult Children do not need to know *details*. (We will revisit infidelity in Chapter 7 when we discuss establishing and maintaining appropriate parent-child boundaries.)

Changes in Parents' Behavior and Appearance

Often adult children are struck by their parents behaving and dressing very differently following later-life divorce. Sometimes this involves seeing once sturdy parents become depressed and even suicidal. Naturally, this weighs heavily on their adult children. Briana was heading off to a new job 500 miles from home when her parents separated. The fresh start she was looking forward to was suddenly encumbered with worry.

"My parents were now so depressed that they were both threatening suicide. My mom was partying nightly and getting drunk a lot. I lived in fear of getting a phone call that she'd killed herself. I worried all the time and couldn't concentrate at work."

Other young adult children focus on behavior changes which stood in stark contrast with how a parent was previously viewed. Angie felt her mother seemed like "a different person" since the divorce: "She's changed so much that I can hardly stand to be around her … a new condo, a new boyfriend, a new boob job."

Tyler described his father as "acting like a rotten teenager"—dressing in styles too young for his age and driving too fast. Norah summed this up when she said she saw her parents engaging in a variety of new and unappealing behaviors. She reluctantly described this as seeing them "changing from hero to human."

These brief observations of changes in their parents' behavior reveal adult children's discomfort in seeing their parents operating outside of their familiar roles as Mom and Dad. And parents may feel less pulled to stay in those parental roles when they view their children as adults. Whether their children are worried, disappointed, or disgusted, they are also conveying that they feel their parents are less available to them as positive role models and sources of support.

Diminished Level of Emotional Support and Interest

This parental unavailability is another common theme Emerging Adults report. They may be watching a once very caring parent become less interested in their children's lives and less prone to offer them emotional support. This may happen when a parent is overwhelmed by depression or preoccupied by the divorce process itself. It may also happen when Mom or Dad appears to suddenly change their priorities. They may take up a whole new hobby or cause, start a relationship with someone very different from their former partner, or abruptly move away.

No matter the explanation, the parental support still wanted and needed by Emerging Adult Children appears to be unavailable at a time when it is sorely needed. They are upset if their parents rarely call and generally seem disinterested in their lives. This is quite the opposite of the complaints of other Emerging Adults whose parents are leaning on them too heavily and taking up too much of their time. Neither group of adult children feels their parents show concern for how the divorce is impacting *them*.

Unabashedly, many Emerging Adults I talked to focused on still needing their parents to function in their lives *as parents* throughout the divorce process. Many emphasized their continued need for support.

Speaking emotionally for himself and his younger sister, Kevin said, "We needed them." Another young man put it this way: "Being 30 doesn't make me any less my parents' child." And, leaving herself quite vulnerable, Angie, 26, said, "I'm embarrassed to say it, but sometimes I just need my 'Mommy'—but she's not there anymore."

Increased Responsibility for Parents

Not only do Emerging Adults experience less parental support at a time when the divorce itself may create a greater need for it, many also experience an increased level of responsibility for one or both parents. Generally, younger children are not expected to take on the burden of a troubled or impaired parent, but adult children may find themselves in just that position. Mom or Dad can literally divorce themselves from a mentally ill, physically disabled, or addicted spouse. Their adult children may not be able to do so. Generally speaking, it is far easier to have an "ex-spouse" than an "ex-parent."

Sometimes this burden lands on the oldest sibling. Sometimes on the one still living at home or the one in closest geographic proximity. Sometimes it is determined by the closeness of the parent-child relationship or the roles a particular child has previously assumed in the family. In any event, once an Emerging Adult Child assumes this caretaker role, his or her own life may go on a back burner.

This was the case for Maggie whom I met at a restaurant where my husband and I frequently go for dinner. We recognized her as new on the wait staff, and we learned she had only recently moved to town. When I asked if she were here to attend one of the local colleges, she became very serious and shared that she had moved here to take care of her father following her parents' divorce. Her mother had moved out and left her father living on his own with rapidly deteriorating health.

Her older siblings turned their backs on him, she said, because they were busy with their own lives and she felt she had no choice but to move to town to take care of him. I'll never forget her response when I commented that sometimes your parents' divorce can still really change your life even as a young adult. Shaking her head and fighting back tears, Maggie (much like Brian in Chapter 1) said, "I don't have a life."

Parents' Dating and Re-Partnering

Parents' dating and re-partnering, a common experience for Emerging Adults as well as for Launchers, is often fraught with emotion. Since this will be addressed at length in Chapter 9, we will only touch on it briefly here. Suffice it to say that many adult children's reactions are similar to those of young children. They don't want to meet a string of potential partners their parents are not serious about. Once their parents do introduce a serious partner, they are more comfortable witnessing displays of affection than of passion. They definitely do not want to know intimate details of their parent's romantic activities like one of my clients who cringed when her mother said things with her new partner were "electric in the bedroom."

In summary, Emerging Adults are less dependent on their parents for basic needs than are Launchers. They are further along the continuum to full adulthood and less likely to need their parents to be in the role of caretaker. Nevertheless, they still want and need their parents to function in their lives as parents. They do not want their parents to violate the parent-child boundary, view them as peers, and share inappropriate information about the divorce. In fact, the caretaker roles could be reversed if these adult children feel called into service to take care of a distraught parent. Short of that, they may still not get the parental support they could use for their own struggles when their parents are preoccupied with their divorce-related challenges or invested in dating and re-partnering.

Changing Relationships with Other Family Members

Parental divorce also affects Emerging Adults' relationships with extended family members. Ideally, these important relatives might provide the understanding, emotional support, and validation which their parents, in the throes of divorce, might not be able to give them. This could add stability to the launching platform or base camp in the form of wisdom, perspective, and compassion. While this sort of support could come from older family friends, teachers, or religious leaders, it is especially powerful coming from people in the family's inner circle.

Unfortunately, it is possible that extended family members may themselves be caught up in the acrimony of the divorce. If they have taken sides, adult children will be walking a narrow line in terms of family loyalty. They could end up estranged from one or even both parents' relatives.

A dramatic example of this, but with a happy ending, is the heartwarming story of Brad Ryan and his 92-year-old grandmother Joy which was picked up by the national news media. Their once idyllic grandson-grandmother relationship was fractured when Brad's parents' divorced while he was in college. For 10 years, family rifts kept them from speaking, but they reconnected at his sister's wedding. Since then, Brad and Joy have been featured in the news, visiting all the U.S. National Parks together, reportedly resulting in greatly improved mental health for them both.[3]

Changing Relationships with Siblings

As with all family relationships, there is no one-size-fits-all for how parental divorce impacts sibling relationships. Some Emerging Adults who are only children rue the fact that they do not have a sibling to turn to for support and commiseration, especially during the early weeks and months when the family they knew is coming apart. They talk about having no one with whom to share childhood memories (both good and bad) and no one to validate what is going on now. Even harder, there is no brother or sister with whom to problem solve how to manage a difficult parent, much less to share the burden of any caretaking responsibilities that might need to be assumed. Lonely, indeed, can be the plight of Emerging Adults who have no siblings.

Sometimes parental divorce brings siblings closer at a time when they had been moving out into the world and away from their families of origin. Who else but a brother or sister shares so many of your childhood memories? Who better to check in with to see what you missed if the divorce comes as a surprise? You can comfort and support each other as you grieve the loss of the family you once knew, or you can join in a collective sigh of relief that one of your parents has safely left an abusive marriage. Ideally, you can share information about, and responsibility for, your parents' well-being.

But, having siblings does not guarantee support or shared responsibility. Emerging Adults can feel the pressure to step in reluctantly to fill a void no one else was addressing. As a result, they may feel that they have sacrificed "having a life." Siblings who escape responsibility and are freer to go on with their own schooling, careers, and/or relationships could experience survivor guilt. They may be grateful that their lives are less affected but feel remorse that this came at the expense of their sibling's well-being.

And sometimes the responsibility one sibling takes on is not for a parent but for younger siblings. In the extreme, this takes the form of assuming the role of surrogate parent when both parents have, temporarily or permanently, abdicated that responsibility. This, too, is a life-changing choice. It forces the now "parental child" into adulthood and pseudo-parenthood overnight.

Or an emerging adult may feel pulled in as a co-parent. This happened for one young man I met who stepped in when needed to help his mother manage his younger siblings when they were acting out in response to the divorce. His mother was very appreciative and, true to the myth that divorce is "no big deal" for adult children, she never thought to ask this adult son if the divorce was hard on him too.

Furthermore, siblings can respond quite differently to their parents' divorce. One may get caught up in the drama while the other takes a laissez-faire stance. They might accuse one another of over- or under-reacting, i.e., of taking on too much or refusing to step in to help. Siblings may align with different parents along gender lines or along father-daughter and mother-son loyalty lines. Their resulting estrangements could mirror those of their parents.

This can extract a heavy toll on the bond between brothers and sisters and threaten to create another divorce-related loss. As with the youngest adult children in Chapter 4, this comes at a precarious time. Young and Emerging Adults are in the process of distancing from their families of origin anyway. Parental divorce can exacerbate the growing separation between siblings as they head out in different directions in pursuit of careers and relationships.

Often young adults are relying on their parents to be an information hub, keeping them up to date on their siblings' lives and pulling them back together for holidays at the family home. When their parents divorce at this time, young adults may lose that hub. They may not be ready or able to take it on among themselves. Since there are no longer legal arrangements for adult siblings to move together between parental homes for holidays, things can become chaotic.

That happened in Anna's family. She grew up the only girl with younger twin brothers. When her newly-divorced parents abdicated responsibility for holiday arrangements, Anna assumed the role of event planner. She was determined that the three siblings, now all college students, be together through the Christmas break as they always had been. Little did she know what a minefield she would be navigating.

Her parents were still tightly bound together by lingering divorce anger and refused to speak to each other. Both were adamant that they should have exactly equal time with their children *and* that they should have them on Christmas Day. Anna spent countless hours when she should have been studying for finals mediating between her parents trying to reach a compromise which, it seemed to her, satisfied no one. Neither parent acknowledged the stress they were causing Anna or its potential effect on her academic performance.

Changing Relationships with Romantic Partners

Many Emerging Adults are exploring and choosing not just careers but also long-term partners. While many are taking their time getting married or making the choice to remain single, they are likely to be in and out of a series of romantic relationships during these years. This can be a formidable task since, as we saw in Chapter 3, people are now expecting a lot from committed relationships. They're not only looking for love and romance but also for partners who help them foster personal growth and self-expression.

Whether or not they saw their parents' marriage as a positive model to aspire to or as a negative model to avoid, news of their divorce likely causes Emerging Adults to pause and reflect. Those who were under the impression that their parents had an ideal, positive, or least a good-enough marriage may now be riddled with doubts about their own judgment. One young man who had seen his friends' parents divorce when he was in middle school thought that would never happen in his family. He speaks for those who are shocked when it does: "It's as if your whole world has tilted on its axis."

When Jen's parents divorced after 26 years, she found herself jaundiced about relationships. She had not seen it coming and it undermined her sense that anything can last.

> "So, now it's just me and my mom. I don't have a special someone in my life and I don't know if I'll ever be able to let someone all the way in. They might like you today, tomorrow, and even 20 years from now, but one day they may wake up and not want you like my dad did to my mom and my family."

In a similar tone, one of Barbara Cain's college students was a disenchanted young man whose ideas about love and marriage changed drastically when he learned of his parents' divorce.[4]

> "Since their divorce, I'm gun-shy about love and spastic about marriage. To me, getting married is like walking over a minefield. You know it's going to explode…you just don't know when."

Lynette's Story

My client Lynette was wary of relationships. She was briefly married in her 20s, which coincided with the time her parents were separating, getting back together, and eventually divorcing after her father had an affair. Lynette was riddled with jealousy and suspicion that her new husband was also unfaithful. Ironically, the two couples divorced in the same year.

When I met her in her late 30s, Lynette was ready to look at her inability to trust people as friends or romantic partners. She identified a pattern of constantly seeking stability in relationships but often committing to unreliable partners. Very soon she found herself waiting for the other shoe to drop which drove away partners that might actually have been appropriate.

Lynette was surprised when I urged her to back up and talk about her parents' divorce before focusing on her own failed relationships. As she began to talk at length for the first time about their divorce, she doubled over, sobbing. She had told herself she shouldn't have been much affected by this event at her age (that is, as an adult who was already married at the time). Now that she gave herself permission to feel its impact, she began to make many connections with her young adult struggles including her problems with trust. She was starting down the path to healing at last.

Like Lynette, it is not unusual for Emerging Adults already in committed relationships to begin to second guess them. They become hyper-alert to a partner's flaws or to possible signs of irreconcilable differences or infidelity. For others, intense grieving over their parents' divorce may cause them to pull away or make enormous demands for support from a partner who is unable to meet their needs. Still others may press their partners for commitments at a pace faster than the relationship was heading. All of these grieving adult children are likely unaware that their reactions are normal and valid in response to their parents' divorce. They may keep their feelings to themselves, isolate, or appear detached or depressed.

A romantic partner whose parents are still married likely can't imagine what their grieving loved one is going though. They may take their behavioral changes personally. One distraught young woman I met reached out to an online support group for adult children of divorce asking for advice and hoping to get sympathy: "My boyfriend of three years just found out his parents are divorcing after 30 years. He's completely shut down emotionally and has no desire to be romantic or intimate."

Several adult children on this online site responded with sympathy—not for her but for the boyfriend, saying that they, too, needed to put their relationships on hold while they dealt with the divorce fallout. One said he had put his own wedding plans on a back burner and told this young woman to be prepared for this to happen.

Not all adult children become jaundiced about marriage and relationships after their parents' divorce. For example, Henry's persistent positive attitude shows quite a different reaction. His parents' marriage ended when his father, after years of sobriety, relapsed and was unable this time to find his way back to treatment and recovery. Since this occurred when Henry was out of college and enrolled in dental school, he had not witnessed the deterioration of his parents' marriage. He was determined to hold onto his childhood memories of two people very much in love:

> "I saw a great marriage my whole childhood. Mine were the only parents who walked over to our soccer games holding hands. They were the perfect model of a loving relationship. I want what they had. The way their marriage ended doesn't erase those good memories. They were ripped apart by alcoholism but they always loved each other."

At the time he said this, Henry was still in denial over any sad feelings about the divorce. When he did get in touch with his feelings and allowed himself to grieve, he also got in touch with the fact that he tended to use alcohol to "numb out." Henry was determined that his marriage would have a happier ending than his parents'. After an honest conversation with his wife, they decided that theirs would be an alcohol-free home.

Changing Relationships with Friends

If family members and romantic partners underestimate, discount, or overlook the impact of parental divorce on Emerging Adults, then it is no surprise that their friends may do so as well. Perhaps the most likely reason for this is that Emerging Adult Children dealing with their parents' divorce may share very little about it. If they have gotten the message that because they are adults they should be able to handle this, they will try to take it in stride. Unfortunately, this only perpetuates the myth of "no big deal!"

Chloe's Story

Chloe, 25, opened up to her three housemates after learning of her parents' plans to divorce. Tearful and shaken, she let her feelings out and immediately got hugs and support which felt good. She was surprised, however, at how quickly her housemates moved on and seemed to forget that Chloe felt like her world had turned upside down.

> "One of my housemate's parents had divorced when she was 12 and she was quick to assure me that it was much harder then. It made me feel a little stupid and even selfish. Another reassured me that I'm strong and can deal with this so not to let it get me down. Only Marianne, who I'm closest to, kept checking back in with me to see what was going on at home and how I was doing. I really appreciated her for that."

It is also possible that friends may be more aware than they let on that divorce at this time in one's life is significant. Alec's friends initially responded much like Chloe's. Later, however, one friend told him that he'd realized that if Alec's parents could get divorced, he worried that his could also. He added that he didn't even want to think about it, which Alec realized meant that his friend actually thought it *was* a big deal.

MILESTONE EVENTS

Emerging into full adulthood is marked by many milestone events and rites of passage. These occasions could be complicated by parental divorce even if it occurred when the children were quite young, now years ago. However, when divorce occurs after the children are adults, less time will have passed before these occasions arise—less time for acrimonious feelings to have resolved, less time for grieving the family as it used to be, and less time for new family formations to have developed and become the new norm. Thus, at these special times when family members come together to celebrate one of their own, emotions may still be raw.

Despite growing trappings of independence, most Emerging Adults still expect and want their parents to be present for their important milestones. Actively divorcing or newly divorced parents may still be grieving and healing. The last thing they may want is to spend time with their former spouse. It can be even harder if that former spouse is now with a new partner who will also be attending the milestone event.

It is common for Emerging Adults to spend a considerable amount of energy worrying about how their parents are going to behave at their graduation or their wedding or their baby's first birthday. These are times of celebration where the adult child (or new grandchild) should be the focus of attention. Too often an anxious cloud hovers overhead, dampening these supposedly festive occasions.

The stories that follow illustrate a range of ways these important events can be negatively impacted by parental divorce. It was precisely because so many of these stories began to accumulate in my office that I knew there needed to be a way to alert both parents and adult children to these potential minefields. I hope this book will be a step in that direction. Chapters 9 and 10 offer ways to avoid these negative situations and ways to handle them when they cannot be avoided.

Graduations

Graduation from college or vocational school should be the time for the whole family to acknowledge and celebrate the hard work and accomplishment of the graduate. Every spring in Ann Arbor where I live, the campus is filled with proud families walking around with their cap and gown-clad grads, hugging and posing for photos. Restaurants and hotels are booked months in advance to be sure that the celebration goes off smoothly. While it can appear idyllic to the outside observer, the inside story may be more complicated.

Ethan's Story

My client Ethan had begun to worry if anyone from his family would even *be* at his graduation. Having two older siblings, he remembered accompanying his parents to their graduations. Since then, much had changed. His mother had filed for divorce two years previous. She had a new partner but had not remarried. His father, still bitter from the divorce, had hastily remarried. He told Ethan he would not attend if his mother would be there even if she came by herself.

It was up to Ethan to figure out how to deliver this message to his mother since his parents were not speaking. While his friends were having fun hanging out together before they graduated and went their separate ways, Ethan was preoccupied with figuring out some sort of solution to his parental dilemma. He worried that he could end up "celebrating" his graduation alone.

After many texts and phone calls, a compromise was reached. Both parents would come but had to promise to keep their distance. Ethan scrambled to find them separate hotel accommodations, and he had to negotiate dining options such that each parent thought he or she was the one hosting the "special" meal. It was a real role reversal from that of his friends whose parents had made all these arrangements.

Needless to say, Ethan was on alert all weekend, trying to make sure each parent felt they'd gotten the better half of the time with him. His smile for those graduation photos was strained and underneath his gown his shirt was wringing wet. Vigilant and emotionally exhausted, he was embarrassed to find himself fighting back tears. He couldn't decide if he was feeling anger or fear or sadness … or, most likely, all three!

Samantha's Story

Samantha had started a serious relationship early in her senior year of college and she was planning to move in with her boyfriend, Justin, at the end of the summer. She and Justin had both been accepted into graduate school programs in another state and she was feeling optimistic about her life. Then a few months before graduation her parents told her that they had decided to go their separate ways. They assured her that it was an amicable and mutual decision, that they both loved her very much, and would be fine coming to her graduation together.

She really hadn't seen this coming and was shaken to her core. Like many others in her situation, she entertained new doubts about her relationship with Justin, but she told herself she didn't have to decide that now. Her biggest issue was embarrassment. She was embarrassed to tell him that her parents "weren't going to make it," since they had frequently discussed how lucky they both felt to be from happily married families.

Samantha was also afraid that Justin might view her differently now, perhaps somehow as a less promising prospective partner. Even more, she was embarrassed because she would be meeting his parents for the first time at graduation and they had plans for a joint dinner with both their parents. Suddenly, Samantha's thoughts about graduation turned from eager anticipation to shame and dread.

Weddings

Divorce issues arise at almost every phase and in almost every aspect of an Emerging Adult's wedding. First, as noted above, are thoughts about whether to get married at all, given that these adult children have recently witnessed their parents' marriages fail after decades together. Some unfortunate brides and grooms are in the process of planning their weddings at the same time their parents' marriages are coming apart. There are also forward-thinkers like Elyssa who had no immediate plans to marry but knew they would later be impacted by her parents' divorce. She was furious with her father for leaving her mother but decided to not to show it because, "One day I may want him to walk me down the aisle … and to pay for my wedding."

Matthew's Story Continued

Luckily, Matthew, the Yale student we met earlier in this chapter who dropped out when his parents divorced, was able to return to school. His mother's close-knit, affluent social network rallied around her and provided the money for both Matthew and his younger brother to return to school. A few years later, they showed the same generosity when Matthew got married to a woman from a family of modest means, pitching in to provide an almost storybook wedding weekend at multiple venues with elaborate catering.

Matthew was uncomfortable as it almost seemed unreal. He knew it was important to his mother and her friends, and he felt he owed it to them. Causing even greater discomfort, however, was his fear that the animosity between his parents might come out into the open with so many events and so much time in each other's presence. This would also be the first time since the divorce that relatives on both sides of his family would come into contact.

Things went surprisingly smoothly through the wedding where his parents even sat together at the ceremony. However, they began to create a buzz later at the reception, detracting attention from the young couple who should have been the central focus of their own wedding. Matthew's parents appeared to drink too much and danced together quite intimately which made many of the guests, familiar with this family's history, uneasy.

Then they were unaccounted for when guests ceremoniously sent the bride and groom off at the end of the evening. And, as a final insult to the newlyweds, they showed up late and disheveled at the brunch the next day still wearing their formal attire from the night before. Sadly, their behavior had created a distraction from the young couple who should have been the center of attention.

Grace's Story

At 29, Grace and her fiancé Andrew had just started making wedding plans when Grace's parents announced they were separating not long after their 30th anniversary. Fortunately, she knew this was going to be very difficult and she reached out for support from other family members as well as her future in-laws. Grace was furious at her parents' timing and not afraid to vent her strong feelings to them even though they were too caught up in their own issues to really listen to her.

Nevertheless, deciding every detail of her own wedding was hard. Juxtaposed with the unraveling of her parents' marriage, it felt like a farce to be carefully planning flowers and venues as if making the right choices would make her own marriage more sturdy. Then there were the seemingly endless decisions of whom to invite to which showers and whom to seat where at the reception given possible divorce-related family rifts.

Stepparents

Sheryl Paul, professional bridal counselor and author of the very pragmatic book *The Conscious Bride*, discusses cases where parental divorce can impact a wedding.[5] In particular, she addresses the potential conflicts involving stepparents. How does a bride include a recently acquired stepmother in her wedding? If she gives the same corsage to her as to her mother, she insults her mother. If she doesn't, will her stepmother feel slighted? Who should be in which pictures? Brides (and grooms) are already worrying about keeping things fair between their two families, and now there is another relationship to worry about.

Sheryl Paul feels that stepparents, and especially stepmothers, become the focus of displaced anxiety in wedding planning. They may be a reminder of divorce wounds not yet healed and grief still unresolved. And even if the bride actually likes her stepmother, how does she incorporate her into her life without feeling disloyal to her mother?

Adult Children and a Parent's Wedding

While most of the stories I heard involving weddings and adult children of divorce were about the adult child's wedding, there were also stressful stories about a parent's remarriage. Sometimes the theme is about secrets. One parent tells their adult child that they are marrying but not to tell the other parent. Or the other parent gets wind of this marriage and presses the adult child for details. These are examples of adult children being caught in the middle which can be awkward, intrusive, and even treacherous. Since Chapters 9 and 10 will delve more deeply into the issues of parents' dating, re-partnering, and remarriage, we will only briefly consider one example here.

Anna's Story Continued

Anna was almost done with college when her parents divorced and sold the family home. She felt stressed and took a break from school and accepted a job out of state, in part to distance herself from the drama. When neither of her parents wanted the elderly family cats, Anna felt compelled to take them on although she could barely afford the vet bills. Both of her parents got involved with new partners within a year or two and were planning weddings around the same time. Her father was determined to get married first. He kept pressuring Anna for her mother's wedding plans and asked Anna to convey to her a long list of dates he wanted to reserve for himself. He offered to buy suits for Anna's twin brothers if they promised not to wear them to their mom's wedding.

Caught in the middle—this time around a parent's wedding, not one's own—Anna felt she was constantly defusing her parents' smoldering anger at each other. She couldn't really look forward to either wedding although she liked the people her parents were marrying and felt they were likely better matches. Add to this how difficult it was for Anna and her brothers, all living in different states, to get time off from their jobs to attend both parents' weddings in the same month. In recalling the two weddings, Anna's memories of the two events focused on stress and exasperation rather than joy.

With all of the logistical concerns of a parent's remarriage, the actual feelings of Emerging Adult Children are often overlooked—by themselves and by their parents! What level of involvement do they want to have in a parent's wedding? What choices do they have? As noted above, we will explore these important issues in greater depth from their and their parents' perspectives in Chapters 9 and 10.

As for Anna, she needed to find a way to extract herself from her divorced parents' contentious and competitive relationship. As their first-born child and only daughter, she was playing out an old family pattern—offering herself up as a go-between with her parents as well as a shield protecting her younger brothers from their conflict. After the stressful weddings were over, she knew something had to change. She realized she was sacrificing her own well-being and sought help. Now with a therapist's strong encouragement, Anna began setting clear limits on what her parents could expect of her. Almost immediately she began to resent them less and felt an enormous sense of relief.

The Arrival of Grandchildren

Marie, the survivor of severe domestic abuse whom we met in Chapter 3, received sufficient legal and psychological support to safely leave her violent marriage. She ended up making drastic financial concessions in order to extricate herself from the seemingly-endless divorce proceedings. Nevertheless, she was cautiously optimistic about starting a new life.

Her ex-husband, Mitch, held on to his anger at Marie for leaving him and refused to speak to her even on matters involving their young adult children. He kept the children trapped in the middle of this toxic scenario using large financial incentives and punishments to garner their loyalty. Additionally, he insisted that they make sure he never run into their mother.

This reached a peak of absurdity even years after their divorce. Now married, their daughter went into labor after a difficult pregnancy with their first grandchild. Both Marie and Mitch showed up at the hospital to be present for whatever was needed, but this time their daughter was unavailable to run interference. Mitch began screaming at Marie in the waiting room, threatening to hit her if she did not leave immediately. His behavior frightened other people as well, and security showed up and took Mitch off in handcuffs. This piled humiliation and stress on the parents-to-be who were already dealing with as much as they could handle. It also foreshadowed years of painful encounters involving grandchildren.

Mitch was a very toxic guy—as husband, father, and grandfather. There was precious little Marie could do beyond trying to avoid running into him. But even more benign stories of problematic divorced grandparents can create hardship for their adult children and their families. It is all too common for a divorced grandparent to insist they cannot attend a grandchild's birthday party if their ex-spouse will be there. Young adult parents can't simply plan the celebration that works best for their child. They have to focus on whether to throw two parties or even alternate shifts and years. Their energy should be on their child's needs, not the grandparents'.

And then there are simply young adults who are grieving that their own children will not experience their grandparents as an intact unit. When one young mother heard in July that her parents were divorcing, her thoughts went immediately to her son who was weeks away first his first birthday. But she was also thinking ahead to Christmas. She agonized about how she could consider both her parents' feelings and the needs of her son:

> "I don't want to get so wrapped up in their needs that I ruin my son's first birthday as well as his first real Christmas. And then there's the feeling that it won't be a real Christmas anyway, without their house to go home to. This colors everything I had been looking forward to."

In Summary

I want to end this chapter with a vignette that illustrates and summarizes the difficulties Emerging Adults face when their parents divorce. In this case, the adult child is not someone I knew and worked with, but a well-known sports celebrity who has written about the impact of his parents' divorce on his young adult life. It is a reminder that even widespread acclaim and success cannot protect an adult child from being thrown off balance by parental divorce. It also reminds us, as did Chris in the previous chapter, that given sufficient time and resources, Emerging Adult Children and their families can achieve a healthy and positive resolution even after what had seemed to be a devastating divorce.

Tennis great Rafael Nadal was too busy with his tennis career to go off to college.[6] He had already won the French Open, Wimbledon, and the Australian Open by the time he was 22. In the Spanish tradition, until he married, he was expected to live in his childhood home on the island of Majorca with his tight-knit family. In his book *Rafa,* he claimed to have had "a fairytale childhood." He grew up in what he felt was a warm, happy family, free of conflict. He was emerging into adulthood from a secure homebase which allowed him to focus on his tennis career.

On a long flight from Melbourne to Dubai, his father mentioned that he and Rafa's mother were having problems. Nadal immediately (and correctly) knew his father was talking about separation and divorce after a nearly 30-year marriage. He felt he had been delivered a shocking blow which he couldn't assimilate and chose not to speak for the remainder of the flight.

Fortunately for those of us who want to dispel the myth that divorce is no big deal for adult children, Nadal chose to speak up about his feelings in his book. His openness about the pain he went through over his parents' divorce and how it affected his career does a lot to highlight this phenomenon. I hope it encourages other Emerging Adults to speak up also.

Nadal was unaware that his feelings and reactions were normal. He felt other people might have taken their parents' divorce more in stride than he and his sister were able to do. He'd considered his parents the pillar of his life and now the pillar was cut in half. His "happy family portrait" was shattered. He felt that his entire extended family of uncles, aunts, grandparents, and cousins was destabilized, and relationships between members of his family system became strained.

The momentum of the winning streak he had been on carried Nadal through a couple more months, so his tennis game did not immediately suffer. As he recalled, his body still went through the motions, but he became increasingly depressed and gloomy. People around him felt he had become a different person, and they knew something was going to give. First it was his knees and later an abdominal muscle. Rafa knew he could not go on. He needed to take time out to recover from his physical ailments but also to deal with what he called the new reality of his family situation.

It took nearly a year and a half for Nadal to recover from the devastating impact of his parents' divorce. Likely this happened as quickly as it did because he observed his parents regaining their equilibrium individually and in relation to each other. This freed him up to once again focus on his tennis game. Perhaps Nadal's parents worked as hard as they did to get past their initial acrimony because their son's devastation was so visible and so public, but Nadal made a direct connection between stability in his family circle and stability in his tennis game.

By the time his book came out in 2011, Nadal's splintered family had come a long way in its healing. He felt that his parents had become friends to the extent that they were able to come to his tournaments and watch him play. He admired and appreciated their civility.

Nadal's story illustrates how Emerging Adults—even those who are already highly successful out in the world beyond their families—are very much affected when their parents divorce. He grew up in a warm, seemingly conflict-free home absent trauma or abuse. This gave him a solid inner core, but it also produced shock and disbelief when his parents divorced. For a while, Nadal and his sister did not know how to interact with their extended circle of family and friends.

Despite Nadal's success as well as the support of many people around him, he eventually had to pull back from his career to heal physically and mentally. While most people cannot afford to quit their jobs when their parents divorce, it was clear that Nadal had to take a serious step back. His parents' decision to take responsibility for their own healing and to behave in a civilized manner with each other probably hastened his recovery.

And what better metaphor of a positive outcome for an adult child of divorce than to have both parents *seated in the same family box,* putting their differences aside and rooting for their child to succeed. It is a good reminder that divorce, as noted earlier, needs to be viewed as a process, and not merely as an event. No matter the circumstances, families need time to grieve but they can eventually reconfigure themselves into new, and perhaps healthier, forms.

Chapter Five Notes—*Taking Off From Base Camp: Emerging Adults in Their 20s and 30s*

1. Jeffrey J. Arnett is credited with coining the term "emerging adulthood." You can read further about this in his book *Emerging Adulthood: The Winding Road From the Late Teens through the Twenties (3rd Edition)*, 2024, Oxford University Press. You can also listen to his Ted Talk on YouTube: "Why Does It Take So Long To Grow Up Today?" April 28, 2015. There Arnett focuses on four explanations: the technology revolution, birth control and the sexual revolution, the women's movement, and the youth movement. See also: *Not Quite Adults: Why 20-Sometings Are Choosing a Slower Path to Adulthood, and Why It's Good for Everyone,* Richard Settersten and Barbara E. Ray, 2010, Random House Publishing Group.

2. See End Note 1 in Chapter 4.

3. Following his parents' contentious divorce, Brad Ryan was estranged from his paternal grandmother, Joy, for 10 years despite having previously had a close relationship with her. Reunited after meeting up at his sister's wedding, Brad learned that his then 85-year-old grandmother wanted to see the mountains and the ocean for the first time. This led the two of them on a remarkable journey visiting all 63 U.S. national parks and learning a lot about each other's lives in the process. Their adventures have been chronicled by CBS, NBC, CNN, NPR, *People Magazine*, and many other news media.

4. Barbara S. Cain, "The Price They Pay: Older Children and Divorce," *New York Times Magazine*, February 18, 1990.

5. Sheryl Paul, *The Conscious Bride: Women Unveil Their True Feelings About Getting Hitched*, 2000, New Harbinger Publications.

6. Rafael Nadal, *Rafa,* 2012, Grand Central Publishing.

-6-
The Lighthouse Goes Dark:
The Oldest Adult Children

Long ago having left the port for their own destinations, the oldest children of divorce are nearing, or solidly in, middle-age themselves. Still, they may see their parents' marriage as a lighthouse, guiding them safely from a distance and providing a reassuring landmark when things get rough. What happens when the light in the lighthouse goes dark? Will they lose their bearings and be thrown off course, at least for a while?

In this chapter, we look at the oldest adult children of divorce. Their numbers are also growing, but they have received even less attention than the Launchers in Chapter 4 and the Emerging Adults in Chapter 5. These adult children are approaching, or solidly in, Middle-Age when their parents divorce. From their mid- to later-30s and well into their 40s, 50s and even beyond, they have been out on their own.

They no longer consider their parents' residences "home" or even "base camp." Unless they have had significant setbacks up to this point (serious physical or mental illness, job loss, bouts with substance abuse, or perhaps failed relationships), even the youngest in this group have likely moved beyond primarily working on the challenges of identity and intimacy. They are facing, or beginning to face, the mid-life challenges of Generativity (Erikson's Stage 7). They are focusing on guiding the next generation at home and at work and hoping their lives will have a positive impact on their world.

All are somewhere in the peak years of middle adulthood. They are raising and supporting their own families, working to hold onto (or advance in) their jobs and careers, and succeeding or failing in their own relationships and marriages. People at this age are considered fully-formed

121

adults, but when their parents' marriages fail, they, too, are *children of divorce*. They are still very much impacted by this important family event. However, the struggle that parental divorce poses for these oldest children is rarely acknowledged, understood, or studied.

The lighthouse metaphor rings more true for those oldest children who saw their parents' long marriages as happy, good enough, or at least non-toxic. Even if their parents stayed together in unhappy marriages, their enduring partnership likely provided predictability in the present and continuity with the past. Still together under one roof, they continued to symbolize a home base for their children to visit.

While it may have seemed surprising that the divorce rate has *doubled* for people over 50, it has *tripled* for people 65 and older. That means that the number of middle-aged adults who join the ranks of children of divorce has also tripled. The myth that adult children should not be affected by their parents' divorce keeps this group especially quiet, almost invisible. After all, their friends are dealing with parents dying, but they are *only* dealing with divorce.

As we will see in Chapter 8, death generally casts a "rosy glow" over the life of a loved one as well as over their marriage. Divorce, by contrast, more often brings up disparagement and negativity. Furthermore, when a middle-aged adult loses a parent, grieving rituals are in place which friends and acquaintances follow by sending sympathy cards and attending funerals or memorial services.

There are no rituals to follow when middle-aged adults are facing their older parents' divorce. For them this is the death of the family they have known for 30, 40, 50 years. Their friends and acquaintances may not even know that this significant event has occurred so there is no opportunity for them to offer the support and understanding that could be very helpful.

The absolute number of couples divorcing at this age is modest even though their numbers have tripled in recent years. Still, it is shocking to encounter older couples who choose to end their long marriages in their final stages of life. As one woman in her mid-forties put it when she learned her parents were divorcing:

> I was just bragging about the fact that my parents were still
> together. I felt proud when so many of my friends' parents were

not. They made it through the valley and were ascending to the golden mountaintop that every married couple wants to achieve. The big 5-0. Why now? It sucks!

For parents in or approaching their final life stages (Erikson's Stages 7 and 8, Generativity and Ego Integrity), divorce poses unique and significant issues emotionally, financially, and logistically. In addition, it can pose unique and significant issues, and even burdens, for their middle-aged children. These oldest adult children were already beginning to worry about their parents as they watch them growing older. Now they have to be concerned about them growing older apart.

If you are a Middle-Aged Child, many of the challenges we discuss below will feel familiar to you. However, you may not have allowed yourself to acknowledge the extent to which your parents' divorce has impacted your life. You may have thought that, at this stage, you should be able to handle whatever comes your way even though your life may already feel beyond full.

As an older, perhaps even elderly, parent reading this chapter, you may think your middle-aged children are beyond being affected by your divorce. This is understandable since you have viewed them as adults for years. But they are still your children no matter their age, and the mid-life stage they are in is as busy and challenging for them as it was for you. Quite likely they have been reluctant to fully share with you the extent to which your divorce has impacted their lives.

There are three main explanations for why the rising divorce rate for older and elderly parents is especially problematic for their middle-aged children. First, because of their status as mature adults, a great deal may be expected of these oldest children when their parents divorce. Second, if they have families of their own, *three* generations are now impacted by later-life divorce. And, finally, as noted above, the needs of parents divorcing in these later-life stages pose unique, and sometimes daunting, challenges for their middle-aged offspring whose time and resources are already spread thin.

MORE MAY BE ASKED OF THEM

Because the oldest children of divorce are the furthest along in establishing their own adult lives, divorcing parents may have even greater expectations of them than they would of a younger adult child. This could involve different expectations about the parent-child relationship itself. Now that all parties are clearly well into adulthood, boundaries for appropriate behavior may even more likely be violated than with younger adult children. It could also involve different expectations about allocation of resources. Adult children at this life stage may have accumulated as many (or even more) resources, such as money or housing, as their parents.

The Parent-Child Relationship

Middle-Aged Adult Children are seen indisputably as adults. Their parents are more likely to view them as peers or even confidantes than they would their younger counterparts. Parents may reason that these mature adult children are familiar with the ups and downs of relationships and marriage. As such, Middle-Aged Adult Children should be able to listen to the details of their parents' marital troubles, including sexual difficulties and incompatibilities.

While this may seem to make sense at first glance, maintaining appropriate and comfortable parent-child boundaries never loses its value and importance. Even when it does make sense to share sensitive or personal information, it is often better done at a general level without specific details. At no age do children want or need to hear unnecessarily negative or highly personal information from one parent about the other.

Marty's Story

Marty was 35 when her parents ended their 46-year marriage. Looking back three years later, she was surprised they lasted as long as they did since things had been, in her words, "sallowing" ever since she and her older sisters were teenagers. That was when their stay-at-home mother went back to school and then took a job in college administration. It was also the time that their father was fired from his well-paid job and could only find part-time work. Along with this role reversal in who was the breadwinner came a lot of arguing, and Marty feels her parents' drinking escalated in order to cope. In fact, it only made things worse.

They finally hit a breaking point when her mother suggested a trial separation and her father insisted she had kicked him out. Always seen as the good child who didn't need anything, Marty—no longer a teenager but now a 35-year-old adult—was pulled into the middle. Both parents used her as a go-between and secret keeper as well as a sounding board, opening up to her about intimate details of their relationship. Equal parts sad and disgusted, Marty told me, "I know everything about their marriage."

These oldest adult children are also more likely to take on the role of mediator between their parents. Jeopardizing their role as children, they may step in and go to great lengths trying to convince their parents to reconcile or at least to divorce more amicably. They are often the ones to suggest their parents seek marital counseling as well as legal and financial advice. Some of them spend considerable time researching and locating these options and even offer to attend these meetings with their parents.

Shona's Story

Shona, a seasoned mental health professional herself, was dumbfounded when her father informed her that he and her mother were going to divorce. She dropped everything, drove 100 miles to their house and cried, "You can't do that!" When this had no effect, she began searching for a marriage counselor in their city.

She was relieved to find one with an excellent reputation. She then sat down with each parent and explained who this counselor was, how well-respected he was, and that he took their insurance. Her mother promptly stated that she wouldn't talk with a man as she was sure he would just see things from Shona's father's perspective. So, Shona spent more hours searching until she found a well-credentialed, highly respected female counselor. When she presented this professional to her father, his response was, "Nope, she'll only see your mother's side."

Shona's parents became increasingly demanding. They went on to pursue an expensive and acrimonious divorce, using up a fair amount of the money they had planned to pass on to their children. Shona had to cut back on her work schedule to be available to put out fires, and she made frequent trips to her parents' homes to see if they were okay. This created stress in Shona's own family.

Her husband had to step up at home and thought the whole thing was ridiculous. Her kids were disappointed when she missed several of their soccer games and her daughter's eighth grade play. Her parents never once asked how her involvement in their divorce was affecting her and seemed oblivious to her increasing distress. Shona found herself angry at all of them as well as at her sister who refused to get involved.

Even though her parents refused counseling, Shona eventually came to see me. She began to recognize that her involvement in her parents' divorce was part her long-standing role as "over-functioner" in her family of origin. She invited her husband into sessions and the two of them worked together on how Shona could set limits in responding to her parents' demands. With great relief, Shona realized that she could not stop her parents from divorcing, but she could protect her own marriage from much of its negative impact.

Allocation of Resources

Adult children at this life stage are likely to have accumulated more resources than their younger counterparts. They may find themselves offering (or being asked) to loan or give their parents money despite the fact that their own finances may be tight while raising children and paying for childcare, housing, and other expenses. If they have their own (owned or rented) residence, they may find themselves taking in a divorcing parent who cannot make it on their own.

Trish's Story

This happened to Trish, the older daughter of Tillie whom we met in Chapter 3. Tillie had married right out of high school, as was expected of girls in her large Catholic family. Bright and optimistic, she wanted more for her daughters. First-born Trish graduated near the top of her high school class and got a four-year scholarship to college. After working for a few years, she went on to get a Master's degree in business, much to Tillie's delight. Aware that marrying young didn't turn out so well for her mother, Trish focused on advancing her career. She didn't consider marriage until she was in her 30s. Like her mom, Trish was smart with money and already owned a modest home when she met her future husband, Greg.

Trish and Greg had barely returned from their honeymoon when Tillie asked her abusive husband to leave. Always her father's favorite, Trish was reluctant to fully believe her mother's complaints about the extent of his drinking and abuse, but she could not ignore his recent run-in with the police which made the front page of the local newspaper. Despite all this, Trish's anger was directed at her mother when her father showed up on her doorstep with no place to stay. She felt she couldn't refuse to take him in, but she was furious at her mother's timing. This was not how she and Greg had hoped to start their married life together.

Mason's Story

Mason (Larry's adopted stepson whom we met in Chapters 1 and 3) had not only a spouse but children when, in his mid-30s, he found himself responsible for his mother. His mother Emily had left Larry without explanation, but their divorce was put on hold when she was declared mentally incompetent due to severe depression. Discharged from the hospital and unable to live on her own, Mason became Emily's legal guardian even though he was ill-equipped to do so. He already had all he could handle at work and with his own family which was quickly outgrowing their small home.

Ted's Story

Millie and Irv's three adult children were even older when Irv surprised everyone with news that he was filing for divorce. Their 40-year-old son, Ted, had also been surprised when his wife left him a few years back. He identified with his mother's situation, took her side, and refused to speak to his father. Almost immediately his mother began to rely on Ted to fix everything that needed fixing in the family home.

He generally seemed happy to do this even though his own home was in need of a fair amount of repair which he never had time for. It got more complicated when his mother needed him on the days he had custody of his four children, and it interfered with his time with them. Ted was hesitant to bring them with him to his mother's as she constantly voiced her resentment of their grandfather at a level even Ted found uncomfortable.

Initially, Millie had panicked when Irv left. He had always handled their finances so she had no idea if she could afford to stay in the house. Ted's sisters were better off financially than he was, so Millie turned to them when she needed money. Increasingly, this began to create strains in their relationship with her and with each other as they each had their own expenses to worry about and hoped the other might be more forthcoming.

One daughter, Sarah, 44, was married and saving for her children's college education. The other daughter, Charla, 37, and her husband had incurred considerable expense from costly infertility treatments and were finally expecting their first child in a few months when her parents' marriage fell apart. Until Irv filed for divorce, all three adult children had been the recipients of small financial gifts from their parents. They were unprepared for the tables to be reversed, but neither could they turn their backs on their mother.

MULTIPLE GENERATIONS ARE IMPACTED

Second, the shock waves from these later-life breakups may now affect not only the divorcing couples' adult children but their grandchildren as well. As noted, these oldest adult children (in their later 30s, 40s and beyond) are likely in the peak years of child-rearing as well as work and other responsibilities. Their own lives may be challenging enough, whether married or single. If married, their marriages may be strained by the demands of the life stage *they* are in. In common with younger adult children, these oldest adult children are likely hoping that their parents' marriages, even if not ideal, form a steady backdrop allowing them to focus on their own lives.

Sandwiched Between Two Generations

These oldest adult children may have been relying on their parents for various kinds of support from childcare to occasional or regular financial advice and help. With news of their parents' divorce, they become sandwiched between trying to keep their own families afloat and dealing with the messy unraveling of their parents' marriages. As one man in his 40s recalled:

> "The week before my parents' 45th anniversary, my dad told my mom that he was in love with another woman and wanted out of the marriage. I felt heartache and disbelief. I had difficulty trying to be some semblance of a husband and dad to my two daughters. I went to sleep every night exhausted from trying to be brave for everyone else and woke up each morning afraid that

I might not have another day of bravery left."

This is precisely the time when these older adult children may be looking to their parents' long marriages as evidence that hard times can be overcome and committed relationships can prevail. But instead of celebrating their parents' Golden Anniversary, they are witnessing an example that marriage as an institution can be precarious and may not last. They may seriously question the viability of their own relationships.

Grandchildren

When these oldest adult children of divorce are parents themselves, there will be grandchildren of divorce as well. Younger grandchildren may feel confused that "Grandma and Grandpa" are no longer a unit. One or both grandparents may, at least temporarily, seem different or troubled, and they may be less involved in their grandchildren's lives. Grandchildren will also be affected by their parents' reaction to, and preoccupation with, what is going on with the oldest generation. Like their parents, grandchildren are likely experiencing a significant loss as well as a major upheaval to their sense of their family's foundational stability.

The familiar grandparental home and traditions may also cease to exist. This was a concern of Charla, Irv and Millie's younger daughter who, after many miscarriages, was in the final trimester of her first pregnancy. For years, she had observed her parents putting on big, happy holiday celebrations for her siblings' children. Now she realized her own child would never experience such events.

Younger Grandchildren

Harriette was furious with her mother for leaving her father abruptly and wanted to cut off contact with her. However, she chose to continue their relationship for the sake of her young daughter, Ava, who missed her grandmother. Their times together were less comfortable than they had been, and it became obvious that Harriette's mother was more invested in fostering her relationship with a man she was seeing than spending time with her granddaughter. When Ava announced that she didn't think her grandma liked her very much anymore, Harriette tried to be reassuring, but she knew at least for now that Ava's assessment was probably correct.

Other middle-aged children have noted how their parents' post-divorce behavior impacted their ability/willingness to play supportive roles in their busy lives. For Nancy, in her late 30s, this became apparent when she had a difficult labor resulting in a C-section for her second child's birth. Her parents had been very involved in offering support and care when their first grandchild was born. Now that they were in the middle of a divorce, they were unavailable to help with the new baby, the three-year-old, or their own daughter recuperating from surgery. The contrast was striking—and very disappointing—to Nancy.

Not surprisingly, grandchildren of all ages may begin to worry about the stability of their own parents' marriages. If "Grandma and Grandpa" can cease to be an entity, then so could "Mom and Dad." Although they may not say anything, younger grandchildren may be hyper-alert to adult conversations about the divorce in order to understand the significance of what is happening around them.

Likely this occurs at a time when the adults' own emotions are running high, causing them to be less aware of their children's needs and worries. Sarah (Millie and Irv's older daughter) had to shuttle her children between both parents' homes whenever she came to town, which was exhausting for her and for them. Like her brother Ted, Sarah tried to shield her children from negative information spewed by their still-bitter grandparents. Sometimes, however, she was too frazzled to remember and later learned that they had overheard hurtful things about their beloved grandparents.

Older Grandchildren

Older grandchildren may be the same age as the youngest and Emerging Adult Children discussed in Chapters 4 and 5. They may be beginning to focus on forming long-term partnerships of their own. They are likely more aware of problems in their grandparents' marriage than younger grandchildren are, and they may have been making mental notes about what works and doesn't work in marriage. Like their younger siblings, they may not ask questions or express their feelings. Nevertheless, they are aware of, and impacted by, this major change in their extended family whether their parents realize it or not.

Mac's Story

Mac's story gives voice to some of the complicated feelings, including denial and sadness, which young adult grandchildren experience when their beloved grandparents divorce. He was on Christmas break from college and joined his parents for a visit to his grandparents in Arizona. Early in the visit the grandparents called a family meeting, including Mac's Aunt Marsha who lived nearby. Mac was in the kitchen making himself a sandwich when he heard the word "divorce" and decided, "It wasn't my place to be there."

He jumped in their golf cart and called his older sister who said she'd have left too. When he returned later, he thought it looked like everyone had been crying. The adults assumed Mac left because he was upset, but when he insisted that wasn't the case, no one inquired further. Neither did Mac.

When I spoke with Mac in my office it was more than three years later, and his grandparents' divorce was only mentioned in passing. I filed it away but eventually brought it back up. When I asked Mac how he felt about it now, he quickly brushed it off as having no effect since he'd known they "had issues." Then he sat quietly and let his tears well up. When he regained his composure, he admitted, "I guess I was shocked. You expect your grandparents to stay together after almost 50 years."

Once Mac allowed himself to say he had feelings about his beloved grandparents' divorce, his emotions started bubbling up. For the next several therapy sessions this was his main focus. He was trying to figure out what "went wrong" in their long marriage and wondered it was realistic to expect any marriage to last. With my encouragement, Mac decided to talk with his parents and was relieved when they took his feelings seriously and appropriately shared some of their own feelings and concerns. Even though it had been three years since the grandparents divorced, Mac and his parents still had some grieving and healing to do.

Lydia's Story

Lydia was also in college when her grandparents made a mutual decision to divorce. She was never one for wild spring break trips. Instead, she opted each spring for a quieter visit with her grandparents in Florida. They were adamant that they still wanted her to come this year even though their long marriage was over. She accepted their invitation with considerable trepidation.

To their credit, Lydia's grandparents worked hard to make her feel comfortable. They came together to pick her up at the airport and the three of them did a lot together during the day and always had dinner together. Lydia felt awkward about choosing to sleep at her Grandma Lily's, but she had more room in her condo. Throughout the visit, Lydia was conscious about dividing her time evenly so as not to hurt her grandfather's feelings.

One night when it was just the two of them, Grandma Lily gently brought up the divorce and offered to talk if Lydia wanted to. Lydia was embarrassed at first but ventured a couple of very general questions. To her relief, her grandmother answered in a matter-of-fact, and also general, manner. She stressed that she and Lydia's grandfather had grown apart and were happier pursuing their separate interests although at times she felt sad that things had ended this way. This allowed Lydia to express her own sadness, and the two ended up sharing hugs and a box of tissues. Throughout this conversation, Lydia heard nothing negative about her grandfather.

Lydia's grandparents' attempts to present a familiar united front where they could was comforting but also a little confusing. When I asked her if her grandparents' divorce had affected her feelings about relationships, she insisted it hadn't.

"I still dream of falling in love and finding my soulmate and staying with them for the rest of my life." As she said this aloud, she looked surprised as if the idea just hit her. "Oh, but old people can get divorced. My parents didn't get divorced." Lydia quickly added the fact that her parents were still married as if it were somehow a guarantee against divorce.

Comforted by how smoothly the visit had gone, Lydia summed it up, "I still get to visit my Grandma and Grandpa,"—as if nothing significant had changed. However, when I asked if either were dating or seeing new people, she seemed surprised. "Truth be told, I'd never thought of them re-partnering. Oh, my God! That would be so weird. It'd be very strange," she replied.

The thoughtful way Lydia's grandparents handled their mutual decision to split has so far lightened the impact for Lydia. She still envisions them dancing together at her wedding but clearly that could be more difficult if one (or both) begins seeing other people.

Rosie's Story

A different grandchild, Rosie, was a little older when her grandparents divorced. She recalled them cutting quite a figure at her wedding five years earlier. One final dance invited all married couples to join the bride and groom on the dance floor and then asked them to stay on if they'd been married five years, then ten … until only the longest married couple was still dancing with the newlyweds. Rosie remembered bursting with pride that these were *her* grandparents and felt it was an omen that her own marriage would be long and happy.

When she heard that they were divorcing, she was shaken to her core. It happened at a time that she and her husband were facing some hard choices about jobs and finances, and it made her doubt the viability of her own marriage.

> "My grandparents were cemented together in my mind … on a pedestal as the best people ever. I didn't see any flaws in their marriage. Walking away from their vows after more than 50 years shattered that. I still think they're amazing people. This makes them more human, I guess, and it sure makes me wonder if anything is made to last. I worry that my parents could be on the brink of divorce. They seem okay but my grandparents seemed even more than okay. Who knows?"

PARENTS ARE WELL ALONG IN ERIKSON'S STAGES 7 AND 8

And third, parents divorcing when their children are in the Middle-Aged Adult stage is particularly problematic simply because these parents are nearing or in the final stages of their lives. Likely, they and their children were already facing or considering challenges posed by aging before divorce entered the picture. Now, all are poignantly aware that time is running out for these parents to be able to land on their feet following the inevitable disequilibrium of divorce.

Stage 7: Parents Growing Older

The divorcing parents of the younger two cohorts of adult children (Chapters 4 and 5) are likely to be younger themselves. For the most part, they are in the early and middle years of Erikson's next to last stage (7, Generativity). Warding off stagnation and looking for satisfaction and meaning in their lives when they divorce, they are hoping they still have the time and resources to put their lives back together.

Many are likely still young and healthy enough to make changes in careers and relationships and begin new lives, if that is their wish. Some will remarry or re-partner and introduce stepparents and stepsiblings into their adult children's lives. Hopefully, once they have had time to recover from the divorce itself, they will be able to reinvest in their roles as parents and grandparents.

All of these divorce-related changes pose significant challenges. They also hold out the possibility of positive growth for the new family formations, with greater health and happiness on both the individual and family level. Over time, when there *is* time, more satisfying and functional outcomes can unfold.

In contrast, the parents of this oldest cohort of Middle-Aged Adult Children likely have much less time remaining after they divorce. The youngest of them are in the latter phases of Erikson's Stage 7 (Generativity) at best. With time itself the ultimate finite resource, they have fewer opportunities to recover from divorce and begin new lives than do the parents of the younger cohorts of adult children. They and their children are aware that they are growing older, if not yet old.

Their children, already middle-aged themselves, could be on the brink of their own mid-life crises at the same time their parents are experiencing theirs. Their parents' decision to divorce can feel like an overwhelming intrusion into their already full lives. They had good reasons for hoping that concerns for their parents, at least temporarily, remained in the background. Now they are front and center.

Barb's Story

Barb's parents had been married for 43 years. She and her mother talked daily, and her mother had never once mentioned being unhappy in her marriage. Mostly their calls focused on the stresses in Barb's life: a demanding job, a husband who worked a different shift, and the logistics of a growing family. Then, shocking everyone, her mother announced she wanted to be alone. Barb experienced disbelief that her parents who were near retirement, with financial security and time to do the things they loved, instead were "throwing it all away."

Not yet qualifying for Medicare, her mom would no longer have health insurance, and her dad was afraid she would get half of his pension and he would have to sell their paid-off house during a downturn in the market. Both Barb and her brother felt their parents were putting them in the middle, but they found themselves taking different sides. Barb summed it up:

> "Who waits until they are older and needs someone around to help them with life in general to pack up and decide to be alone! On top of everything else, my dad has blood in his urine and is undergoing some pretty extensive tests. I keep thinking *WHY NOW?*"

Barb needed to ask for time off at work to get her dad to his appointments. And there were losses as well as worries. Barb and her husband had considered her parents among their very best friends, people they played euchre with regularly. In addition, the once much anticipated holiday gatherings were now viewed with dread.

Stage 8: Parents Growing Old

It is even more likely that the divorcing parents of middle-aged children will be in Erikson's eighth and final stage of life—Ego Integrity vs. Despair. Whether their parents are married, widowed, or divorced, adult children of elderly parents worry about how long they will be able to live on their own. They worry about their parents' declining physical, mental, and cognitive health. They worry about their vulnerability and safety.

Children's universal worry about their parents "growing old" is somewhat lessened when they are "growing old together." If they divorce at this final stage when their functionality is winding down, it is much less likely that they can or will re-partner. So now, in addition to the logistical concerns of how long one's parents will be able to live on their own, comes the double duty of addressing these concerns for each parent separately.

Likely no new income is forthcoming so whatever marital assets there are may be stretched thin to provide two separate packages of care and residence. And, needless to say, the older adult child's time is also spread thin. Instead of feeling responsible for a widowed elderly parent, there are now *two* elderly parents to consider—all on top of heavy commitments to one's own nuclear family.

Hank's Story

Hank was an only child in his late 40s. His mom was moderately disabled, unable to work, and dependent on her husband for many things. His dad was retired and involved in volunteer activities, some of which took him out of town. Lately, his mother's disability had prevented her from traveling with him.

When Hank's dad returned from a recent trip, he told his wife he no longer loved her but insisted there was no one else. At first, she was crushed. Then she was angry, and during a heated argument, she ordered him to leave. Hank was called in at this point. He was overwhelmed with the logistics of his parents living separately after 48 years, but they were determined. He could only imagine how much this was going to fall on his shoulders, and they refused to pursue any of the counseling options he had found for them.

On his wife's wise suggestion, Hank pursued counseling for himself. With a lot going on at work as well as three adolescent children still living at home, he knew he needed a place to sort out his options for dealing with his parents. What role was he willing and able to play in assisting their efforts to live apart without jeopardizing meeting his own life's challenges? He was pleasantly surprised to find that counseling also gave him a chance to sort out strong feelings of anger and sadness which his parents' divorce had triggered. Hank was determined to use his new insights to take care of his marriage in the hope that his own family could avoid what he and his parents were going through.

And what if an elderly parent is showing signs of cognitive decline? While always a reason for concern and sadness, this becomes particularly problematic when divorce is added to the picture. Now, in addition to concerns about appropriate care, there are fears that this parent is particularly vulnerable to abuse and scams.

Sometimes these fears arise specifically around an elderly parent's decision to hastily remarry someone their children hardly know. Was this a rational decision? Who is this new partner? Is the parent safe? Is the inheritance (if there is one) safe? We will return to these issues in greater depth in Chapters 9 and 10, but Serena's experience illustrates these concerns.

Serena's Story

Serena questioned her mother's mental stability when she up and left her dad after nearly 50 years. She hadn't seen this coming and found out her mom had immediately moved in with a man whom neither Serena nor her father had ever heard of. Even more unsettling, this strange man would only allow Serena to talk to her mother when he was present. Understandably worried and feeling protective for her mother's safety, she felt powerless to intervene as every attempt seemed to result in creating further distance from her mother. Without concrete evidence of her mother's mental incompetence, she was unable to enlist outside support, and her siblings were too busy with their own lives to get involved.

JoAnna's Story

JoAnna's story illustrates many of the points made in this chapter. In addition, it provides a longitudinal perspective and brings to light how events unfolding in both parent and adult child generations might lead to divorce. It clearly demonstrates the surprisingly powerful impact of parents divorcing even when their children are "all grown up."

JoAnna appeared to all the world to be a happy faculty wife living an enviable life. Tall, attractive, and athletic, she had never quite found a career path that fit her. Since her husband supported them comfortably on his academic salary, she didn't want or need to work outside the home.

Her first two children, both boys, were good students as well as excellent athletes, and JoAnna got great satisfaction out of being their mom. She volunteered in their classrooms and coached their soccer teams when they were in elementary school. She was also well regarded for her talent at entertaining. With equal ease, she could create a formal French-inspired dinner party for her husband's colleagues and students or, on the spur of the moment, pull up extra chairs to the kitchen table, inviting neighbors or friends to join the family for a simple spaghetti supper or pot of stew.

While the other moms in her circle, stay-at-home moms as well as professionals, thought she had it all, JoAnna always felt something was missing. Privately, she cringed at seeing herself as a dilettante but admitted that probably described her as she dabbled in the latest causes of the day but never really invested much energy in them. Her husband publicly proclaimed his adoration of her, but he was so busy with his work, and the travel that entailed, that she often felt they were growing apart. Consciously or unconsciously, she's not sure, she hit on the idea that a third child might bring them closer. The arrival of a baby girl did seem to bring new life to the marriage for several years.

Then, out of the blue, or so it seemed at first, JoAnna got word that her parents' marriage was coming apart. Like hers, their marriage had been fairly traditional. Her mother's role was subservient to her husband's career, the norm for her generation, and she did not share his interest in outdoor adventures. They had lived an affluent lifestyle in a small midwestern town for years and were highly regarded in their Episcopal Church community.

But now JoAnna's mother had come upon evidence that her husband had been having an affair which likely had been going on for decades. She would not stand for it, and he wouldn't promise to end it. So, with her children grown and mostly married and settled, she straightened her back, held her head high, and filed for divorce.

This left JoAnna reeling, shaken to her core. Clearly, her mother being a dutiful wife and mother had not been enough to keep her dad from straying. Being athletic like her dad, JoAnna found herself siding with him and identifying with his desire for something more than a perfunctory marriage. Looking back a few years later, she recognized this as a time when she might have seriously explored a career or persuaded her husband to go to marriage counseling. Instead, she ended up having an affair of her own. She recalls thinking, *If my parents couldn't make it after all those years together, then maybe marriage isn't meant to last.*

At the time their grandparents divorced, JoAnna's children ranged from early elementary school age to adolescence. All three seemed sad and confused by this news but only her young daughter openly expressed any feelings. JoAnna didn't pursue this as she was busy sorting out her own. The joyful annual summer reunion in The Smoky Mountains with all the cousins never happened again as the grandparents sold the family cottage. The cousins, once close and comfortable with each other, grew apart.

As divorce proceedings became increasingly contentious, JoAnna and her siblings felt increasingly stressed. In addition to their already busy lives, they were now forced to worry about how each of their parents, now in their late 60s, would manage their post-divorce lives. The siblings also frequently found themselves at odds. JoAnna was the most sympathetic toward her father and felt her mother had let her marriage fail. JoAnna's older brother staunchly defended his mother as the injured party although his own marriage fell apart shortly after his parents'. Their much younger sister hastily married a staunch Catholic and declared her determination never to divorce.

Both of JoAnna's parents remarried within a couple of years. Her mother married a well-off childless widow who was attracted by her wifely skills, so JoAnna was relieved not to have to worry about her for the foreseeable future. JoAnna gradually developed a fondness for this man and eventually considered him a stepfather. He embraced his new wife's children and grandchildren although he was awkward and formal around them. Still, there were times when he seemed to revel in his new role as grandfather, especially around the holidays.

Her father married the woman he'd been involved with. After that, he seemed to make little effort to connect with JoAnna and her siblings who experienced him as having changed. They never liked his new wife and considered her a "homewrecker." She had a rather distant relationship with her own children, and no one attempted to blend the two families or to develop any new family traditions.

Before long, it became apparent that their father's new wife was mainly interested in his money. The three siblings tried to pull together to protect their interests when they felt their father was becoming incompetent at handling his affairs. They were only modestly successful in this endeavor and alienated him in the process. This created a rift which JoAnna, especially, experienced as a loss.

As for JoAnna's own marriage? When her husband found out about her affair, he began one of his own. For a while they thought that evening the score might save their marriage, but that seemed unlikely.

What can we learn from JoAnna's story? First, it illustrates several points about the impact of parental divorce on Middle-Aged Adult

Children. When their parents' marriage failed, all three adult siblings questioned the viability of marriage each in their own way. Relationships among them were stressed when they sided with different parents. Extended family traditions changed when the grandparents sold the summer home that had brought their far-flung children and grandchildren together each year.

Concern for their mother lifted when she remarried a man who supported her continued involvement with her family. Overtime, he blended in as a stepparent and grandparent. Concern for their father, however, grew over time. His new wife never attempted to bond with them and took advantage of his cognitive decline to gain control of his finances.

It is possible JoAnna's marriage may not have lasted even if her parents hadn't divorced. Her husband's investment in his career to the neglect of their marriage added to her sense of unfulfillment. Looking back, JoAnna realized she could have insisted on marriage counseling, and she could have sought help in finding work or volunteer activities which would give her a sense of purpose once her children were older. Her "choice" of an affair became a self-fulfilling prophecy that her marriage would go the route of her parents.

In Summary: A Joke and a Eulogy

Much has been studied and written about the effects of divorce on young and very young children. Young adult children, those in their late teens, twenties, and even early thirties are at least beginning to get the attention they deserve when their parents divorce. However, the children of older and elderly parents whose marriages end in divorce have essentially been ignored altogether. They are approaching, or have entered, mid-life themselves when their parents are in Erikson's final life stages.

As noted above, for parents who divorce in Erikson's Stage 7, there may still be time and opportunity to make changes in both their work life and personal relationships. But when divorce occurs in Erikson's final Stage 8, parents are likely to be elderly, and time, as well as resources, are running out. Their middle-aged children are left to deal both with the shock and the reality of their parents' situation.

Precious little has been written about either parents or adult children of couples who choose to end long marriages in the final life stage. It may be because their absolute numbers are small relative to the numbers of divorces at earlier ages, but as a phenomenon on the rise it needs to be better understood. However, there is no question that divorce at this final stage has a powerful and dramatic impact on the couple's children whose lives are already busy and full.

The Joke

The realization of this impact can be seen in the dark humor of a "joke" which has made the rounds on the internet. It has taken on different specifics in different cultures and countries. I include it here because it illustrates several important points. The following is a composite version.

> Retired to Sun City, Arizona, 85-year-old Herb dials up his son Isaac in New York. He is surprised when his son answers since he is often too busy to take his dad's calls. "I hope this doesn't spoil your day," he says, "but I need to let you know that your mom and I are getting divorced."
>
> "Dad, this is crazy. You've got to be kidding me. You guys just celebrated your 60th anniversary."
>
> "I'm not kidding," Herb says. "It's been 60 years of hell and we've both had enough. We can't stand to be in the same room with each other, and I need you to break the news to your sister in St. Louis." Before his son could speak, Herb hangs up.
>
> In shock, Isaac calls his sister. "Over my dead body they're getting a divorce. Let me handle this!" she insists and immediately calls her parents. Choked up and screaming, she emphatically tells them that they are NOT getting a divorce. "Sit tight and don't make a move till I get there. I'm calling Isaac and we will both be there tomorrow. Is that perfectly clear?"
>
> The old man hangs up. Smugly, he turns to his wife and says, "Well, they'll be here for Thanksgiving after all. Now, how will we get them here for Passover?"

Clearly for adult children, hearing that their elderly parents are contemplating divorce is a powerful activator. Often too busy with their own lives to spend the holidays with their aging parents, they still spring into action at the drop of the word "divorce." Such shocking "news" can stimulate siblings in faraway places to pull together with a common purpose—trying to avert a potential disaster.

The power of this "joke" rests on universal concerns adult children have about their aging parents' ability, physically and mentally, to go it alone. Additionally, deciding to divorce at this late stage may seem rash and indicate cognitive decline, poor decision making, and an inability to consider consequences. Their parents' divorce at this stage of life would spell extra work and burden for these mid-life children whose lives and resources are already stretched thin. Perhaps even more important, it would also threaten the turn their sense of their family history upside down. If they can keep their parents' marriage intact, their childhood memories remain intact as well![1]

The Eulogy

In a 2020 New York Times opinion piece, Allyson Hobbs, Director of Stanford's African American Studies program, provides a serious and poignant account of the impact of her elderly parents' divorce. Entitled "When 80-Year-Old Parents Divorce," Professor Hobbs describes the ending of her parents' marriage after 60 years.[2] Their marriage had survived the death of one of their children along with a string of other deaths in the extended family. She felt their relationship only grew closer through adversity:

> They were unbroken; their bond was indestructible. My parents told the same stories of growing up on the South Side of Chicago hundreds of times. They anticipated the punch lines of jokes that they already knew, sometimes bursting into laughter before the joke was complete… They seemed to relish sharing the smallest and most mundane moments of life: running errands to the grocery store, the post office, the mall.

Despite Hobbs herself having achieved many external trappings of successful adulthood, she was surprised at how deeply affected she was by "the spectacular collapse" of her parents' marriage:

I am undone, untethered, dysfunctional. I am in a small boat, too fatigued to pick up an oar, lost at sea. The lighthouse that never failed to guide me home is now out of service. I think of my friends whose parents divorced when they were children or teenagers. I am an adult. I don't have to shuttle between two homes, I won't have to endure remarriages, I don't believe that I am at fault. I should be able to stanch the wound, but I can't. I'm bleeding out.

She struggled to find an explanation for why they could no longer live together. The one she seemed to find most convincing is almost paradoxical:

Or perhaps in their mid-80s—after all the joys, the stories, the sorrows, after all of the life that they have lived together—my parents find this final act too frightening and too disorienting. Is it possible that it might be easier to live without each other by choice, to break that once indestructible bond now, rather than to wait until it is broken cruelly, against their will? ... I've been perseverating over my parents' mortality for years. It must be terrifying for them.

In Summary

As a mature, Middle-Aged Adult Child, you likely have a number of legitimate concerns when you hear that your parents are divorcing in the final decades of their lives. Most of your worries will be about them. You may worry that they are making a big mistake and wonder if they are of sound mind. You may worry that their finances will run out. You may worry whether they can live on their own if they are declining physically or mentally. You may worry that they will be lonely. You may worry that they may re-partner with someone who doesn't have their best interests at heart.

Other worries will be about yourself. Will you have enough time or resources to take care of both of them in addition to your own mid-life responsibilities? Will attempting to meet their needs put a strain on your relationships at home? At work? How might their divorce impact you financially? Could they commit to new relationships that do not have room for you and your children? Is your own marriage or relationship going to last if theirs could end after all these years together?

These issues and concerns are significant and legitimate. They have, however, been almost completely ignored even by those who believe that divorce can impact younger adult children. By virtue of your age and maturity, people mistakenly assume you can and will simply take your older parents' divorce in stride along with everything else you have responsibility for. I hope this chapter has convinced you that this is nearly impossible. As we will see in the next chapter, you need to shore up your boundaries and take care of yourself!

Chapter Six Notes: *The Lighthouse Goes Dark: The Oldest Adult Children*

1. Similar to the theme of the online "joke" is Bess Wohl's Tony-nominated Broadway play *Grand Horizons,* first performed in 2019. It, too, portrays a family turned upside down by a later-life divorce. When octogenarians Bill and Nancy announce that they want a divorce after a fifty-year marriage, their adult sons rush to their senior living community to talk them out of it. The parents appear unfazed, but their sons are shaken to the core and reexamine what they thought they knew about their parents' marriage. It was billed as a comedy—"both hilarious and heart-breaking."

2. Allyson Hobbs, "When 80-Year-Old Parents Divorce - I Thought Their Bond was Indestructible. Now I'm Mourning People Who are Still Alive." *The New York Times,* Opinion Piece, February 13, 2020.

PART IV

Key Concepts

-7-
Boundaries and Compassion

Boundaries signify that two things are separate. They designate where one thing—a person or place or concept—ends and another begins. A river, a fence, or a line on a map indicate a point or a limit where two areas become different. Boundaries are also expectations or rules about the limits of acceptable behavior. They refer to lines that should not be crossed, things that should or should not be done.

Overview

The importance of establishing and maintaining appropriate parent-child boundaries throughout the divorce process has been a strong thread running through the previous chapters. In fact, having healthy boundaries is important enough to deserve its own chapter. But what do we mean by a boundary?

As noted above, the word boundary has two important meanings. It indicates where one thing ends and another begins. Applied to human interaction, healthy contact and connection among people requires us to be clear about where we end and another person begins. We are separate beings with our own thoughts, feelings, and needs. But a boundary also refers to limits defining acceptable behavior. There are expectations and sometimes rules about how we should and shouldn't act, about lines that should not be crossed.

Here we will primarily focus on the importance of parents and adult children remaining acutely aware of their familial roles even while going through the throes of divorce and its aftermath. We will see that it is not uncommon for parents to lose sight that their adult children are still their children who are rightfully experiencing their parents' divorce from their own perspective. We will also see that while adult children may want to fully grasp what is going on, they need to respect the healthy boundaries their parents set around the divorce itself.

The distress experienced as marriages unravel naturally produces strong feelings and reactions. Fear, sadness, and anger are common as are their more extreme versions—terror, depression, and even rage. Not surprisingly, when these feelings are at a peak, parents may be overwhelmed and show lapses in judgment. At such times, they are more likely to involve their children in the divorce in unhealthy ways.

Lapses in judgment about appropriate parent-child boundaries also occur for adult children as they react to their parents' divorce with their own intense feelings. In an attempt to make sense of what is happening, they may be open to, or even press for, information beyond what is necessary or healthy for them in their role as children. They may feel flattered to be trusted with intimate details, but they could end up learning things about their parents they wished they did not know.

The experience of Abby, a young woman in her late 20s, starkly illustrates the negative consequences of poor parent-child boundaries during the divorce process.

> "My parents were so wrapped up in their own problems that they forgot how to be parents. Everything was about them. Sometimes I felt like I was babysitting two five-year-olds who needed to be sent to separate rooms for time-out. I got so caught up in their issues that I lost touch with my own feelings. It was like I was watching a train wreck and the only way I could stop it was to throw myself down on the tracks. They both kept trying to pull me over to their side and never asked how I was doing. Eventually I just had to cut off my relationship with both of them in order to save myself."

Parents are generally aware that *young* children need to be safeguarded from all this as much as possible. However, even in well-handled cases of divorce, young children will still have some exposure to their parents' intense emotions, including anger at and negative feelings about the other parent. Under ideal circumstances, family members, school personnel, neighbors, and one's community or "village" will recognize the need to step in to address the needs of younger children when their parents are temporarily struggling and too needy themselves to do so. With sufficient resources and support, an appropriate parent-child relationship is more likely to be preserved—albeit with occasional lapses.

But when the "children" are adults, that parent-child boundary is more often violated. Now, in addition to the intense emotional climate, divorcing parents are more likely to view their adult children as peers and even confidantes. Shielding them from adult issues and adult scenarios may seem less important. One might reason that they are grown up, after all, and should be able to take it all in stride. This is rarely the case as one young woman's experience illustrates:

> "Because I was an adult, I wasn't shielded from any of the sordid little secrets like my younger sister was. I was put in the middle and felt like I had to take sides, but that's impossible. It was awful to suddenly become a sounding board for all my father's faults. Whatever they are, he is my dad, and I love him. Whatever my mom's faults are, she is my mom, and I love her too."

Yet, despite the greater likelihood that parents will violate boundaries and share too much with their adult children, adult children may have some advantages over their younger counterparts. If they are no longer living in the family home, they may have less exposure to the angst their parents are going through during the early days and even years of divorce. Being older, they may be better able to recognize inappropriate sharing and have a larger skill set for setting and maintaining healthy boundaries. As such, adult children have a greater chance of protecting themselves when their parents step over the line into over-sharing and boundary violations. This also means they shoulder some of the burden for avoiding and addressing these uncomfortable situations.

This was the experience of Sally, a 31-year-old woman, whose mother turned to her as her primary support.

> "At first I wasn't able to set limits with my mom when she wanted to tell me all the gory details of the divorce. I was just broadsided by the shock of it all, and I guess I felt really sorry for her when she was crying really hard. But then I felt

something shift inside and I realized I just didn't want to hear any more about it. I started crying, too, and I told her she needed to stop. I asked her to find someone else to dump on—her sister or a friend or someone, anyone but not me! She looked really surprised but she got it. I really thank her for that."

Initially, both Sally and her mother were too distraught over the divorce to set limits on her mother's inappropriate sharing. Luckily, when Sally tuned into her gut reaction, she was able to voice her discomfort and ask her mother to stop. Equally fortunate, Sally's mother heard and respected her daughter's request. Sally's ability to recognize and assert her needs and her mother's willingness to honor them reestablished a healthy parent-child relationship.

Boundaries in Context

Although we will be talking about healthy parent-child boundaries in general, I first want to acknowledge that there are many individual and cultural variations. What constitutes appropriate personal space differs by culture, type of relationship, and social context. The same is true of appropriate boundaries.

What one culture or family considers a healthy level of connection among family members, another might consider too close, enmeshed, or even smothering. Similarly, one culture or family may prize a high level of independence and autonomy in their adult children whereas another might see this as too distant, detached, or even estranged.

Even within cultures, families vary widely along a continuum in how physically close they are, both geographically and in terms of physical contact when they get together. They also vary widely in how they communicate, both how often they talk to each other and the depth of their sharing of feelings and events when they do. For example, in some families it is normal for mothers and their adult daughters to talk on a daily basis, sharing the minutiae of their daily lives. Other families still feel sufficiently close when they live far apart, talk, or get together much less frequently, and primarily share only the highlights of their lives.

These different cultural and family norms for what constitutes appropriate sharing of feelings and information have been in play long before parental divorce enters the picture. Thus, what families consider appropriate sharing about divorce may also be quite subjective and differ widely. Nevertheless, whether families share a great deal or very little, members recognize when a different level of sharing occurs. They identify this as something outside their usual experience and likely feel uncomfortable.

Boundaries and Compassion

Popular writer and podcast host Brené Brown has strongly emphasized the importance of personal boundaries for one's own mental and physical well-being. Having clear boundaries means prioritizing your own needs and practicing self-care without feeling guilty. The alternative, as she sees it, is "losing yourself," as we saw with Abby at the beginning of this chapter.[1]

Being clear about where you end and another person begins allows you to interact safely with them. It allows you to connect with other people without fear of enmeshment. When your own boundaries are clear and firm, you have enough distance to feel compassion and empathy for others.

When boundaries are blurred it is difficult to differentiate your own feelings, thoughts, and needs from those of others. Being overly involved in another person's life—or they in yours—robs you both of your individuality and autonomy. You may find yourself focusing on the other person's needs to the neglect of your own.

Brown recognizes that taking care of yourself by setting clear boundaries may be met with disappointment, resistance, or even hostility. Nevertheless, she remains convinced that it is still best for all concerned. In fact, since strong boundaries reduce resentment, they are a prerequisite for feeling generous towards others and accepting them as they are without judgement. Almost paradoxically, Brown asserts that the most compassionate people have "boundaries of steel."

This is a very important point! One of the goals of this book is to help parents and their adult children recognize both their own and each others' needs as they navigate the process of parental divorce. When each generation takes care of themselves during this challenging time, they will be more likely to have compassion for the other's experience. And all this hinges on having firm, clear personal boundaries.

In her 2021 book *Set Boundaries, Find Peace,* Nedra Glover Tawwab[2] delivers much the same message and offers what some have called the "boundary bible." She defines boundaries as expectations and needs that make people feel safe and comfortable in their relationships. As such, they promote mental and emotional well-being. An essential part of comfort in relationships is learning when to say "no" and when to say "yes."

Her book is an excellent resource for assessing the health of one's boundaries in different kinds of relationships, understanding why they are so important for one's well-being, and learning how to set and maintain clear boundaries even when met with push back. Tawwab's focus is not on a family crisis such as divorce nor on setting limits with what parents are sharing about their lives. However, she highlights that it is particularly difficult to set limits with one's parents.

When young adults stand up to the people who have likely been the most influential force in their lives, it signals a change in the relationship. Tawwab feels that you become an adult when you are able to set boundaries with your parents. And this is exactly what adult children of divorce need to do to take care of themselves and preserve a healthy parent-child relationship!

Boundary Violations

If someone crosses over a line, verbally or behaviorally, in a way that causes another person to feel uncomfortable, a boundary may have been violated. The boundary may or may not have been stated explicitly, and the boundary violation may have been accidental. If so, the situation can easily be rectified. Often, however, it is not so simple.

When a person feels something inappropriate or unacceptable has happened, they may initially be in a quandary and not know how to react. The sooner they can recognize what is happening, the sooner they can state or reinstate their boundary (the limits of what is acceptable) and trust that it will be honored. Both the recognition as well as the honoring can be influenced by a power differential between the two persons.

The person in the lower power position may be less likely to realize they have a right to set limits with a person of greater power. They may be hesitant to assert this right even when recognized. On the other hand, the person in the higher power position may feel justified in challenging any limits placed on their behavior. More likely than not, when there is a power imbalance in a parent-child relationship, it is the parent holding the greater power.

Marty, whom we met in Chapter 6, identified boundary violations by both of her parents as the hardest thing for her about their divorce. Because she had been aware that they were not happy together for much of their 46-year marriage, their split came more as a relief than a shock. However, at 35, she was surprised to find herself caught in the middle and used as a sounding board, a confidante, a go-between, and a secret keeper. All of these uncomfortable roles ignored that fact that Marty was a loyal daughter who hoped to maintain an appropriately close relationship with both parents. As a result, her anger began to grow, and flip flopped between her mom and dad, depending on which one was making the latest inappropriate request.

As a sounding board and confidante, Marty heard hateful accounts from each parent about the other. By the time she realized she needed to set limits she had already heard things she never wanted to hear. Sadly, she told me:

> "Unfortunately, I know everything about their marriage. At first, I felt like I had to listen to my mom because she was so upset and she'd been there for me when I was going through a break-up. By the time I realized it was just too much, I already knew so much bad stuff about my dad. You can't just erase it. When I tried to stop my dad from venting about mom, he threatened to cut off my inheritance. He told me he'd been there for me, paying for college and everything, and now I needed to be there for him. It's just not the same. You know, it hurts like hell when your parents hate each other. I try to keep love at the core of my relationship with each of them, but this rocks your core."

Marty's parents also used her as a go-between. Ever since their bitter divorce three years ago, they had refused to speak to each other and would not be in the same room. This made it impossible to hold events with the whole family and, initially, it forced Marty into being a message carrier.

After hurtful emails between her parents didn't resolve urgent financial matters, Marty's mother asked her to deliver sensitive tax papers to her father. Seeing the box of papers as representing the marriage, her father blew up at her, screamed obscenities, and accused Marty of siding with her mother.

And then there was Marty's role as secret keeper. She and her older sisters supported the divorce and expected that both parents might be happier apart than they had been together. They anticipated they could "still have 25 more years left on this earth." However, the sisters were not prepared for their father's remarriage less than a year after the divorce was final. He made them promise not to tell their mother about the wedding or, again, he would cut them out of his will. Marty felt trapped, caught in the crossfires of a no-win situation. Neither she nor her sisters attended the wedding but that summer when one of the grandchildren let it slip that there was a "new grandma," Marty's mom felt devastated and betrayed by her daughters.

With both of her parents committing glaring violations of healthy parent-child boundaries, the only feelings Marty experienced were exhaustion and resentment. Her fundamental loyalty to, and sacrifice for, her parents went unnoticed and unappreciated. Until she could shore up her boundaries, there would be no room to experience empathy or compassion for what they were actually going through.

If you are an adult child feeling uncomfortable about a parent's behavior, how do you know if a boundary has been violated? It is often important to pay attention to your "gut" because sometimes the body registers discomfort sooner than the mind. Ask yourself how you are feeling about being put in this particular situation or being party to this particular information:

> **➤Do I feel confused? Overwhelmed? Nauseous?**
> **➤Do I feel unsafe?**
> **➤Do I feel numb? Disconnected?**
> **➤Do I just want to disappear or get away from it all?**

In addition to paying attention to your gut feelings, here is list of questions to ask yourself. Affirmative answers likely indicate that the parent-child boundary is being violated:

Do you feel your parents may be using you as:
> ➤ **A sounding board?**
> ➤ **A witness to their loss and grief with no concern for your feelings?**
> ➤ **A mediator or go-between?**
> ➤ **A message-carrier?**
> ➤ **A secret-keeper?**
> ➤ **An emotional caretaker?**
> ➤ **A therapist?**

Do you feel your parents are:
> ➤ **Asking you to take sides?**
> ➤ **Giving you information about each other's shortcomings?**
> ➤ **Sharing intimate details about their marriage, including details about their sex life or lack thereof?**
> ➤ **Providing uncomfortable information about affairs or relationships?**

Barriers vs. Boundaries

When boundary violations continue or accumulate to the point where an adult child just wants to "get away from it all," they may resort to erecting *barriers*. This can happen because *boundaries* were never clearly set in the first place, because attempts to maintain them have failed, or because they were never respected. By actively creating concrete obstacles that obstruct access or passage, barriers go beyond setting limits and asking them to be honored. They signal that a more desperate step is considered necessary to keep oneself safe emotionally or physically. In terms of family dynamics, this can result in serious cut-offs, temporary or permanent.

We saw this with Abby, the young woman who described her parents' impending divorce as a "train wreck" and felt compelled to throw herself on the tracks to stop it. She had allowed herself to become too involved in the drama of her parents' divorce. When she realized this was harming her physical and mental health, she began to set limits or boundaries. She told her parents she would not take sides and would be pulling back from her involvement in their divorce drama for the sake of her own well-being.

Unfortunately, neither parent chose to respect her position of neutrality or her decision to take care of herself. She felt a cut off was the only choice remaining. Almost apologetically, she told me, "If your parents won't respect your boundaries, you may need to cut off contact with them. I hope someday down the road we are able to have a relationship again, but I know, for my own health, it can't happen now."

In families or relationships where boundaries are respected, barriers aren't necessary. Take a simple example: if it is known that a closed bedroom or bathroom door signifies a desire for privacy, members of families with healthy boundaries will knock and ask for permission before entering. In families where this boundary is not respected, a person may need to lock or barricade the door in order to ensure privacy. In extreme cases of boundary violations, family members may feel the need to literally cut off contact in order to preserve their own well-being.

Adult children still have many kinds of barriers they can erect short of cutting off all contact which Abby felt she needed to do. They can simply end an uncomfortable phone call. They can refuse to answer future calls from a boundary-violating parent. They can walk out of the room or house. They might stay in touch but on a much less frequent or friendly basis or temporarily refuse to have contact. It is only in the most extreme cases that an adult child feels the need to physically move away or terminate the relationship for an extended period or even permanently.

Divorce nearly always comes with losses. Parents and children losing their connection is a heavy loss even if only temporary. Generally, it is not a necessary loss except in the most extreme and toxic situations where efforts to maintain healthy boundaries are repeatedly violated. Unfortunately, Abby's was one of those.

When parents have had a generally positive relationship with their adult children prior to divorce, it is likely their relationship will endure. It is even *more* likely when clear parent-child boundaries are established, maintained, and respected so that barriers do not become necessary. There may be lapses and struggles, but when parents remain in their roles as Mom and Dad, their adult children can remain in their role as children, not confidantes or peers.

Rectifying Boundary Violations

What happens if a parent-child boundary is violated, intentionally or inadvertently? Hurtful as it is, can it be rectified? The three stories that follow will illustrate successful resolutions that avoided cut-offs and increased the likelihood that adult children with firm and respected boundaries would emerge with greater compassion for their parents' struggles during the divorce process.

Molly's Story

First, with Molly, whom we met in Chapter 5, we saw how much harm parents' boundary violations can cause an adult child. She described her mother as an "over-sharer" who "kept no secrets." Within hours of her parents' decision to separate, her mother showed up at her apartment sobbing incoherently. Molly felt she had no choice but to let her in, comfort her, and try to figure out as best she could what was going on—all this despite being in a difficult place in her own life. Looking back, she realized her mom "completely dumped on me," but at the time she felt it was normal. Very soon, Molly's dad sought her out with his version of things. In an effort to be fair, Molly listened to him and comforted him too.

As she recalled it when we met:

> "I was following every emotional blow by blow. At 25, I didn't have the personal wherewithal to say, 'Knock it off!' They were supposed to know what was best, so I guess I deferred to them and their judgement. There's a huge power differential between parents and kids and I was sort of flattered to be let in on things. I think I also felt a lot of responsibility for both of them even though I was really just learning how to take care of myself."

When extended family members asked how she was doing, Molly said she was okay. She didn't want to speak poorly of her parents out of family loyalty, and she assumed she should be handling things better. Reconstructing this time in her life after nearly a decade had passed, Molly said:

"I think I was embarrassed about my parents' behavior and I thought it was my fault that I had so much information about their marriage. Now that I'm more of a fully baked person it seems obvious to me. Your kids are not your therapist. I wish my parents hadn't used me in that way. It's not fair. I wish somebody had told me it was okay to back off."

But Molly *did* have the wherewithal to get herself into therapy eventually. We discussed her need to take care of herself and her right to assert her boundaries with her parents—issues which were still unresolved since their divorce almost 10 years earlier. For a while, she still kept a cautious distance from them until she felt she could really trust them to respect the clear limits she was now able to set.

Molly was one of the fortunate ones. She held firm and both of her parents eventually came around to respecting her boundaries. This was a huge relief as well as an indication of significant progress. Still, she often wondered how her younger adult years might have been different if she had been able to do this earlier.

In addition to respect for her boundaries, Molly also wished her parents might someday apologize to her for having put her in such a difficult situation for so long. It took a few more years before she could ask for this, but by the time she did, both of her parents had done their own healing and knew what Molly needed. Their words of apology still had a profound effect. This is yet another reminder that *divorce is a process and not an event.* Deep healing can come even after a decade or more.

Like Molly, many adult children love their parents very much. When they see how sad or troubled they are, they are tempted to drop their own concerns and try to take care of them. However, most of the time the parents have more appropriate places to turn for support. The sooner their children are able to step back into their appropriate role as adult children dealing with their own divorce feelings on top of their own developmental challenges, the sooner they can release the burden of managing their parents. The sooner their parents recognize and respect the need for this, the sooner a healthy parent-child relationship can be resumed.

Travis's Story

Travis was a brilliant young man. When his parents' 40-year marriage began to unravel, he was away at law school and his considerably older brother Garrett was in the Army, stationed in Germany with his wife and three children. Growing up, Travis had been close to both of his parents and had always imagined that they were happily married. Lately he had his hands full with his heavy class schedule and a part-time job, so he chose to ignore the increasing tone of discontent in his mother's emails and texts. She persisted until he felt he had to call and see what was going on at home.

Always an open book, his mother poured out an account of his father's increasingly problematic drinking and her plans to divorce. Part of the time she was crying so hard that Travis couldn't even understand what she was saying. When his father didn't return his phone calls, Travis decided he had better go home for a long weekend to see for himself what was going on. What he found was far worse than he had anticipated and he ended up staying for a week, returning to law school poorly prepared for the exams that were soon to follow.

But things with his parents did not settle down and Travis began to feel his present life was becoming unmanageable and his future dreams were beginning to look unattainable. He found himself on the phone with his parents on a daily basis even though he told them he really didn't have time for this and felt they never followed his advice anyway. For his own survival, he abruptly cut himself off from everything but school, his job, and calls with his parents.

He felt he no longer had time to get together with Julie, a psychology graduate student he had been seeing and really liked. After all, he was thinking, relationships are a lot of work, and they don't last anyway. Although she was hurt and confused, Julie insisted they meet to discuss what was happening. She listened empathically to his distress, didn't take his seeming rejection personally, and convinced him to see a psychotherapist.

That's when I met Travis and we immediately identified his need to firm up his boundaries with his parents and get more support for himself. First, he reached out to his brother Garrett in Germany who was willing to get involved and do what he could at a distance to share the burden with his younger brother. At the very least, Garrett felt he could contact their parents and tell them to get help for themselves and to stop leaning on Travis. As the older son, more established in his adult role, Garrett commanded more respect from their parents who agreed to follow his requests. He also set up regular times to talk with each of them and asked them not to involve Travis.

Then Travis laid out his own boundaries with his parents. He told them he needed to concentrate on school and would call them when he could take a break. He asked both of them not to call him except in an emergency. When his mother violated this boundary and called over something minor, Travis said he needed to end the call and did.

During the calls which he initiated, he rigorously applied the *broken record* technique. With this type of assertiveness behavior, the speaker conveys a clear and firm message. If met with resistance or argument, the message is simply repeated, unchanged, as often as necessary. For Travis, this meant he repeated his firm recommendations that each parent get professional help, thus closing off their efforts to go over their same litany of complaints. Furthermore, he decided to call when he had a definite time constraint which he clearly conveyed and held to. Eventually, Travis's parents turned to other sources of support and, perhaps at his brother's urging, more often asked Travis how things were going for him, including school.

Travis's mother contacted an attorney and a counselor, and his father entered an out-patient substance abuse program. Travis felt it was unlikely they would reconcile, but he was at peace with whatever outcome they chose knowing they both had appropriate supports in place. What mattered most was that he was once again able to concentrate on school and to cautiously resume his relationship with Julie, who seemed to understand and respect his need to proceed slowly.

Now, instead of dreading contact with his parents and resenting their demands on his time and energy, Travis had room for compassion. He experienced sadness for each of them and the difficulties they were going through, now from a much healthier distance. The only choices he once felt he had—sacrificing his own young adult plans or cutting off from his parents altogether—had greatly expanded. This was due to the firm boundaries Travis and his brother put into place as well as to his parents' willingness to seek appropriate help and support.

These two examples demonstrate that boundary violations can be rectified after weeks/months (like Travis) or even after years (like Molly).

Travis's story also illustrates how helpful it can be when siblings support each other's efforts to establish firm boundaries with their parents. Let's turn now to a third example of setting clear boundaries, this time after decades. As we will see, all three stories support the connection between healthy boundaries and greater compassion.

Jody's Story

Jody, now a Midwesterner seen in Chapter 3, visited her mother in California several times a year. Although her mother divorced more than 30 years ago when Jody was in college, she never remarried. Neither did Jody's father, a Methodist minister who came out as gay. Now in his late 80s, he moved to the town where Jody and her family lived and required a fair amount of caretaking.

In recent years, somewhere during Jody's visits in California, her mother would pull out her (now quite old) wedding album and want to reminisce with her. Mainly, however, she used this as an opportunity to disparage Jody's dad, recalling how he behaved "like an asshole" around their wedding and how she should have known then that the marriage was a mistake.

Anticipating her next cross-country visit, Jody got in touch with how badly this little ritual made her feel. She made plans to take better care of herself. This time when her mother reached for the album, Jody was prepared: "Mom, I don't want to look at your wedding album again. It just makes me feel bad about Dad. You divorced him but I still have to deal with him."

Her elderly mother was surprised and hurt that Jody would draw this line. Briefly she tried to make Jody feel guilty, saying she had no one else to talk with about this. But Jody held firm, repeating her position and sitting with a serious expression. Valuing these visits from her daughter, Jody's mother backed off in the moment and later surprised Jody with a heart-felt apology at the end of the visit. For her part, Jody felt relieved to have her boundary respected and almost immediately experienced more compassion for her mother than she usually felt.

In all three of these stories where boundary violations were eventually rectified, the adult children had greater success when they conveyed their concerns using "I messages" rather than "You messages." "You messages" are experienced as blaming or criticizing another's behavior and likely produce defensiveness and shame. "I messages" convey one's own feelings which are not debatable. To be able to effectively deliver an "I message," you need to be in touch with your feelings and that requires good boundaries. You need to know where you end, and the other person begins.

We see this clearly in Jody's firm statement. She could have attacked her mother's behavior as annoying or stuck. She could have said something like: "You say all the same old negative things about Dad every time I'm here." That would have likely led to an argument. Instead, Jody had identified the feelings that came up when her mother reached for the wedding album. She was clear that she didn't want to hear negative things about her father because they made her feel bad and she still had to deal with him on a regular basis. Her mother tried a little push back, but Jody held firm and they both moved on to greater empathy for each other's experience of the family divorce.

Can Adult Children Violate Parents' Boundaries?

Of course they can! In an effort to understand what is going on, adult children may be the ones who cross the line and ask for information which is inappropriate. This can happen any time during the divorce process as well as when a parent starts to explore or establish a new relationship. This time, it is the parents whose guts register discomfort. They are the ones who need to set firm limits on what their adult children should and need to know in order to preserve a healthy parent-child relationship.

When Sophia, whom we met in Chapter 1, recovered from her hysterectomy she decided it was time to leave her loveless marriage. She expected this to come as no surprise to her son and daughter who were both married. However, perhaps because Sophia and Ted's marriage had been lackluster for years, their children assumed that's how it would continue on into the sunset. They had not witnessed any arguments, and neither parent had vented any dissatisfaction to them.

In his usual taciturn manner, Ted never tried to change Sophia's mind about seeking a divorce. Nor did he openly complain to his children about how unfairly he felt he was being treated, although they could discern this from his passive aggressive behaviors toward their mother. They were well aware of his thwarting her efforts to reach a divorce settlement and get the house ready to sell.

For her part, Sophia was eager to extricate herself from Ted, but she felt a twinge of guilt over leaving. She knew she had a better chance of moving on to a good future than Ted did and didn't want to turn his children against him. Sophia thought Ted would benefit from their support as he had no close friends or family and she had a strong network. She was in therapy by this point, and we had discussed the importance of not putting the children in the middle.

Sophia was determined to keep her personal issues with Ted to herself. She was not prepared for her children's pressure for explanations. Having witnessed no overt hostility or toxicity, they wanted to know why she decided "out of nowhere" to leave their dad. They anticipated he would be relying on them for basic needs since he'd never cooked a meal or run a vacuum. They also anticipated he would want to spend more time with them than they had available in their busy lives. For a while they tried to convince their mom not to go through with the divorce.

Sophia tried to placate them with general explanations. Her daughter Shannan would have none of it. She demanded to know more about what was lacking in her parents' relationship than her mother was comfortable sharing. Hard as it was for Sophia to hold back from revealing a litany of complaints and disparaging assessments (including evidence over the years of Ted's lukewarm emotional investment in his children), she was determined not to paint Ted in a negative light. She held firm even when Shannan tried to bait her with negative things Ted had supposedly said about Sophia.

Eventually, Sophia firmly told both of her adult children that she was divorcing Ted for her own personal reasons of incompatibility and growing apart but she wanted them to continue to have a close relationship with him. Sometimes Shannan still pushed for more and put herself in the middle carrying messages to Sophia from Ted.

By this time in our work together, Sophia was adamant about setting boundaries. She told me:

> "I had to let her know that her father could contact me directly and I would be happy to discuss whatever he wants to discuss. I think the pressure on her … the feeling of

responsibility she now has for her dad … was really getting to her and I felt bad that he was now leaning on her instead of me. I told her I had a therapist to talk to about these things and that she might want to do the same, but she got kind of angry about that. I told her that it isn't her responsibility to take care of her dad or me and that I really miss spending time with her without her dad always being the focus."

Over time, Shannan was able to find her way back to a warm relationship with her mom, but it took patience and persistence on Sophia's part. Ted's continued self-imposed isolation and leaning on Shannan strained her marriage, and Sophia wished she weren't the only person encouraging Shannan to set limits with her dad. Still, with her own clear boundaries in place, Sophia was able to listen with compassion and neutrality to Shannan's problems with her dad, focusing on Shannan's well-being not Ted's. When Sophia's gut told her even this was too much, she would reiterate her suggestion that Shannan find other people to talk to. (Again, the broken record technique.) As she held firm, Sophia sensed Shannan was becoming more receptive to looking for additional support.

A Dilemma

Sophia and Shannan's story illustrates the important dilemma which adult children and their divorcing parents face. Over the years as I listened to adult children expressing distress when their divorcing parents stepped over the line into inappropriate sharing, the solution seemed simple: parents need to say as little as possible about why they are divorcing. But that solution ignores the fact that adult children may desperately want to know what went wrong in their parents' marriage. They want sufficient information to make sense of what is happening in their family now, and they may also feel that this could help them avoid mistakes in their own marriages in the future. They, like Shannan, may be the ones pressing their parents for information.

There is a strong urge to gain mastery over confusing, highly emotional, and seemingly out-of-control situations. Parents' later-life divorce can present just such a situation. One way for adult children to gain mastery is to gather as much information as possible about what went wrong in their parents' marriage—the "who did what when?" Should they have seen it coming years ago? More recently? Is one parent to blame? Could the divorce have been prevented? Is there any hope of reconciliation? Was there a time when their parents *were* happy together?

Herein lies the dilemma: while adult children may press for information, they generally do not want to hear specific details that would portray one or both parents as people they can no longer respect. They do not want to know details of their parents' intimate marital problems. They do not want to know about a parent's most unappealing qualities. Neither do they want to be let in on personal information one parent shared privately with their spouse when things were better between them. These are the types of details which most adult children would experience as "too much information." These are the details they wish they had not been told.

How can this dilemma be resolved? When does information cross over the line from providing adult children with a healthy understanding of what is happening into over-sharing or information which makes them uncomfortable? We noted earlier that there are significant cultural and familial differences in how much is too much, so we can be sure there is no one-size-fits-all solution.

Parents and their adult children share responsibility for setting clear boundaries and expecting them to be respected. Parents, first of all, need to take several deep breaths and think about *what* they want to tell their children about the divorce as well as *why.* Is this information that their children need in order to understand what is going on or is it meant to rally their support for oneself and turn them against their other parent? These are tough questions to ask of oneself—tough enough that a parent would likely benefit from talking this through with a trusted friend, family member, clergy member, or therapist.

In addition, parents need to check in with their children, initially asking them what they want to know and continually assessing their children's comfort level. They need to specifically invite their children to tell them when what they are sharing no longer feels appropriate. In short, they need to give their children permission to set boundaries. And once these limits have been stated, parents need to respect them even if they do not agree.

For their part, adult children need to know they have the right as well as the responsibility to set clear boundaries with their parents. To do so, they need to listen to their gut reactions as well as to their rational thinking. They need to speak up as early as they can when what their parent is sharing begins to feel inappropriate.

We saw with Sophia and Shannan that this works both ways. Parents need to be prepared to tell their adult children when the information they are asking for is more than the parent wants to, or feels they should, share. Whether they agree or not, adult children need to respect a boundary set by a parent.

Where There is Infidelity: A Special Case

When infidelity is part of the reason for divorce, emotions are likely running particularly high and that is when boundary violations most often occur. Infidelity involves the breaking of a promise to remain faithful to a committed partner or spouse. It can involve emotional as well as physical or sexual violations. Even when discovered, unfaithfulness may not result in divorce, but, when it does, the partner who feels they have been wronged may use it to rally family and friends to their side and against their spouse. They may harness their anger and hurt in an attempt to bolster their case as the victim.

We saw that in Chapter 3 with Jan and Justin. They initially stayed together after Jan discovered Justin's affair with a colleague at work. But, after five years of Justin's recommitment to their marriage as well as couple's therapy, Jan still could not reengage in their relationship. She generally withheld all forms of affection, including sex. Both were miserable but hoped to avoid divorce for the sake of their children. After all three children were out of the house, Justin was ready to move on in the hopes of finding a loving relationship. He feared Jan's anger since she had said she never wanted to be divorced.

Up to that point, Jan had kept Justin's affair secret. Now he worried she would use it against him, and he was right! Even though the affair was five years in the past, Jan told everyone who would listen. Their young adult children were shocked and also embarrassed as everyone in their small town seemed to know about their father's indiscretion. All three rallied around their mother as the injured party. For several years, they had little to do with Justin except to accept his financial help with college and, later, weddings.

For his part, Justin continued in individual therapy, hoping to improve his relationship with his children. Much as he wanted to counter Jan's negative depiction of him with hurtful information about her, he resisted. Instead, he told his young adult children that there are two sides to any story. He said he hoped someday they might be more open to believing that he had once worked hard to make his marriage work. Justin owned responsibility for the affair but gave no details about it nor about the marriage before or after it occurred. When the children let him know that even that was more than they wanted to hear, he respected their boundaries although he had hoped for more support.

Eventually, his patience paid off. Both Jan and Justin were attractive people in their 50s and found new partners within a few years. Jan continued to hold animosity toward Justin and tried to interact with him as little as possible at their adult children's important milestone events. Their children noticed this and the stress and discomfort it created.

Justin's new partner (unrelated to the affair) was warm and supportive and didn't attempt to push herself onto his semi-estranged children. Over time, his older son began to notice this and appreciated his father's non-problematic presence at family events. His two younger siblings gradually followed suit and began to spend more time with Justin and his wife. The arrival of grandchildren seemed to usher in a new phase—almost a fresh start—where Justin and his wife were invited to play a greater role in his children's lives. The children remained close to, and protective of, their mother. However, they grew increasingly uncomfortable when she spoke negatively of Justin and now asked her to stop.

There can be considerable stigma and moral outrage attached to infidelity which makes it particularly difficult to talk about. What, in general, do children want to know about a parent's infidelity? What do they *need* to know? I have heard a range of opinions from clients over the years. One young man wished he knew nothing at all: "I heard that my dad was cheated on by my mom, and I feel like I was too." Similarly, a young woman was shocked by finding out that the father she idolized had been "cheating:" "I've lost trust in all guys, and I push them away."

However, another young man, Ben, was furious that he couldn't get answers: "Both my parents have been lying about seeing other people. Until they can respect me enough to tell me the truth, I am done with them. It's a tough decision to make but you have to do what's best for you and what will keep you healthy and sane."

Ben's gut told him that no one was being honest with him. He felt helpless to get enough solid information to make sense of what was going on at home. He'd previously felt he could trust both of his parents. Now he felt he didn't know either one of them. He found the whole situation "crazy making" and chose to distance from both of them until things settled down.

Honesty is always important. But that doesn't mean that a parent's only options are to say nothing or open up entirely! Parents can honestly admit to an affair without offering further details or they can honestly say that they do not want to talk about it at this time. They can also acknowledge that this may not be the answer their children want but it is all they are ready to say. Their children may not be satisfied with this boundary but at least they do not feel lied to. Further trust has not been broken.

These last three brief and varied examples give a flavor of the complexity of reactions that adult children have when infidelity is part of their parents' divorce. The longer vignette involving Justin and Jan's adult children illustrates that, even with infidelity, there are changes over time. The initial ripple effects can die down and make way for new perspectives and greater compassion. And by now it should be clear that a positive outcome is more likely when parent-child boundaries are clear and firm. Justin's commitment to honoring his children's strict boundaries about acceptable information was hard at times, but it was eventually rewarded.

In Summary

Parent-child boundaries are at risk of being violated in the emotionally-charged climate of divorce. Sometimes these violations take the form of oversharing. It is not just hearing about a parent's infidelity and sexual behavior that adult children experience as crossing the line over into "too much information." They also don't want to hear highly personal information about a parent's unappealing habits and qualities. An angry parent hoping to gain sympathy and support from an adult child may be eager to share such information to justify the decision to leave or to emphasize the unfairness of being left especially if their adult child seems to want to know more. Sometimes only one parent is the violator while the other parent's decision to maintain firm boundaries leaves their side of the story untold.

It can be a fine line to draw. How much information do adult children need in order to make sense of what is going on? They are likely to want and be able to handle more information than a younger child could. Still, when they indicate that enough is enough, a wise parent knows it is time to stop. And if the adult children are the ones asking for inappropriate information, parents need to set their own limits.

Over-sharing of information is only one way of crossing a parent-child boundary in the throes of divorce. As we saw with Molly and Travis, parents can lean too heavily on their adult children by relying on them for emotional support when their children are dealing with their own feelings as well as their own life stage challenges. And we saw with Marty that parents can put their children in the middle as messengers or go-betweens, and they can burden them with heavy secrets to be kept from the other parent. Most of these reflect boundary lapses which would less likely occur with younger children.

Setting and continually enforcing clear boundaries preserves an appropriate parent-child relationship and allows parents and adult children to feel compassion for one another's experiences. Firm boundaries protect this important relationship from becoming yet another divorce-related casualty. Below is a summary of the key points of this chapter with reminders for both parents and adult children. Despite some considerable overlap, there are also unique concerns for the two generations.

Reminders about Boundaries for Both Parents and Adult Children

- Having boundaries is healthy and normal in all relationships, including the relationship between parents and their adult children.

- Having strong personal boundaries (knowing where you end and another person begins as well as knowing your limits as to what is acceptable) will allow you to be less judgmental and have more compassion for other people.

- Boundary lapses or violations may be more likely to occur during highly emotional times such as divorce and re-partnering.

• Both parents and adult children may notice when their relationship is becoming uncomfortable due to a breakdown in boundaries.

• At such times, it is critical to speak up as soon as possible, stating or restating boundaries clearly and consistently with the goal of preserving a healthy parent-child relationship.

• If boundaries are not respected after repeated requests, it may be necessary to erect a barrier, at least temporarily.

For Parents

• It may be a new experience to have your adult children set limits on what they see as acceptable behavior from you. They have evolved, or are evolving, into adults with their own thoughts and feelings.

• You may find it upsetting and even disrespectful when your adult children set limits on your behavior. However, it is actually a healthy sign that they are taking care of themselves, and, as such, it should be honored. Eventually you may be able to see this as a positive sign of your child's strength and maturity.

• You may be tempted to share negative and/or highly personal information about your marriage or ex-spouse with the aim of eliciting your adult child's support, but this is not appropriate.

• You may also be tempted to share highly personal information as you begin to date or re-partner. Your adult child may find this inappropriate or may simply not be ready to hear it. Respect their limits.

• Likewise, if your adult child pushes you for details about your divorce that you feel would be inappropriate or harmful, or if they later show too much interest as you begin to meet new people, *you* are the one to put a firm boundary in place. Eventually, your child will likely recognize your wisdom and maturity and be grateful that you stayed in a healthy parental role.

For Adult Children

- It may seem new to both you and your parents when you set a firm boundary with them, so it could be difficult for you and may be met with resistance. Remember, this is also a process, so be patient and resolute.

- Insisting on respect for the limits you set with your parents during their divorce process increases the likelihood of a positive outcome both for yourself and for your relationship with your parents.

- By taking care of yourself during this challenging time, you will likely emerge from it with not only a healthier relationship with your parents, but also with greater compassion for what they have gone through.

- Be wary of feeling flattered or "special" when a parent shares highly personal information. Instead, recognize it as a time to strengthen your boundaries before you get drawn into an unhealthy situation.

- If your parents set limits with *you* when you ask for details about their marriage or about their starting to meet new people, respect their boundary. It is a sign that they are staying in a healthy, appropriate role as your parent.

Adhering to these reminders is a tall order for both parents and adult children—especially at a time when everyone's emotions are running high. We have repeatedly encouraged the two generations to have compassion for their own and each other's struggles brought on by later-life divorce. But now we seem to be asking them to put strong emotions aside and behave in a very rational fashion. Likewise, we have asked both generations to have empathy for the other's experience as well as one's own. Now it may appear that we are encouraging them to focus on themselves, even giving them permission to be "selfish." Yet we have repeatedly seen that when people—both parents and adult children—take care of themselves and insist that their boundaries be honored, their capacity for empathy and compassion increases.

Consistently putting forth, maintaining, and respecting strong boundaries requires a lot of effort. Few individuals and families will be able to live up to this ideal without occasional lapses or violations. However, acknowledging and understanding the importance of strong boundaries reminds both parents and their adult children of their appropriate roles vis-à-vis each other. For any particular family or situation, it could take a while to figure out what feels comfortable and appropriate, but healthy boundaries can be established or reestablished at any point in the divorce process.

Chapter Seven Notes: *Boundaries and Compassion*

1. Brené Brown has written and spoken extensively about healthy boundaries. See Brené Brown, *Atlas of the Heart: Mapping Meaningful Connection and the Language of Human Experience*, 2021, Random House. See also her numerous podcasts and YouTube videos such as "Boundaries, Feelings, & Core Emotions," February 6, 2023.

2. Nedra Glover Tawwab, *Set Boundaries, Find Peace: A Guide to Reclaiming Yourself*, 2021. Tarcher.

-8-
Lost and Found
Grief and New Beginnings

Things aren't what they used to be and probably never were.
Will Rogers, performer, humorous social commentator

New beginnings are often disguised as painful endings.
Lao Tzu, ancient Chinese philosopher

Divorce at any life stage entails significant loss. This is true for divorcing couples as well as their children and extended families. It is easy to imagine the losses when the children are young and will no longer be growing up in a home with both of their parents. Losses on a day-to-day basis. Losses at holidays, on vacations, and at special occasions.

But what about later-life divorces when the parents are in, or approaching, their final life stages and their children are already adults? Shouldn't families—adults and children alike—experience fewer losses at that point? After all, the children have essentially grown up in an intact family, not one split apart by divorce. And the parents didn't have to miss out on precious time with their children in their formative years as might have happened even with shared custody arrangements.

While the losses are somewhat different for parents and adult children experiencing later-life divorce, they are still very much losses as must be clear if you have gotten this far in this book.

**All losses must be recognized and grieved in order
to move forward.**

When we downplay them or ignore them altogether, we do an enormous disservice to older divorcing families. We thwart their

177

opportunity to fully grieve, heal, and move on to healthier new beginnings for individuals and healthier new formations for families. Unfortunately, this is the legacy promoted by the myth that divorce in later life is "no big deal," especially for adult children.

The basic message of this chapter distills down to this:

•	When you adhere to the myth that divorce in later life is "no big deal," especially for adult children, you are denying that it entails significant losses.

•	When you deny these significant losses, you miss out on the opportunity to grieve them. Without the opportunity to grieve, you cannot truly heal.

•	In the absence of deep healing, both parents and adult children are likely to stay stuck in a negative place and/or repeat prior mistakes.

On the other hand, put in *positive* terms:

•	When you recognize that later-life divorce poses important challenges that have often been overlooked, you will be open to the fact that it comes with significant losses.

•	Once you acknowledge and accept that there will be significant losses for both parents and their adult children, you will be able to grieve them.

•	When you allow yourself sufficient time and opportunity to grieve, you will be able to heal.

•	With deep healing comes the possibility of growth, compassion, resilience, and new beginnings for both individuals and families.

WHAT INTERFERES WITH EXPERIENCING DIVORCE-RELATED LOSS?

When couples take the vow "for better or for worse," most are hoping their relationship will weather the inevitable ups and downs that will be coming their way. Likely, this is especially true once children are added and the couple becomes a family. Most divorcing parents, therefore, experience sadness when their marriages end.

Something significant has changed resulting in a sense of loss. It may even feel much like a death. No matter how negative a marriage may look at the time it ends, there can still be grief for the loss of happier times in the past as well as dreams for the future. There is grief for the loss of hope that things might have improved, and divorce could have been avoided. In short, most couples, including those in the later stages of life, experience divorce as a significant loss.

Denial

This is important since, in order to lean into grief, a person must acknowledge that there has been loss and, thus, that there is something to grieve. While this normally happens for most family members when divorce occurs, it cannot happen as long as there is denial. But isn't some denial a normal reaction to loss?

Initially, denial helps us carry on when the shock and pain of what is transpiring seems almost unbearable. For divorcing parents there may be times in the process when one or both think reconciliation is still possible. This can happen even after they have hired attorneys and filed for divorce. However, eventually if things move forward and the divorce is finalized, denial no longer works.

In some ways, this tendency to deny is even more complicated for their adult children who may remain hopeful that their parents will change their minds. They may continue to encourage them to go for counseling well after the parents know it is too late. It is not uncommon for children of all ages to hold out hope for years that their parents will remarry even after the divorce is final. Sometimes it is not until one or both parents re-partner that they may relinquish their denial once and for all.

But eventually the reality of divorce for parents and children cannot be denied. What is worrisome is that they may deny their feelings about the divorce, not the fact that it is happening. We'll look here at three circumstances that can block acknowledging and experiencing feelings of loss and sadness. Two of these apply to parents and children no matter their age or life stage, although here we will focus primarily on parents divorcing after long marriages. The third circumstance applies more often to adult vs. younger children and, by now, should come as no surprise.

Anger

Some divorcing individuals and couples focus almost exclusively on anger. They deny or are unable to experience the sadness that accompanies the end of their marriages. Instead of acknowledging loss, they see themselves as victims. They feel they have been wronged by their partner's behavior and have difficulty moving beyond anger. Ironically, anger can keep a couple emotionally bound together as strongly as love once did. Stuck in this negative emotional experience, they do not grieve and so they cannot fully move forward to a healthier new life.

Anita and Stan

In earlier chapters, we saw some poignant examples of how anger is an obstacle to healing. Anita (in Chapter 3) eventually gave up on her marriage to Stan when he refused to go to counseling with her to save their empty-nest marriage. Even though the divorce was her idea, she knew she needed to give herself time to grieve the ending of a long marriage to a man she had once loved deeply and the life they had built together, including their four now-adult children.

Stan, on the other hand, never forgave Anita for ending their marriage, and refused to ever speak to her again. When he remarried Carolyn almost immediately, he never gave himself the opportunity to feel sad or to understand what had gone wrong in his first marriage. Consequently, instead of this being a chance for a new beginning, Stan continued to focus on his bitterness toward Anita. He insisted that Carolyn also refuse to speak to Anita. He also told his children he was afraid Carolyn might leave him too.

Acknowledging loss and leaning into grief at the end of her decades-long marriage allowed Anita to heal. With time and psychotherapy, she came to terms with how her marriage failed. Eventually she found herself open to meeting someone new and starting a fresh chapter in her later years. From the outside, it looked like Stan had recovered more quickly from the divorce, but his anger at Anita prevented him from grieving as well as examining his role in their divorce. It was likely that his hasty "new beginning" could remain colored by anger and distrust.

Marty's Father

We saw a similar dynamic with Marty's father (Chapters 5 and 7). Like Stan, he also remarried quickly, although he tried to keep it a secret from Marty's mother. Never giving himself a chance to feel anything but anger, he continued to present himself to his daughters as the victim rather than a happy man beginning a new life.

Charles

Charles' wife Miriam's rage attacks (Chapter 3) eventually led him to divorce her after their children were all adults. Charles and his children each grieved the loss of their family in their own way, but Miriam refused to admit to any sadness. When her grown children mentioned any sense of loss, Miriam went off on a rant of Charles' shortcomings.

Fear

Other divorcing parents may focus primarily on fear. Like anger, fear can get in the way of experiencing sadness and being able to grieve. This may be common when parents divorce at or near Erickson's final life stage, resulting in despair. With less time and fewer resources to put together a new life, they may fear that their lives will draw to an end with a sense of chaos and lack of control rather than a sense of being meaningful and well-lived.

Some who are fearful of being able to survive on their own, financially or logistically, are overtaken by panic. Fear of simply managing alone in the final stages of life can be paralyzing and rob one of the time and opportunity to grieve and heal.

Helen

Helen was in her 80s when her husband left her for a woman half his age. Surprisingly, she didn't feel anger at being left nor did she feel the sadness she might have felt if he had died and left her a widow. Her children described her as appearing in shock and numb with terror. She'd never handled financial matters, didn't understand the mechanics of their home, and didn't know how she could adapt to the reality of divorce at her age. All this despite the fact that she had been quite healthy physically and cognitively up to that point.

The reactions of Helen's middle-aged children illustrate that anger and fear can keep adult children from grieving as well. Helen's adult children were furious with their dad and worried about the inheritance they were counting on. They, too, were out of touch with any sadness over the end of their parents' long marriage. Instead, they focused on anger at their dad and fear for their mother's ability to manage on her own.

Marie

And for those who divorce to end an abusive situation, there could be realistic fear of the partner's retaliation. Marie (in Chapter 3) was eventually able to leave her physically and emotionally abusive husband, Mitch, but she lived in fear for years that he would seek her out and harm her. She was terrified when she had to face him in a series of long, drawn-out court battles even with many other people present.

This terror made it hard for Marie to empathize with her children's sadness over the divorce, let alone feel any of her own. Again, the grieving process was obstructed, this time by fear. Perhaps not surprisingly, she quickly chose a new partner who seemed strong enough to protect her from Mitch. What she didn't see was that, while he did not physically abuse her, her new partner used his "strength" to control her activities. Like Stan, Marie's impulsive "moving on" did not allow her to process her past choices and behaviors. That left her likely to repeat past behaviors rather than have a chance for a genuine fresh start. While her physical safety was no longer at risk, she was still not in control of her own life.

Once Again, The Myth of "No Big Deal"

As we saw with Helen's children, anger and fear can prevent adult children as well as parents from experiencing and grieving losses related to divorce. Some adult children may focus on anger at the parent who initiated the divorce. Others may be angry that their parents didn't take better care of their marriage or that they didn't seek help to prevent a divorce. Still others could simply be furious that the timing of the divorce interferes with their own young adult needs and plans.

Similarly, with fear. Some adult children's feelings of loss could get blocked or dwarfed by worries about how one or both parents will manage on their own. Others may be afraid that their own needs for parental support—material and emotional—will no longer be met.

But anger and fear are probably not the biggest obstacles to adult children being able to experience their legitimate feelings of loss when their parents divorce. For them, it is the "myth of no big deal." The failure of society to acknowledge that their losses are both real and substantial thwarts their grieving process. When we don't give them permission to experience grief, they may struggle to even recognize it. Consciously or not, they may deny their gut feelings. They are likely to carry on with their own adult challenges and/or take care of their parents' feelings to the neglect of their own.[1]

Some may initially register loss and grief upon hearing their parents' plans to divorce. However, if they sense that they should be taking things more in stride, they may quickly "correct" themselves and downplay their feelings. Early feedback questioning the validity of their experience will quash their legitimate feelings. Societal "shoulds" and "should nots" can block adult children's ability to grieve. Over and over in my office I heard them chastise themselves with some version of the following:

~ I'm an adult already so I shouldn't be bothered by my parents' divorce.

~ I should be grateful that my parents didn't divorce when I was much younger.

~ I shouldn't care if my parents sell the house I grew up in since I haven't lived there in years.

~ I should be able to handle it when my mom wants me to listen to how upset she is about my dad.

~ I should be able to function better at work/school even though I need to help my dad figure out how to live on his own.

In this chapter, we will outline important losses for parents and adult children at different developmental life stages and walk through the grieving process. Leaning into grief promotes healing over time. We will end the chapter with what can eventually be found in the form of growth and the opportunity for new beginnings.

Whether you are the parent or the adult child reading this book, you can begin to do some healing on your own even if the timing is not yet right for your other family members. As with all the dances we do, we can only control our own steps. But you can begin to hear the music differently and decline to repeat the old familiar steps that have only left you feeling stuck and miserable. You can start dancing in a new way even if others are not ready to join in.

WHAT HAS BEEN LOST?

At one extreme, divorce is experienced as the death of a family. It shatters the portrait of the family carrying on intact until death alters the picture. It entails the loss of what has been familiar and often cherished, much as does the death of a loved one. But divorce uproots the past as well as the present. It ushers in disillusionment and negativity and requires a revision of one's family story even if the "ending" could have been predicted.

A caveat: Even reading about death, loss, and grief can be painful. Having read this far, some of you may want to take a break—at least for now. Understandable as that is, eventually the realities and feelings of loss must be faced in order to heal and move forward. Perhaps you are feeling the urge to put the book down and do something to take care of yourself—call a friend, go for a walk or a run, put on some comforting music, take a bath, or fix yourself a healthy snack. If that's how you are feeling, go right ahead. Taking good care of yourself is a top priority.

But sooner or later, you need to nudge yourself to get back to addressing your own painful experience with divorce-related loss and grief. When you do, be sure to surround yourself with as much support as you can from both personal and professional networks because with grief the only way out is through. For many people, this is the time to seek out a therapist or counselor you trust and feel comfortable with. When you give yourself sufficient time and support you can heal and come out on the other side, stronger and healthier than you were before.

So, what specifically *are* the divorce-related the losses? Early in my clinical training, I came across a drawing called the "Divorce Onion." It graphically depicted "divorces within a divorce" or the many layers of loss associated with the ending of a marriage. I was never able to track down its source, but it poignantly labeled layer upon layer of losses from roles and identities to friends and family, from hopes and structure, to companionship and sex.

Below we combine the ideas inherent in the onion analogy with Erikson's life stages. The outline shows the layers of potential loss accompanying later-life divorce for both parents and adult children. Since these experiences of loss are discussed in detail in the body of earlier and later chapters, this table serves primarily as a summary. It is important to remember that not everyone experiences all of these losses, although everyone experiences at least some of them.

POTENTIAL LOSSES FROM LATER-LIFE DIVORCE

Potential Losses For Parents Divorcing When in Erikson's Stage 7 (Generativity)

- Economic losses
- Loss of security
- Loss of companionship
- Loss of home
- Loss of friends
- Loss of in-laws
- Loss of routines and traditions
- Loss of shared history
- Loss of place in one's community
- Loss of future hopes and dreams
- Loss of identity

- Loss of sexual relationship
- Loss of dignity
- Loss of purpose/sense of failure

Potential Losses for Parents Divorcing When in Erikson's Stage 8 (Ego Integrity)

(All of the above plus....)
- Loss of opportunity to find a new relationship
- Loss of a potential partner to help with issues of health and aging
- Loss of confidence of being able to manage on one's own
- Loss of a sense of final accomplishment

Potential Losses for *ALL* Adult Children

- Loss of the family home
- Loss of an idealized sense of one's family and one's past
- Loss of ordinary times and gatherings with one's nuclear family
- Loss of traditions
- Loss of confidence in one's own perceptions, questioning of happy memories
- Loss of extended family if rifts develop
- Loss of relationships with siblings
- Financial losses when parents' financial situations change
- Loss of trust that committed relationships last, questioning the sanctity of marriage
- Loss of emotional support from overwhelmed/self-absorbed parents

Potential Losses Specifically for the Launchers

- Loss of a firm platform for launching
- Loss of a moratorium or opportunity to try out adult roles before making decisions
- Loss of a primary home/residence
- Loss of a place to store one's belongings

Potential Losses Specifically for Emerging Adults

- Loss of a "base camp" to return to
- Loss of the final phases of a moratorium
- Loss of an intact family at milestone events
- Loss of ease of functioning at milestone events
- Loss of grandparent involvement in their young children's lives

Potential Losses Specifically for the Middle-Aged Adult Children

- Loss of an anchor as one enters middle-age
- Loss of confidence that marriages can endure in the long run
- Loss of supportive services such as childcare and advice about childrearing
- Loss of grandparent involvement in their children's lives
- Loss of possible inheritance
- Loss of peace of mind about aging parents
- Loss of time and resources due to increased responsibility for one or both elderly parents

Looking over these long lists of potential and substantial loss can be overwhelming. Some parents will experience more of these than others, and the same is true of their adult children. But, unless they are stuck in denial, none will escape experiencing at least some significant loss when there is a divorce in the family. The sorrow that is caused by this sense of great loss is called grief.

GRIEF

Grief plays an important role in healing from loss, including divorce-related loss. The form it takes as well as its duration are unique for each griever and for the particular losses incurred. There is no clear timeline for healing or navigating grief. No "one size fits all." The only real answer for the duration of one's grief and healing is: "It takes as long as it takes!"

In her ground-breaking book, *On Death and Dying*, Elisabeth Kubler-Ross taught the world about five stages of death and dying: denial, anger, bargaining, depression, and acceptance.[2] In the years since, these five stages are now more often seen as five common *responses* which do not necessarily flow in any order. Furthermore, no longer is there assumed to be a typical response to loss since no loss is typical.

David Kessler worked with Kubler-Ross to apply the five stages of dying to the grieving process itself.[3] Again, they cautioned against rigid application, affirming that all grief is individual. In later writings, Kessler emphasized two key concepts which are particularly valuable for our understanding of grief in response to later-life divorce—acceptance and witnessing.

Acceptance

Kessler knows that we don't like loss. Still, he insists that in order to heal from it as much as we can, we must accept it as our reality. The only way to protect ourselves from ever experiencing loss and grief would be to totally detach from all feelings including positive feelings such as joy, love, and happiness. But it is important not to confuse acceptance of loss with being okay with it. Kessler says that most people never feel "okay" or "all right" with a significant loss but they eventually come to accept that the new reality is permanent.

With divorce, like the death of a loved one, it can at first feel like things will never again be okay. But, unlike a death, as long as everyone is still alive, there remains hope that things will feel better, albeit different, in the future. With enough time, support, and compassion, perhaps most family members will come to feel "okay" or "all right" about the divorce. But to get there, they have to accept that some things have permanently changed.

Witnessing

A second key concept is the importance of witnessing.[4] Kessler feels strongly that *grief must be witnessed.* Everyone needs to have their unique loss and grief be heard in all its magnitude. They need someone to be fully present and to listen without attempting to lessen or reframe it in a more positive light. They need their grief to be heard by someone who does not try to "fix" it or tell them that "everything happens for a purpose" or that "everything will be okay."

This important witnessing can be challenging for parents and their adult children if boundaries, as emphasized in Chapter 7, are to be carefully respected. Both generations need their divorce-related loss, pain, and grief to be witnessed in order to heal and move on. But by whom?

How much of their parents' distress do adult children need to witness in order to understand how hurt and devastated a parent may be feeling? How much can they bear witness to and still maintain appropriate boundaries and prioritize taking care of themselves? Adult children cannot and do not need to be totally shielded from their parents' pain, but they should not be expected to be either parent's primary support person.

They need to be able to tell their parents if and when they are feeling overwhelmed by parental needs and demands. They need to be able to draw the line, set a boundary, and have that be honored. Even if disappointed by this, a parent needs to accept it and make a decision to find a more appropriate witness—a friend, a sibling, a mental health professional, or a clergy person—who can hear their suffering with more distance and objectivity.

Adult children clearly need their grief to be witnessed too. Timing is important here. When news of the divorce first comes out, adult children may see their parents as particularly fragile or vulnerable and appropriately choose not to add their own strong emotions to the mix. They may also be in a state of shock and are not yet aware of how they will be affected and how they are feeling.

With time, if they are fortunate enough to accept that their strong feelings about their parents' divorce are normal, most adult children will want their parents to have some awareness of how their lives have been impacted. If these were the people who comforted you in the past when you were sad or worried, then it makes sense to want to turn to them for reassurance and support when something of this magnitude is happening. Now it is the parents' job to set boundaries if this is more than they feel they can handle.

Eventually parents and their children may want to talk to each other about the divorce. But, early on when feelings are particularly raw, it makes more sense to seek out a witness who is not as intimately involved. This is often a time when people seek the support of trained mental health professionals.

Meg's Story

The experience of Meg and her daughter Kelsey illustrates some of these complexities. Meg, a very insightful woman who was soon to become my client, had just sent her daughter, Kelsey, back to college after spring break. During the visit, Meg and her husband had gathered Kelsey and her siblings together to tell them they were getting a divorce. This was something Meg's husband was initiating and Meg didn't want, although that was not emphasized in their joint announcement to their children.

Kelsey reacted more strongly than her parents had anticipated and was either furious with them or almost inconsolable for the rest of the school break. She spent as much time as possible holed up in her room or out with her friends. Kelsey rejected her mother's tentative attempts to reach out to her and seemed disgusted by her mother's weary and tearful appearance. As soon as she got back to school, she began sending angry texts to both parents about how they were letting her down by getting divorced and how it seemed that nobody cared about *her* feelings anyway.

Caught up in her own feelings about the divorce, Meg was still able see through this angry exchange without defensiveness. She realized that Kelsey was crying out for support and understanding for her own hurt and fear which the divorce brought up. She was asking for support from the people she had turned to in the past for nurturing and comfort, although now in an angry manner. Messy and upsetting as Kelsey's reactions were, Meg instinctively recognized that they were legitimate and that it was healthy for Kelsey to be able to express them.

However, Meg also recognized that she was too overwhelmed by her own strong emotions to fully assume her usual maternal role. Even before she entered psychotherapy, she had been able to tell Kelsey her own limitations as a mom while still validating Kelsey's legitimate needs, including the need to be heard. Later Meg showed me some of her early texts and emails to her daughter. They reflected a remarkable ability to take care both of herself and the mother-daughter relationship even in the midst of the initial stages of divorce. For example:

"Kelsey, I hear what you are saying. You are probably in as much pain as I am, and I wish I could say something to make you feel better. Right now I'm a bit of a mess and I need to keep functioning. I'm afraid if I open up too much to what is going on for you, I'll just fall apart completely. Can we agree to talk about all this in a couple of days? I'm going to reach out to your Aunt Nancy and get the name of the therapist she saw who helped her get through her divorce. Maybe you can get into the counseling center there [at her college] ASAP. Please know that I really do think I'll be in better shape soon and be able to be a better mom to you. Please take good care of yourself. It's crazy right now but we're all going to be okay. I love you no matter what!!"

Weeks, not days later, Meg *was* able to more fully hear her daughter's grief about the divorce. She bore witness by simply listening, although at times it was very painful to hear how much her daughter was hurting. It was also difficult to just listen when Kelsey called her out in ways she felt Meg let her down even though the divorce was not Meg's idea. In short, this amazing mom acknowledged her daughter's pain without downplaying it or trying to fix it. And she let her daughter tell her how she had disappointed her while neither trying to defend and explain her behavior, nor putting the full responsibility on Kelsey's dad.

Needless to say, this was very healing. Kelsey had the gift of her mother's being willing and able to witness her grief without sharing too much about her own. Meg was back in role as mother which felt good to both of them. Likely, without fully realizing it, Kelsey was feeling relief that she could trust her mother to maintain appropriate boundaries.

She was also likely feeling relieved that her mother was getting help and support for herself and didn't seem to need much from Kelsey. This freed Kelsey up to focus on school and friends. By the time summer rolled around and Kelsey was assured that her room at home was still available, she expressed her gratitude for Meg's acceptance of her early strong reactions. She even apologized for having been overly critical of her as she now appreciated how challenging things had been for Meg too.

Unfortunately, Kelsey's dad was less comfortable with the expression of strong emotions. He was judgmental of Kelsey's outbursts and accusations. He felt she was being selfish at a time when he could have used her support. When Kelsey didn't want to hear his complaints about the marriage, he was disappointed and thought she was taking her mother's side. Kelsey's positive interaction with her mother had given her the confidence to hold firm to healthy boundaries with her father while still hoping things would get better with him.

Not everyone is able to handle things the way Meg did. In large part this was because she surrounded herself with plenty of support. As a result, Kelsey didn't have to adhere to the myth that her feelings didn't matter or weren't appropriate, and she didn't have to worry about her mother.

Meg could have taken advantage of her favored position and increased Kelsey's distance from her father by sharing negative things about him. This might have drawn Kelsey further to her "side," but Meg knew it would be hurtful to her daughter who would benefit from a healthy relationship with both of her parents. So, during a fairly-amicable divorce mediation meeting when her husband mentioned feeling estranged from Kelsey, Meg told him Kelsey missed him and encouraged him to reach out to her and ask her how she was doing.

He immediately invited Kelsey to dinner and found out some of her worries were about finances and whether he had room for her in his new condo. He assured her she would be able to continue in college. Then they went to see his condo, and he pointed out the futon in his study where she was welcome to sleep any time she wanted to. The two ended up crying together and hugging, reassured that they had not lost their connection. In fact, Kelsey told Meg that she thought she and her dad would be getting to know each other at a new level since he'd always counted on Meg to be the more involved parent.

How the Grieving Process Works

To reiterate, with grief the only way out is through. You need to lean into your grief. Lean into your feelings and let yourself fully grieve your losses. Whether you are a parent or an adult child, if you don't get stuck in anger, fear, or in denial of the extent of your divorce-related losses, you will begin to confront and accept them no matter how big they feel. Allow yourself to grieve them for as long as you need to. There is no time limit on grieving since all grievers are unique, and all grief is unique. In your own time, you will begin to heal and move on emotionally from the sadness that once felt almost unbearable.

Find Support

Everyone needs and deserves support when they are grieving, and people find support in different places. Because grief needs to be witnessed, finding someone who will really listen to you is very important. This needs to be someone who can hear your pain without judgement or a need to "fix it." That may be a family member or a friend, but it needs to be someone who has more distance from the divorce than those who are directly involved. Throughout the divorce process, parents should not rely on their adult children as their primary support system, nor should adult children expect that their grieving parents can reliably fulfill this role for them.

Fortunately, there are many other resources available. Divorce is frequently a time when people seek out counseling or psychotherapy. Trained therapists and counselors are able to listen with compassion as well as boundaries to their clients' strong feelings, and thus are able to support and guide them through the difficult times during and after divorce. This is an especially important step to take if you are feeling stuck or if people close to you feel you could use more help and support. There is no stigma in seeking professional help at this time, and it well may result in personal growth far beyond just surviving the divorce itself.

Whether you are the parent or the adult child of divorce, if you decide to seek professional help, do so with care. Get recommendations from people you respect and trust your own gut in early sessions before deciding if this person is a good match for you. In addition, I hope this book has convinced you that you would likely be better served by a therapist or counselor who takes a family systems perspective. Does this professional, while primarily attuned to your needs, also see you as part of a family where all are being affected by the divorce? Does he or she seem to be considering the developmental stages and challenges that you all are dealing with?

This is also the time to seek out additional resources for comfort and support. My resource section lists books which you may find helpful. There are also some online self-help groups and chat rooms of varying degrees of usefulness, although they tend to be sporadic. Some of you may prefer to turn to your religious community. Many religious institutions offer divorce support groups for their members as well as for the larger community. It is important to seek out support from multiple sources, and your needs for these may change over the course of your own grieving process.

For parents, I am a firm believer in seeking out a well-run divorce recovery/support group. Over the years, I observed clients benefitting enormously from being in the company of others while they were going through divorce. I also had clients who benefitted from involvement in a group even when their divorces had occurred many years before they joined. In fact, these groups may benefit from having members who are at different stages of healing from divorce. Feelings are most raw early on in the process and those members are reassured when they see others further along in their healing. Likewise, those further along are reminded of how far they have come and how well they are now able to cope when they see members who are just beginning to deal with divorce.

Well-run groups tend to have enough structure to keep sessions from becoming stuck in complaints and strong emotions. While they allow individuals to tell their stories and have them witnessed, they also are time-limited, have topics for each session, and often invite outside experts in to speak on legal and financial aspects of divorce. Generally, they have trained facilitators who were previous group members, and participants are allowed to re-enroll for an additional cycle if they feel it could be helpful. As we have said, people grieve and heal at different paces.

Perhaps one of the greatest benefits of attending a divorce recovery group is finding a new group of peers—others going through what you are going through. If there is a stigma surrounding divorce in your family or social network, here are people who aren't going to judge you for being divorced. I watched clients who came from a predominantly couples-oriented world form lasting friendships with other newly-single people, both men and women. This became a new circle of friends with whom to go to dinner, movies, or sporting events. Some went further and celebrated holidays together if they were going to be alone. Others agreed to check on each other if they were ill.

Unfortunately, comparable groups for adult children experiencing their parents' divorce are rare or even non-existent. If they were still legally children, they might have been referred to a divorce group at school where they would have realized that they were not the only ones whose home life was in upheaval. Adult children, however, have to turn to online groups for validation of their feelings which the "no big deal" myth downplays. These online groups can be helpful, but they are neither reliably available nor do they substitute for in-person interactions with others dealing with your same concerns.

In addition, unlike their parents, the reality of divorce is often not part of an adult child's public identity. Depending on their life stage, two adults could be sitting next to each other in a college classroom, operating in adjoining workstations, or co-chairing a PTA meeting and never know that they both had parents who were divorcing after 20, 30, 40 years of marriage. If they bought into the idea that they shouldn't be affected by this important family event, they are not likely to talk about it. Thus, they lose the opportunity to find out they are not alone and/or to get support.

I see no simple solution for adult children to get the support they need and deserve while grieving and healing. If this is your situation, the most promising source of support is finding a good therapist who will help you see that your grief is normal. In addition, hopefully books such as this will give you permission to speak up with friends, family, and coworkers about how your parents' divorce is affecting you. Honest conversations with important people in your life will go a long way in legitimating your grief and promoting your healing.

Grieving Rituals

There are many more rituals around marriage than there are around divorce. That doesn't mean you can't create your own if that sounds appealing to you. Rituals give us a way to acknowledge that something is important and to take action on its behalf. They can give us a sense of agency and mastery which we miss when we only grieve passively or silently.

A grieving ritual can be formal or casual. It can be something you do on your own or with other people. It can happen only once or more often such as on the anniversary of a significant event. What is important is that the ritual feels meaningful to you and gives you a sense of comfort.

Since rituals are highly personal, I won't attempt to be exhaustive about the possibilities. Included below are a few examples that clients and others have shared with me over the years. These are rituals that divorcing parents as well as adult children have created and found meaningful as part of their healing process.

Parents' Rituals

Rod had documented nearly every event in his life with a photograph. No surprise then that he asked his wife Phoebe to pose for a picture together as they left the courtroom where their uncontested divorce was finalized. He placed it on the final page of an album documenting their marriage, beginning with their wedding photo taken 30 years earlier. Every year he looked through this album on the date of their divorce and was pleasantly surprised to find that fewer tears and more warm memories came up as the years accumulated.

Rod's experience demonstrates that even a small, and in his case, private ritual can be very helpful. He used his creativity as well as a familiar activity (photography) to develop an annual ritual that helped him mark progress in his grieving. Every year it helped him lean into whatever sadness remained.

Amanda from Chapters 1 and 2, was married for 43 years to a man who never treated her as special. She had put on weight over the years, and by the time she finally decided to end her unhappy marriage, she could not remove her wedding ring. When her divorce was final, she made an appointment with a jeweler near the courthouse to have this simple band removed.

When she apologized for her plump fingers, the jeweler assured her she had beautiful hands. That compliment as well as seeing her ring finger looking bare got Amanda to thinking. Her husband had rarely given her any gifts, and she was never one to indulge herself. However, she made a bold decision to buy herself a modest but pretty new ring.

Each year thereafter, on the anniversary of her divorce, she purchased a simple piece of jewelry to remind herself that she was "worth something." Amanda had come a long way in her healing from being in a marriage where she was often ridiculed and seldom valued. She had leaned into her grief and landed back on her feet.

Adult Children's Rituals

Karl and his two younger siblings had for years set aside a week in the summer to vacation with their parents on a nearby lake. This continued as an annual event even after they had all graduated from college. This summer's plans changed, however, when their parents announced they would be getting a divorce and selling what had been the family home. Needless to say, the family vacation was canceled. At Karl's urging, the siblings agreed to use the week to gather at the family home one last time and assist their parents who were at various stages of moving to separate condos.

One stipulation they made was to have time alone with each parent to reminisce only about happier times in the past and to discuss how they would get together in the future. The other stipulation was to ask for time in the house without their parents. This allowed the siblings to go from room to room sharing highly individual memories both positive and negative, taking time for hugs and tears.

Karl and his wife had come to my office when they learned of his parents' divorce. I encouraged them to set firm boundaries, ask for what they needed from the divorcing parents, and fortify the sibling bond despite any differences in reactions to the divorce. The specific stipulations were their own creation.

This strong and creative couple was determined to deal with Karl's parents' divorce in a thoughtful manner. Within healthy parent-child boundaries they wanted to better understand why the parents were divorcing. They also wanted to find ways to hold onto what had been many positive aspects of Karl's childhood and family life. Along the way, they wanted to let themselves feel the losses and sadness that came up.

Victoria was initially devastated by her parents' divorce. Unlike Karl, she was an only child so there were no siblings to share her sadness when her parents split. She had spent her junior year in college in Mexico and was touched by the altars which her host family created for deceased relatives on Día de (los) Muertos. She decided to build a little altar in her small apartment to commemorate the "death of my family."

At the outset, she included photos of her mom and dad holding her as a baby as well as photos and tiny souvenirs of family trips they had taken. In the early months after the divorce announcement, when her feelings were quite raw, she would add fresh marigolds, a favorite food she and her family used to enjoy, and other objects that held symbolic or sentimental value. Sometimes, when she got home from her stressful job as a middle school math teacher, she would sit in front of her little altar and let herself cry. She said these sad moments felt "bittersweet" and helped her lean into her grief.

Parent-Child Rituals

In my experience, it is infrequent for parents and adult children to jointly establish a grieving ritual after divorce. This may be because they are grieving different losses. Or they could be at very different stages in their grieving process. Still, there can be times when it makes sense for parents and children to acknowledge together the one-year, five-year, etc. anniversary of the divorce with what might resemble a ritual. When this happens, it is important for them to remain comfortably within their parent/child roles.

This happened for Charles (from Chapter 3) two years after his contentious divorce. He invited his four adult children (now dispersed throughout the same state) to attend a family therapy session in my office. The goal was to process how all were faring two years after his divorce from their mentally ill mother, Miriam. This would be the first time all had been together since the divorce although Charles had kept in touch with each of them individually.

Charles hoped this would foster constructive conversation among them and perhaps repair some sibling bonds which had been damaged. He also wanted to use the meeting to acknowledge and consolidate the individual healing he felt each of them had done. At first, Charles' children rejected his invitation, but his low-key and straightforward responses to their questions and comments brought them around.

We were able to schedule a very productive three-hour meeting. All four young adults were remarkably forthcoming about how the divorce had affected them. As they spoke, they discovered both similarities and differences in their experiences.

Carefully and respectfully, Charles answered their questions about why he had left their mother. He expressed very little negativity. Mostly he conveyed deep compassion both for her struggles and for his children's concerns about her. He offered to help them find the support they needed to deal with their mother as she did not want Charles involved in any way.

Throughout the meeting, Charles bore witness to his children's pain. He did so without judgment or downplaying, and he chose not to mention his own struggles during these difficult years. In the end, all four shared tears as well as hugs and agreed that they wanted to schedule another family session in a year to assess further progress. They now anticipated having contact with each other in the interim which they hoped would not focus on their mother. Still, they felt it could be helpful to set aside a time once a year to acknowledge and grieve their common losses.

Charles' story touches on some of the special concerns when the divorce involves a mentally ill parent. What if there is an addicted parent? An abusive parent? What if a parent moves away or moves on to a new family and has minimal contact with their children?

We will consider these difficult situations at the conclusions of both Chapters 9 and 10. They entail significant losses that need to be grieved in all their complexity. However, even with instances involving major challenges and losses, positive aspects may still be "found." The nonimpaired parent may well be better off following divorce. They now have the chance to create a more functional family for their adult children to be part of, whether they remarry or remain single. As long as the burden of managing the impaired parent is not passed on to the adult children without sufficient resources, the whole family in its new formation may stand a much better chance of being happy and healthy.

When a parent abandons his or her children even when they are adults, the experience of loss is highly dependent on the specific circumstances. The non-abandoning parent may be able to help their adult children reach closure and get appropriate support. The bottom line remains: having one healthy, functional, and hopefully, happy-enough parent is likely better than two who were unhealthy, dysfunctional, and unhappy together and it is certainly better than none!

FOUND

It may not have taken much convincing to see that divorce *at any stage of life* can result in significant losses. It may be harder to be open to the possibility that divorce can also have some significantly positive outcomes. With sufficient time, support, permission, and opportunity to grieve, all members of a later-life divorce family can eventually feel strong and happy again. The more fortunate ones may even emerge stronger and happier than they were before, especially if the divorce occurred because of trauma or serious dysfunction. And how can that be?

Happier Parents, Happier Kids

For the parents, the best outcome following divorce at any life stage is for both parties to move on from the initial pain and carve out healthy new lives. To do so they need sufficient resources (both monetary and social) to at least live comfortably. This is true whether they re-partner or remain single.

Most will be forced to make major changes. Having to do things differently presents the possibility of learning from new experiences and discovering new aspects of themselves. Parents who are no longer in abusive relationships may encounter a whole new way of being in the world without fear, shame, and constant vigilance. Both they and their children will feel and welcome this difference.

The best outcome for adult children is seeing both parents land on their feet following divorce whether they remain single or re-partner. Adult children can breathe a sigh of relief if they see that their parents are happy enough, able to take care of themselves emotionally, physically and financially, and are engaged in meaningful pursuits and relationships. This allows them to concentrate on their own lives and life stages.

Hopefully, they will remain in contact with both of their parents and feel like they are "still family" with each of them. If so, adult children will emerge from the divorce process now with a sense of being in a binuclear family. A binuclear family is a post-divorce family with children. It consists of the original nuclear family now divided into two families, each headed by one of the parents. The two new families may be either single-parent families or stepfamilies.

Constance Ahrons' groundbreaking book *We're Still Family* challenged the earlier grim view that divorce always destroys families.[5] In fact, the research she reports on adults who had grown up as children in divorced families tells a very different story. As adults (aged 21 to 52), they felt that what impacted them was not divorce itself but how their parents related to each other. Parents who can maintain a civil relationship with each other following divorce contribute not only to the health of their families but also to their own sense of well-being. We clearly saw that with Kelsey's parents earlier in this chapter.

Ahrons makes a strong case that there can be "good divorces" despite the media's portrayal of bad divorces as the norm. Good divorces, according to Ahrons, leave meaningful family relationships intact. Children continue to have ties to both of their parents and their parents' extended families. This includes the families that a parent acquires when they re-partner or remarry. The parents, despite their decision to divorce, maintain a working relationship which allows them to focus on their childrens' needs.

While the adults in Ahrons' study were young children when their parents divorced, much of what they told her applies to adult children of later-life divorce. They, too, benefit from having a strong sense of family. And families these days can take many forms including stepparents and stepsiblings, half-siblings, cohabitating partners, and exes.

If the parents divorcing in later life can maintain at least a civil relationship with each other, there is a much greater probability that their adult children (as well as grandchildren) can continue to feel a positive sense of having and being a family. Ahrons feels there can be a huge benefit from having these new, larger family formations. She calls this having a "tribe," and feels this is generally preferable to being in a family with two parents staying together without love.

I have often seen this with my own clients. Some young adult clients spoke of the advantages of acquiring stepsiblings who broaden the expertise available from having a larger tribe. Now there may be someone to turn to for help with a plumbing issue, a health concern, or a tax situation. They may compare notes on childrearing and even babysit for each other on occasion.

Lessons Learned from Taking Care of Yourself

For divorcing parents and adult children alike, steps made to take care of themselves throughout the (perhaps lengthy) divorce process often result in personal growth. Under reasonably positive circumstances when you have to let go of the old ways of doing things and come up with new ones, you have the opportunity to construct healthier patterns for your life. Never underestimate the benefits of learning to adapt to change no matter how long it takes or how old you are when you have to do so.

Parents

For parents, along with the need to adapt to change, comes the opportunity to reevaluate your former, married lifestyle. Obviously, as a person divorcing after a long marriage, you are significantly older than when you got married. Likely you've learned a fair amount during this time whether you realize it not. You probably know yourself better than you did in your 20s and 30s. You have a better sense of what gives your life meaning. Hopefully, once you move beyond anger and grief, you will be able to think about what is really important to you and seek out those things that matter most.

If you are in Erikson's Stage 7, Generativity, you still have the time to construct a purposeful life and to feel good about leaving a legacy that fits your values. You can put into practice what you have learned about what makes partnerships and marriages work and not work. You may be freer to move to where you can find a meaningful job or volunteer opportunities. You can strengthen your ties with friends and relatives. This may hold true especially with your adult children and grandchildren. Ask yourself, what kind of parent or grandparent do you want to be? And then, start putting that into practice if you are not already doing so.

That is what Linda did. She had held onto her marriage for a number of years despite suspecting that her husband Jack was having affairs. Finally, with her self-esteem in tatters, she found her way to my office. Looking back on our first encounter several years later, she said:

"I really can't believe I put up with this for as long as I did. I guess I didn't know I deserved better. I can see now how Jack appealed to me. He was handsome, dashing, risk-taking. Very appealing to a little Goody Two-Shoes girl like I was—looking for adventure. But he turned out to be a terrible provider and mediocre father, and I didn't want to admit I'd made a mistake. And I guess I still loved him.

At this point in my life, being single feels fine … safer. But I've seen a lot of marriages by now between my brothers and my friends and my co-workers and I know if I ever decide to date, I'll be looking for an entirely different type of man. There are a lot more important things than what you see on the surface.

Right now, I'm still focused on my work where I am hoping to make some important contributions. And my kids still need me even though they're young adults now. That's where I'm going to put my energy and it feels just right."

Linda has learned a lot over the 35 years since she married Jack. She's seen marriages that seem to work and marriages that don't. Her priorities have changed as she has come to know herself better. She feels she still has time to make a difference at work and with her children and their young families.

If you are in Erikson's final Stage 8, Ego Integrity, you may feel that divorce—initiated by you or not—leaves less time to get your life in whatever order you want it to be in. Nevertheless, it is still possible to put your time and energy into what you deem to be of utmost importance. In fact, feeling this urgency may make it more likely that you will dust yourself off and act now!

You have accumulated a lot of valuable life experience, and likely, wisdom. With whom can you share it, in person or in writing, both inside and outside of your family? To your children and grandchildren, you may well be a role model of resiliency and integrity for being able to adapt to change even in your elder years.

Margot was in her 80s when she divorced. She explains:

"At first, I was totally lost. Who was I now? I had been a wife for nearly 60 years but now that role was gone. Honestly, I would have rather been widowed. Then you still have that identity. You were someone's partner until they died so you can still wear your ring and be treated like someone who had been in a loving relationship.

I felt pretty worthless for a while but my sons kept reminding me how many friends I had and how important I was to them and their families. I made sure I kept taking care of myself and I found a therapist who respected old ladies like me (chuckles). At some point I realized that I had a lot more time now that I didn't have to attend to my demanding husband.

Looking back, I now see it all as a blessing. I got back in touch with some of my old talents and started writing poetry again. Maybe it's not the greatest poetry, but my family and friends keep asking me to write poems for special occasions and I'm loving it. I'm also collating stories from my family history and making copies for my children and grandchildren. I've started a book group with my neighbors and joined a quilting group where I'm making baby quilts for my great grandchildren who have started arriving. Honestly, I can't remember being this happy and busy."

Being in good health was a great asset for Margot, but she still knew she had a limited number of good years left. In her therapy sessions she thought a lot about what activities and relationships had been the most satisfying over the years. She prioritized these, held her head high, and began a poignant new chapter of her long life.

Adult Children

If you are an adult child and have experienced the necessity of building and maintaining healthy boundaries with your parents during their divorce, you have acquired a very valuable skill. Strong boundaries and the assertiveness required to ask that they be respected will serve you well in your other significant personal relationships as well as in the workplace. If you have given yourself the right to ask important people in your life to acknowledge and witness the grief your parents' later-life divorce has caused you even if they had thought it was "no big deal," you have learned to value your own experience and to ask for what you need. These are enormous steps in your healthy personal growth.

And as adults yourselves, you have the capacity to learn from your parents' (or grandparents') marriage and divorce. While still maintaining strong boundaries and not being privy to inappropriate information, you have likely formed opinions about what did and didn't work in their marriage. Some adult children of divorce feel jaundiced about the possibility of a happy and lasting marriage, but many others feel they gained valuable lessons to apply to relationships with current or future partners. What follows are brief illustrations of this from adult children I saw in my office over the years.

From Chad whom we met in Chapter 3:

"I watched my dad kowtow to my alcoholic mom, nagging her to stop drinking until she left him. Then he remarried a very attractive woman, and it looked like he was willing to let her run the show rather than risk losing her. I saw myself doing the same thing in my relationships—picking people I thought were more attractive than me and not feeling like I had a right to stand up for myself.

My sister kept talking about how seeing a counselor was really helping her, so I gave it a try. It helped me see some unhealthy patterns I was drawn to. I broke off my relationship with a woman who only made me feel bad about myself, and now I'm determined to never marry anyone unless we feel like equal partners."

In his therapy sessions, Chad was beginning to put his valuable observations into practice. He had set sufficient boundaries with his father to be able to look at his father's behavior in relationships without judgment. He could see the negative effects of some of his father's choices and feel compassion for him. When Chad saw similarities to some of his own choices, he resolved to break the pattern.

Once she'd gone beyond her initial grief, Victoria (an only child we saw earlier in this chapter) used our therapy sessions to start thinking about what had gone wrong in her parents' marriage.

"They were both so caught up in their careers that they

didn't make time for each other. I think I was the glue that held them together because they were so determined to be good parents to me. They each traveled a lot for work, but they made sure one of them was always home with me. Vacations were always the three of us and they always made holidays special for me.

But now that I think about it, they never went anywhere on their own. They almost quit being a couple after I came along. I really respect them as brilliant people, but I know I want more of a romantic partnership when I get married. I have friends whose parents have successful careers, but they also go out together and prioritize their relationship."

Victoria gave herself plenty of time to grieve what she called the death of her family. Once she accepted that her family had forever changed, she could move on. Now she was able to step back and view marriage from a broader perspective. She could begin to see ways she would want her own marriage to be very different from her parents' while still cherishing some very positive aspects of her childhood.

Alan, a middle-aged adult, looked back thoughtfully on his parents' failed marriage and hoped to avoid their mistakes:

"I was a star athlete in high school, and my sister was somewhat of a musical prodigy. Our parents were so completely invested in following my sports events and my sister's concerts and recitals that they had little time for anything else. I sort of feel like they were living through us and sometimes I felt like I had to keep being the "star" for their sake and not mine.

I wasn't really good enough to do sports in college. Maybe I let them down by going someplace where I could concentrate on academics, but as soon as my sister and I were out on our own their marriage seemed to crumble. My wife and I are making sure our kids aren't our 'everything.' We love them and I think we are involved enough in their activities, but they aren't our whole life."

Like Victoria, Alan felt he was learning ways to avoid the mistakes his parents made. Victoria's parents paid careful attention to the demands of parenting and work but neglected their relationship. Alan's parents prioritized their children over everything else. Likely their interest was closer to enmeshment than to healthy involvement. In both cases the children were the glue holding the marriage together. Once they were gone, the marriages were empty shells.

And from Kendra, now in her 30s, who married five years after her parents divorced:

> "My parents fought all the time. I really don't think they ever had much in common and I'm not sure why they married in the first place. When I see how much happier my dad is with his new wife and how much happier my mom is on her own with a lot of friends and a job she loves, I wish they had divorced when I was younger.
>
> Lately, my husband and I have started arguing about money and spending time with our families and I'm afraid we could be headed for divorce. I don't want my kids to see this on a daily basis, so I wanted to get help right away."

Kendra was determined to avoid divorce. She felt her parents were mismatched from the outset and thought she would have had a better childhood if they divorced before she was an adult. At the first sign of "fighting" in her own marriage, she reached out for help. That was a wise decision because her fears about marital conflict were rigid and exaggerated. She needed to air her feelings about her parents' marriage and divorce, but she also needed to learn about healthy disagreements and rules for "fair fighting."[6]

New Families and New Traditions

Eventually, when parents are able to move on and establish meaningful lives for themselves after divorce, there is a strong possibility that they will also be able to create happier families. We have so far seen this happen when parents remain single. But what happens if one or both re-partner or remarry?

These new family formations will be different from, and perhaps more complex and even messier than, the predivorce family. But children at all ages would likely prefer a large "tribe" of people of good will who consider themselves family than a small original family with two parents living together unhappily.

If everyone is realistic as well as patient about blending families, they can come to feel like real additions to one's life especially after experiencing so much divorce-related loss. Increasing the size of one's extended family can lead to more varied available resources. This happened for Dana's adult children who felt fortunate to gain stepsiblings whom they could turn to for legal advice as well as occasional childcare. It was true as well for Sophia's daughter, Shannan, who eventually came to appreciate her stepfather's willingness to help her and her husband make the home improvements they wanted but lacked the time and skill to do on their own. Even living at a distance, when adult stepsiblings have children close in age, there's a whole new batch of cousins to grow up with at holidays and on vacations.

Fran and Gil

Fran (Chapter 3) remained single for eight years after her divorce from her critical and judgmental husband. She dated a few men before she met and fell in love with Gil. This would be her second marriage and his fourth, so Fran took her time before deciding it was a good idea. Gil had two sons and a daughter, one from each of his prior marriages, and Fran had three daughters. The five older children were married and living in different states and the sixth was a student at the local college.

All willingly attended Fran and Gil's wedding. They seemed to enjoy getting to know each other but had minimal expectations that they would be important in each other's lives. This was especially true for Gil's children who had three different mothers. They had grown up in separate households with little parental cooperation around holidays. They liked Fran but considered her yet another stepmother who might not be around for long.

This changed dramatically when Gil was diagnosed with abdominal cancer shortly after the wedding. Living at a distance and with heavy family and work responsibilities, Gil's older two children were deeply appreciative of Fran's solicitous care for their father during a series of surgeries and rounds of chemotherapy.

They kept in close contact with Fran and Gil by phone and came to town when their schedules allowed. Gil's daughter created a group email of all six siblings in order to share information and see what might be needed. Fran's daughters stepped up to help their mother and came to town as often as they could. In so doing, they quickly bonded not only with Gil but with his younger son, a college student who lived nearby.

Long story short, by the time Gil had a near-miraculous recovery, this new family had become more deeply attached than would have happened otherwise. The stepsiblings planned a surprise family reunion the summer after Gil was declared cancer-free. It was such a huge success, they have done this every year since with nearly everyone in attendance. This amazing story is a tribute to the character of these particular family members. It is also an inspirational reminder of the healing process that can come after divorce.

Remarrying in their late 60s, Gil and Fran had had minimal expectations that the families of their widely dispersed adult children (from Emerging to Middle-Aged Adults) would become close. However, Gil's illness and the stress it put on the newly married couple prompted their grown children on both sides to step up where they could. In so doing, their sense of becoming "family" was a happy surprise for them all.

In large part this happened because the adult children on both sides experienced this marriage as far more loving and functional than their pre-divorce families and they wanted to support it. They found it easy to be around Fran and Gil who seemed so comfortable with each other and so welcoming of each other's children with all their idiosyncrasies.

Fran was big on hosting at holidays. This was a breath of fresh air for Gil's children who, coming from three separate marriages, had previously experienced little of this togetherness. And Fran's children relished Gil's jovial style which seemed to suit their mother better than their father's bah-humbug personality had.

This level of blending is less surprising when parents remarry in their 40s and 50s and still have many years ahead for new family traditions to develop. We saw this with Chris (in Chapter 4) who was a college freshman when her parents divorced. Both parents quickly remarried new partners who had their own children. Thinking back on this after decades,

Chris was surprised to find herself not differentiating between stepsiblings and biological siblings in terms of whom she feels close to now, whom she visits more frequently, and with whom she shares more similar political views. The years for her family brought both mending and blending, and the raw feelings she needed to escape from early on seem like ancient history. Thankfully, the process of healing from her parents' divorce had time to run its course and she valued the additions to her "tribe."

With a longer time perspective, stories like these are not all that rare. They are a good reminder that healing and resilience are possible. However, these examples are not intended to create a Pollyannaish perception that all can be a bed of roses even when the later-life divorce is a "good divorce." The intent is to counter the idea that later-life divorce has to be devastating or that the effects of later-life divorce for parents and children alike are always negative.

In Summary

It is important to acknowledge that *all* families—those that have divorce in their history and those that don't—will always be dealing with the challenges inherent in life itself. The effects of divorce on families are not all negative in the long run. The effects of not divorcing are not all positive. All families will face hardships and losses over the years, and all families will experience some more fortunate times. Unless you get stuck in anger, fear, or denial and cannot really grieve and heal, divorce itself does not have to be the defining feature of your family.

Chapter Eight Notes—*Lost and Found: Grief and New Beginnings*

1. In *You Can Heal Your Heart: Finding Peace After a Breakup, Divorce, or Death*, 2014, Hay House LLC, Louise Hay and David Kessler expand grieving beyond dealing with death. Hay and Kessler address finding peace after a breakup or divorce. Their recommendations for "healing the grief of divorce" are aimed primarily at divorcing adults although they briefly mention that young children grieve their parents' divorce as well. The absence of acknowledgment that adult children also grieve their parents' divorce subtly perpetuates the myth that children are not significantly impacted once they are adults. This sort of omission only reinforces adult children's tendency to deny their gut feelings of sadness and loss.

2. Elisabeth Kubler-Ross, *On Death and Dying: What the Dying Have to Teach Doctors, Nurses, Clergy & Their Own Families*, 1969, Scribner.

3. Elisabeth Kubler-Ross and David Kessler, *On Grief and Grieving: Finding the Meaning of Grief Through the Five Stages of Loss*, 2014, Scribner.

4. David Kessler, *Finding Meaning: The Sixth Stage of Grief*, 2019, Scribner.

5. Constance Ahrons, *We're Still Family: What Grown Children Have to Say About Their Parents' Divorce*, 2004, Harper Perennial.

6. There are different versions of rules for fighting fair. All are intended to increase the likelihood of a positive outcome when couples try to communicate about hard or heated topics in their relationship. The following are some frequently considered "rules:"
    1. Establish a limited time (e.g., 30-60 minutes) for this conversation.
    2. If things become too heated, take a time out of at least 30 minutes and no more than 24 hours. The person requesting the time out needs to reschedule the conversation.
    3. Address only one issue or concern at a time.
    4. Take turns and listen when the other person is talking.

5. Avoid using "always" and "never" as these only tend to escalate an argument.

6. No yelling.

7. No name calling.

8. No swearing.

9. No bringing in third parties such as saying, "All our friends think you are selfish" or, "You act just like your mother."

10. Take responsibility for your feelings. Use "I statements" such as "I feel…" versus "You statements," such as "You make me…"

11. Look for ways to compromise and find common ground.

12. Learn to apologize when you realize that you have been wrong or see that you have hurt your partner.

13. Learn how to use a "reset button" and give yourselves a chance for a fresh start.

PART V

Paths to a Healthy Parent-Child Relationship During & After Divorce

What Can Parents Do?

Advice to Divorcing and Divorced Parents on Taking Care of Your Relationship with Your Adult Children

A Caveat: What is "advice" anyway and why do many of us have a strong reaction to the very word? Is it something we want only if it agrees with what we already plan to do? Is it what we ask for reluctantly, knowing we probably won't like the answer? Is it easier to hand out than to listen to and profit from?

While we call the recommendations in the next two chapters "advice," they are really suggestions since every individual's and every family's situation is unique. Any particular recommendattion will fit some situations better than others. That is yours to decide.

This chapter summarizes and reinforces what has come before. In addition, it offers ways for parents to take care of their relationships with their adult children during and following the process of divorce. I hope you will read this chapter with an open mind and open heart. Try on these suggestions. See what does and doesn't fit your situation. And when something fits, pay attention even if it feels uncomfortable.

As a parent, having gotten this far in the book (or even if you skipped to this chapter right away), you are likely concerned about how your divorce has affected/will affect your relationship with your adult children. Hopefully by now, you are no longer under the impression that divorce has no impact on children once they are 18 or older, living on their own, off at college, married, parents, or even middle-aged. You realize that it does. Like yourself, your adult children will experience divorce-related losses and challenges.

Some of you may still be trying to decide whether or not to divorce. You may have waited until your children were no longer at home thinking that their lives would then not be disrupted. Now that you know this is impossible, you may be questioning the decision to divorce. Is it fair to your children? Do you have a right to divorce and upset their lives?

This book is not intended to help you make that decision. Deciding whether to divorce or how to respond when divorce was not your choice are complicated and consequential situations. Hopefully, as we discuss below, you will seek out the resources you need to help you navigate this challenging time.[1]

Our goal here is to remind you that whatever your decision, it will affect not only you and your spouse but your entire family. You need to keep your mind and heart open to how this decision will impact others, especially your adult children.

Your children are attempting to launch their own lives beyond the family of origin. They are trying to forge and maintain their own occupational and relationship identities out in the world. They are dealing with the challenges of the life stages *they* are in just as you are dealing with the challenges your divorce presents at the stage of life that *you* are in. Your children now must add this significant family event—divorce—into the mix of their already complicated lives, just as you must add concern for their reactions and well-being into the mix of yours.

When all this is going on for both generations, how do you maintain a healthy relationship with your adult children? How can you strengthen or repair a relationship that may already be reeling from the impact of the divorce? Is it possible to heal from estrangement caused by, or even preceding, the divorce? Are there ways you can lessen the divorce-related losses for your children?

The recommendations that follow will help you maintain or develop healthy relationships with your adult children during and after divorce. They come with deep respect for the infinite variety of parent-child relationships. It is never a case of "one size fits all." Nuances and tiny situational and personality differences will determine if a suggestion is useful in your situation. It is possible that relationships have become so strained by the challenges both generations are facing that professional intervention is highly recommended. When that appears to be the case, I hope you will seek it and find it beneficial.

For some of you, these recommendations may seem to be coming too late. You may have already behaved in a way you now regret, in a way that hurt your relationship with your adult children. While "what's done is done" and you can't turn back the clock, you can still own your behavior, apologize, and vow to do things differently from now own.

For those of you who skipped ahead to this chapter, you may encounter concepts and references which are new to you. Although enough detail is presented here for this chapter to stand on its own, I would encourage you to go back and read the chapters where these concepts are presented in detail and fleshed out with examples. Recommendations make more sense when you have a fuller understanding of what they are grounded in.

If you have read the previous chapters, these concepts will already be familiar. For you, this chapter will be a review and summary of the issues, challenges, and pitfalls later-life divorce poses for both you and your adult children. With that in mind, let's look at the following recommendations for taking constructive action throughout the divorce process.

TAKE CARE OF YOURSELF

It may seem contradictory but taking appropriate care of your relationship with your adult child *first and foremost* requires that you take care of yourself. Even if your adult child appears to be in significant pain over the divorce, it is still important that you, like Meg in Chapter 8, be as healthy and strong as possible when you reach out to comfort and support. As we hear with every in-flight airline announcement, "In the event of an emergency, secure your own oxygen mask before assisting others."

This directive ensures that you are sufficiently healthy to actually be of assistance. You will be more help to your adult children when your own situation is under control. So, how do you practice self-care during the divorce process?

Seek Support from Appropriate Places

To take care of yourself as you deal with your divorce and all its challenges, you need to seek appropriate social support. You may be tempted to turn to your adult children but, as emphasized in Chapter 7, they should not be your primary support system. They, too, are deeply impacted by the divorce and are going through their own struggles. To rely primarily on them violates important parent-child boundaries.

Instead, reach out to other important adults in your life. If you are fortunate, you may have friends who are able to meet many of your needs for support. Family members—your own parents, siblings, perhaps even in-laws—may also be people you can turn to as you sort out your feelings and your next steps. Clergy members can fill this need for those with a religious affiliation or orientation. Finding a divorce support group can be an enormous asset, providing companionship with others who are going through a similar situation as well as information regarding legal and financial issues. Not infrequently, these groups evolve into a social network of other newly-single people with whom to socialize, perhaps replacing a previously couples-oriented network.

Because divorce entails many changes and losses, it can be a motivation for seeking out individual psychotherapy. Unlike friends and family members who may have their own opinions about your divorce, a professional therapist brings objectivity as well as support during this difficult time. When everything seems to be in a state of upheaval you may be open to examining yourself and your life in a whole new way.

You might end up exploring issues beyond the logistics of dealing with the divorce itself. Issues such as: Why didn't I see this coming? Why did I put up with such an unhealthy situation for so long? Why didn't I take better care of my relationship? Why am I never satisfied with any aspect of my life? You could emerge from the pain of divorce with a stronger and healthier sense of yourself as a person. This, in turn, will make you a stronger and healthier parent.

If you do seek psychotherapy, I hope you will look for someone who appreciates and respects the family system you are part of. This should be someone who is aware of your adult children's issues and needs at the same time they are attentive to yours. Perhaps they would be open to inviting your children in for a family meeting if you think that might be appropriate and helpful. If your therapist is helpful to you but downplays or seems unaware of your adult children's challenges, you can always hand them this book!

Other Types of Self-Care

Seeking social support is not the only way to take care of yourself. Other forms of self-care include spending time alone with a book, listening to a podcast, practicing yoga or mediation, taking a warm bath, working out, going for a walk or a run, or praying at home or in a place of worship. Pay close attention to whatever you do that leaves you feeling replenished and invigorated. Those activities qualify as your own personal form of self-care. You need to make time for them even when you feel you should be doing something more "productive." Unless taken to extremes, taking care of yourself in your own unique ways is an excellent use of your time.

Be Open to Hearing When Well-Meaning People Think You Could Use More Support

Some people are well aware that they need more support in their lives in order to get on with the tasks before them. Others are of the "stiff upper lip" variety. They insist they are doing fine and don't need anything or anyone. Whether you are one of these or anywhere in between, pay attention when well-meaning people in your life suggest you could use more support.

They may be noticing that you aren't acting like yourself. They may be concerned that you are spending too much time alone. They may feel you are pulling away from people who care about you. They may notice that you are drinking more than you used to or that you are making poor decisions about your finances or your personal safety.

Even if they care deeply about you, they may be feeling overwhelmed by your neediness. Friends and family members may feel unable to continue supporting you at the current level while meeting the demands of their own lives. They may be setting limits and establishing healthy boundaries in order to take care of themselves. They may merely be securing their own oxygen masks.

When important people in your life recommend that you seek more support than you have or than they can provide, you are likely to be disappointed. It could even feel hurtful. However, it is important to take time to let their input sink in. If these are people who have generally had your best interests at heart, they may be telling you something you don't want to hear but that may be true. For your own sake, as well as to preserve these relationships, it is probably time to reach out for professional help and support.

This is especially true when it is your adult children who think you could use more support. Likely, this is their way of telling you that they are worried about you and are overwhelmed by your needs. They may be saying that they can't assume the roles they feel you want them to take—confidante, caretaker, or witness bearer to the wrongs you feel their other parent committed.

Instead of being offended, try to hear what may be driving their concern. It may be that they care about you but want to set healthy limits for their own well-being. They could be trying to preserve their relationship with you as their parent and themselves as your child. It is less that your adult child is pulling away and more that they are genuinely concerned about your well-being and pleading for you to get help. This could be the time you, in your role as a caring and responsible parent, suggest that your child could also use additional support like Sophia did with her daughter Shannan in Chapter 7.

If your children are already middle-aged, they have unique concerns when they hear that you are divorcing in the final decades of your life. Most of their worries will be about you. They may worry that you are making a big mistake and wonder if you are of sound mind. They may worry that your finances will run out. They may worry about you living on your own if you have physical or mental limitations. They may worry that you will be lonely. They may worry that you will re-partner with someone who does not have your best interests at heart.

Other worries will be about themselves. Will they have the time and resources to take care of both of their parents as well as their own mid-life responsibilities? How will your divorce affect them monetarily? They may worry whether any new relationship you might form will have room for them and your grandchildren. Many may be worrying that their own marriages might not last if yours could end after all these years together.

Take time to truly listen to your adult children's concerns. If they seem legitimate, continue the conversation even if it is uncomfortable for all of you. Take the appropriate steps to reassure your children that you are taking care of yourself and encourage them to do the same.

Legal and Financial Advice

There are already many books and articles dealing with later-life divorce from both legal and financial perspectives. Some are listed in the Resources Section at the end of the book. These are important considerations for people divorcing at any age, and perhaps more so when you are divorcing in your 50s, 60s, 70s, and beyond. For you, the number of possible income-accruing years are diminishing, and health-related concerns and expenses may be increasing. Gaining good financial advice, whatever your income level, is of utmost importance.

The same is true for legal matters. Using lawyers and/or mediators who have special understanding of the issues and needs of older divorcing adults is crucial for both parties ending up as well off and viable as possible. It is also important to find lawyers who have a family perspective and understand the needs and concerns of your adult children.

Lawyers and financial advisors are in many ways ahead of mental health professions in recognizing the upward trend, as well as the special needs, of parents divorcing later in life. Since they have written more extensively on these issues, we won't focus here beyond mentioning their importance. Instead, we are trying to fill the gaps left by ignoring crucial relationship issues between older divorcing parents and their adult children.

DEALING WITH YOUR CHILDREN AROUND THE DIVORCE ITSELF

How you tell your adult children about the divorce makes a difference in your relationship with them both in the short and long run. The recommendations here are grounded in clinical experience, common sense, and good will. I am well aware that some of these suggestions may not be feasible given the acrimony around the marital split or the emotional state of one or both divorcing parents. In that case, they represent an ideal or best-case scenario. Where this is not possible, the closer to the ideal the better, but you can only do what you can do.

If you are already beyond this early stage and realize now that you might have handled things better, do not be hard on yourself. You can still apologize to your adult child now that you have had a chance to think more clearly. This may not immediately erase the effects of a less-than-ideal way of having handled things, but your child will likely appreciate your stated regret for your earlier behavior. A *sincere apology* along with *clearly taking responsibility* for your behavior sets the tone for healthy and respectful communication with your adult child now and in the future. It can go a long way toward healing rifts in your relationship with them.

When Possible, Tell Your Children as a Family

The best way to tell your children about the divorce is for you and your spouse to call the family together and present a statement you have agreed upon. Some couples find it easier to do this after consulting with a couples or family therapist, but others are able to agree on this on their own. Be clear what you want and don't want to tell your children as well as how you will handle questions that go beyond what you plan to present.

The bottom line is to ask yourself: *What do the children need to know in order to understand why you reached this decision?* But first and last, tell them you love them and will continue to care about their well-being. Reassure them, wherever you can honestly do so, that you will continue to be involved in their lives and be responsive to their needs. In short, let them know that you will remain in an appropriate role as their parent.

All children of divorce, no matter their age, need to hear that the ending of their parents' marriage does not mean their parents do not love them. They also need to hear that they did not cause the divorce. Even if you as parents have argued over the years about how to deal with your children, this rarely precipitates a decision to divorce.

On your own or with professional help, there are important issues to discuss with your spouse prior to this family meeting. How will you provide a home base for your youngest adult children who are not yet living on their own? How will you share responsibility for holiday plans so your children are not floundering about where to go and what to expect? Are there important milestone events coming up in your adult children's lives which could be impacted by the divorce? What additional logistical and financial issues need to be addressed?

You are now aware that your adult children have legitimate needs that will be affected by your divorce. As much as possible, you want to reassure them that, despite the divorce, their age-appropriate needs will be taken into account. This is true for families who have sufficient resources as well as for those where resources are scarce and hardships are anticipated.

You may be wondering how the ideal scenario of a family meeting can take place when young to Middle-Aged Adult Children may be scattered geographically. In previous chapters, we saw examples where this family meeting happened around holidays because that is when the adult children are more likely to be home at the same time. On one level, that makes sense. But, on another, it can forever link a supposedly happy holiday with shock and sadness.

The possibility of a video meeting gives another option. Everyone can be present to hear the news of the divorce at a more neutral time and to see each other's reactions. However, this clearly has disadvantages as well, especially the absence of family members being able to offer tangible physical support to one another.

What to Share with Your Adult Children

You can be honest and authentic and still maintain healthy boundaries with your adult children. You can draw the line and not share personal or private things that would be unnecessarily hurtful for them and for you. There is a difference between something that is "secret" and something that is "private." Private or very personal things between you and your spouse generally do not need to be shared with your children. If there are things one or both of you want to keep secret, you can admit that you are choosing not to share some things at this time without revealing the content. It may be uncomfortable for everyone, but your honesty sets the tone for maintaining healthy relationships. For example:

➢That's a perfectly legitimate question, but it's not something your dad and I are comfortable talking about right now.

➢I want to be honest with you and the honest answer is that part of the reason we are getting a divorce is very personal and private between us. I know you want to know more but this feels like all we want to say at this point. If that feels different in the future, we will let you know. It's not really a big secret, it's just private.

If the divorce is happening because of infidelity which is likely to come out eventually, you can agree on how much to share, sparing your children the details. If mental illness, substance or domestic abuse is involved, again this can be shared without hurtful details. Bottom line: being honest with your adult children does not require full disclosure. They will accept it when you set a limit on what you feel is appropriate to share even if they push for more information. In the long run, they are likely to be grateful that you are modeling clear boundaries.

And if You Cannot Tell Your Children as a Family...

Obviously, it isn't always possible to tell your children about the divorce with everyone present. The most important missing family member may be one of the divorcing spouses. Under many circumstances, emotions are running high and civility and cooperation are running low early on in the decision to divorce. If so, there may be little chance that the parents will be able to hold a "family meeting" to break the news. One or both parents may have already informed the adult children—often in an impulsive, angry, and emotional manner.

If that is your situation you can still take the high road and call your children together for a meeting. It will be a different kind of meeting but, staying firmly in your parental role, you can follow many of the recommendations above. You can reassure your children that you love them and that the divorce is not their fault. You can decide on your own what to share about why the divorce is happening, knowing that your children do not want to hear inappropriate and negative things about their absent parent.

This is a tall order. It may be your first opportunity to show your children (as well as yourself) the type of healthy, single parent you want to be. They will likely respect you for doing the best you can to inform them what is going on while maintaining the parent-child boundary.

If the missing family member is one of the children who can't be present or if none are available for a family meeting, then what? In so far as possible all should be informed about the divorce around the same time. That protects against anyone feeling like an outsider or the "last to know."

STAY IN YOUR ROLE AS A PARENT

When everything seems to be unraveling, it may be particularly challenging to remember that you are still your adult children's parent. Yet it is essential to do your best to continue to function as Mom or Dad. You are losing your role as husband or wife, but you are not losing your fundamental role as parent.

Remembering and appreciating that you still play a very significant part in your adult children's lives can provide much-needed structure and scaffolding during this challenging time. Despite considerable upheaval, something very significant has *not* changed. As much as you can, especially in the early stages of the divorce, keep reminding yourself that even though your children are legally adults, they will always be your children and they will always see you as their parent.

It is especially important to maintain an appropriate parental role with the youngest adult children, the Launchers. They are the least experienced at living independently and taking care of themselves, so they are still quite vulnerable. Your input regarding housing, finances, family relationships, and general decision-making, while still important for the older two cohorts, is critical for them.

Do Not Use Your Children as Your Main Source of Emotional Support

It bears repeating here what we said above and in earlier chapters: Your adult children should not be your primary support system. Their own feelings about the divorce are complicated enough already. They do not need to take on the additional burden of making sure you are okay. Quite likely they care about you and would like to support and comfort you, but they could easily become overwhelmed by your distress and lose touch with what is healthy for themselves. Perhaps even more important, their feelings about their other parent are likely to be very different from yours. Much of what you may want to talk about is not something they want or need to hear.

When your children see you reach out for support from friends and family or from a therapist or clergy member, they are reassured that you are taking care of yourself. They are also likely to be relieved that you are not treating them as peers or, worse still, reversing the roles of parent and child. Your determination to bolster your support system at this time gives them the freedom, permission, and example to take care of themselves.

Do Not Use Your Children as Confidantes

A confidante is someone with whom one shares a private matter or secret. It involves trusting that person not to repeat private or personal information given in confidence. A confidante should be someone whose primary loyalty is to the person sharing with them and not to the person who is the object of the problem or secret.

Entrusting your adult children with private information about personal issues involving their other parent puts them in an untenable situation. They are burdened with a heavy secret which they can neither discuss nor validate. If they do end up sharing this information, they have violated the trust invested in them. It is a lose-lose situation for children at any age to be put into a loyalty conflict between their parents. Other people who do not have such loyalty conflicts are far more appropriate confidantes. It is your job to seek them out.

Pay Attention to Your Children's Well-Being

You are still the parent. Quite likely, you know your own children fairly well. You have knowledge of how they have dealt with previous stressful situations. How do they seem to be dealing with the news of the divorce? Are there behavioral changes? Do they appear to be angry, depressed, anxious, or fearful? Are they isolating themselves from family and friends? While you cannot force your adult child to talk to you or to get help, you may be in the best position to notice, start a conversation, and steer your child to the necessary resources.

What other important things are going on in their lives right now? With everything *you* are going through regarding the divorce, you may have lost track of how your children are doing. As much as you can, try to remain alert to your adult children's well-being. Again, it is particularly important with your youngest adult children who are not likely yet to be in solid relationships with significant others. Without a strong network of caring relationships, you may be the only person in their lives who is truly concerned about their physical and mental health.

Respect Your Children's Perspective

Hard as it may be with your emotions running high and serious concerns about your future, try to step back and put yourself in your adult child's shoes. They are experiencing this divorce very differently from you. I am hoping that this book will help you to be more knowledgeable about, and respectful of, the unique and legitimate challenges which your divorce poses for them at their different developmental life stages.

Your Children will Likely Benefit from a Continued Relationship with Both Parents

Divorce legally ends the husband-wife relationship, but it does not end the relationship between parents and their children. With the exception of some situations involving trauma and abuse, most adult children want to continue to have a relationship with both of their parents following divorce. You may no longer have positive feelings for your ex-spouse, but your children quite likely do.

They may be angry at one or both of you but, if their earlier bonds were strong, their love and loyalty will likely remain intact. Your children do not want to hear your negative accounts of their other parent. The object of your disdain or disappointment is still the Mom or Dad for whom they have loving feelings. This person with all their faults is often half of their genetic make-up, so any insults about that person can feel personal as well.

Continuing to disparage your children's other parent will likely result in their distancing from you to protect against hearing unwanted complaints. Even when your child tells you negative things your former spouse has said about you, you can take the high road and refuse to answer in kind. Better yet, you can ask your child not to relay these comments and release them from an uncomfortable, destructive position in the middle.

Keep Them Out of the Middle.

In general, making sure your child does not feel caught in the middle of acrimony between you and their other parent has significant payoffs. Your child will be more comfortable spending time with you because they are not worrying about being exposed to negativity toward their other parent. If they sense that you respect the fact that they continue to care about, want to have a relationship with, and want to spend time with both of you, they will less likely be caught in a loyalty bind between the two of you. They will feel grateful to you for your maturity and wisdom.

It is also important not to literally put your adult children in the middle. As we saw with Marty in Chapter 6, when parents refuse to speak with each other during and following a divorce, they may try to use their adult children as go-betweens. They may ask them to carry messages back and forth or deliver important papers. They may try to pump them for information about the other parent's activities or well-being. They may share emotionally-laden information which they insist must be kept secret. All of this places an enormous emotional burden on adult children of all ages. If those children are fortunate enough to be able to set boundaries which keep them out of the middle, those boundaries need to be respected by you.

What your adult children desperately want is for you and your ex-spouse to be civil toward one another. They want you to act like grown-ups who can communicate directly about their children's needs when that is necessary. You don't need to like each other or enjoy being together at extended family events, but you need to be able to get along to the extent that any conflict between you is not causing your children distress.

IF THERE ARE NEW PARTNERS

The probability of remarriage is low for the parents of the oldest or Middle-Aged children, but it still happens for some even in the final stages of life. Re-partnering and remarriage are much more frequent for the parents of the Launchers and Emerging Adults. They are younger and have more time to heal from divorce and be ready to move on. They also have a larger pool of eligible partners. For some, the desire to find a new and more compatible partner while there is still time to enjoy many years together was one of the main motives for divorce.

Others are wary of marriage, especially if this divorce was not their first. They may hope to find companionship—someone to go for a walk with, have dinner with, travel with, share intimacy with. Some may hope to remarry or re-partner but it doesn't work out that way. Still others are done with marriage or romantic entanglements and prefer the freedom of living on their own and developing other interests more to their liking. And, of course, it can happen that some people who think they aren't interested in finding a new relationship end up meeting the love of their life.

So, there will be questions about how and when to involve your adult children in any of these scenarios. The suggestions below address how and when to tell your adult children that you are dating or have found someone special. We know that some of you have no interest in "getting back out there" even though your children may eventually encourage this. If that is what works for you, let your children know and ask them to respect what feels right for you. You can, at least for now, skip the next few pages.

As always, the general suggestions below are just that—suggestions. Hopefully, they will give you a way to start thinking about what might work best in your own situation. You are one of a kind. Your divorce has unique aspects. Your relationship with each of your adult children is as distinctly different as their personalities. Try on the ideas below. If they fit, use them. If they don't, don't. And don't hesitate to tweak them a bit to fit your special circumstances.

When to Introduce the New Person to Your Adult Children

No matter how much time has passed since the divorce, children may never be ready to hear that their parents are starting new relationships. For many, this indicates that the marriage is truly over, something they may have denied up till then. Probably at this point all they want to know is that a parent is okay and not too lonely. Just because you are feeling good about getting out on the dating circuit doesn't mean that your children will be happy for you. So, when is the right time to tell them you are interested in dating and possibly a new relationship?

This depends on many factors. Is the divorce final? How is their other parent doing? At the time you are ready to meet new people, your children may be focused on their other parent who may still be having a hard time over the divorce.

Much of the time your children do not need to be aware that you are dating. They really don't need to hear about the different characters you have run into online or in person. These experiences are better shared with friends and peers. They are the best ones to turn to when filling out your online dating profile if you choose to go that route. Asking your children to help you with something like this often feels awkward for them. It can trigger loyalty conflicts about their other parent who may still be grieving the divorce.

Early on, as you are meeting different people, your adult children could be curious. Be thoughtful about how much you choose to share with them. Broad outlines are all they need to know. They definitely do not need to know any intimate details just as it is not appropriate for you to ask them for intimate details of their dating experiences. Remember that while you are all adults, you are not peers.

But what happens when you meet someone where it develops into something serious? When do you let your children know this? Likely they do not want to meet a string of casual relationships, but they probably want to meet someone you are seeing regularly. Maybe you are even thinking about moving in with or marrying this person. You don't want this decision to come as a shock to your children. How your children and this new person respond to each other provides you with valuable information about how they will fit into your family.

Hillary's Story

How and when adult children learn about a parent's new romantic interest matters. At one extreme of what not to do is Hillary's story. She came home from her first semester in graduate school in Massachusetts to spend Christmas shuttling between her recently divorced parents' homes. Both of her parents knew she had found school very stressful and needed a break. She was touched when they jointly bought her a ticket to fly home for the holidays, and grateful that they seemed to have carefully arranged for her to have equal time with each of them as well as minimal conflict.

Starting out at her Dad's home, Hillary felt further well cared for when he presented her with a gift certificate for a massage the next day. All this sense of TLC ended abruptly as she was lying on the massage table, covered only by a sheet, and the masseuse said, "I hope your father told you how special we are to each other." Hillary hadn't known her dad was even dating anyone. As soon as she could gather up her wits and her clothing, she left and called her mother for support. To her further dismay, a man answered and said he was looking forward to meeting her soon.

How to Introduce a New Person to Your Adult Children

There are many thoughtful possibilities here depending on your unique circumstances. Planning a casual meeting with minimal expectations is best if you can do it. Meeting around a sporting event or a simple meal may be a good way to start. Everyone may be nervous (including you) so don't anticipate instant bonding. Let this be a first step that gives important people in your life a chance to get to know each other. Here's an example of how to approach this topic:

> You know I've been spending time with Tom from work. I'm wondering if you'd like to meet him. No big deal. No big announcement or anything, but I'd like you to meet him, and he's heard a lot about you. Would you like to all meet up for dinner at Casey's to watch the game on Saturday?

Be prepared. Your children may not like *any* new person. They may still be loyal to their other parent and hope you will either get back together or find someone just like them. If you get negative feedback from your child after this first encounter, consider it respectfully. If it doesn't fit well with your own feelings, file it away and give yourself more time with this new person before involving your children again.

Equally important at this point is how the new person reacts to your children. Knowing their importance to you, are they respectful of your feelings about your children? Does the new person seem interested in gaining a better understanding of them?

You may end up deciding that this new person is fun to be with but may not become a permanent part of your life. They may meet your needs for now but not for the future. If so, go ahead and enjoy your time together without involving your children in your activities.

But what if you eventually find someone you are ready to make a commitment to? If your children live nearby, they likely will have met your chosen partner. If at a distance, they likely will have heard about them from you or from their siblings. Tell them your plans and reassure them that this new relationship will still leave room for your relationship with them. Children of divorce often value time alone with their parent even when they like and accept a stepparent. For example,

> I don't know if you've already been wondering about this, but Sarah and I are thinking about getting married sometime in a year or so. I'd guess you have some feelings about this so I wonder if we could get together to talk about it—just the two of us. I really want to hear your thoughts.

Give your adult children time to get used to this important new information. There is a good chance that it may trigger a well-spring of old grief about the divorce. So, be prepared for your children to respond with a range of emotions and reactions.

This may be a time that you can witness their grief in a way you weren't able to earlier in the divorce process. If so, it will deepen the healing for all of you. You don't want to deliver this information right before the wedding when there is no time for everyone to process it. And you definitely don't want to tell your children after the fact.

Unfortunately, as we saw with Hillary, some parents are rather insensitive to their adult children's feelings. Perhaps their excitement about finding a new partner blinds them to the possibility that their children will experience this differently or perhaps this insensitivity is part of a broader pattern. Hearing about a parent's new partner should not come as a shock as it did for my client Ella. During the father-daughter dance at her wedding, her highly self-centered dad whispered in her ear that the "date" he brought to her wedding would soon be her stepmother.

And that brings us to remarriage.

If there is a Remarriage, How to Include Your Children in the Wedding

Your specific circumstances will greatly influence decisions here as well. How much time has passed? How do your children feel about your soon-to-be new spouse? How do your partner's children feel about *you*? Has your ex-spouse remarried? If so, what role did your children play in that wedding?

I hope your decision to marry again is founded on deep love and respect. Hopefully, you are not making a rash decision like Ella's father did. Hopefully, you've given yourself sufficient time to grieve your divorce, learn from what went wrong, and carefully assess compatibility with your new partner. Midwestern wisdom advises us to "winter them and summer them"—that is, to not rush into a commitment but rather to give yourself enough time to see how a relationship weathers a variety of situations and seasons.

However, even if you are convinced that you are making a good decision, you may sense that your adult children have very conflicted feelings. If this threatens to dampen your excitement about the wedding, you might be tempted to go off to a romantic island, get married privately, and tell your children after the fact. Appealing as that may be, it is almost never a good way to begin your new life as a blended family. It deprives your children of the opportunity to work through important feelings (both those left over from the divorce and those about this new partnership) and be ready to participate in this new chapter of your family's life.

Start by meeting alone with your adult children without your new partner. Let them know how much you want them to be part of this next step. Meeting alone, they will be more honest with you, and if they have hurtful things they need to say, your new partner will be spared from hearing them. They likely need time to sort out their feelings and to hear what their siblings are thinking. There will be time later to bring your future spouse into the planning circle.

It is important to give your adult children choices about how they are involved in your wedding. Let them know you would value their presence in whatever capacity feels comfortable. Perhaps, initially, one or more of your children will say they do not want to attend. Another might be willing to attend but wants to play no formal role. Try to understand and deal with whatever is behind these positions and, if necessary, accept them even while hoping they might change. Having this conversation far enough in advance of the wedding date gives everyone time to work with and through a range of feelings.

In Chapter 5 we met Anna who was caught in the middle trying to negotiate the Christmas holidays for herself and her twin brothers. She found herself uncomfortably in the middle again when both parents were planning weddings in the same year. Her father wanted her to tell her mother to block out dates that he might want for himself. He offered to buy new suits for the occasion for Anna's brothers on the condition they not wear them to their mom's wedding. Although Anna and her brothers liked the people their parents were marrying, the weddings themselves were marred by anxiety and competition.

Far more fortunate and stress free was Carter's experience under what were rather similar circumstances. His parents were also remarrying just a few months apart. The parents pooled resources to buy their children's wedding apparel and agreed on two dates far enough apart that their five young adult children could all get time off from work and school. Beyond that rather remarkable degree of cooperation, neither parent knew any details of the other's wedding, and if there was any competition between his parents, Carter and his siblings were unaware of it.

Carter spoke fondly of a simple ritual which was a focal part of his mother and stepfather's ceremony. After his stepfather vowed to support and encourage Carter and his siblings in their individual endeavors, he added that he would always be supportive of their special bond with both their mother and their father. The bride and groom together poured colored sand into a clear container representing their new family. Then the five adult children each added sand of their chosen color into the mix. They'd been asked well in advance if they were comfortable with this ritual and seemed to enjoy playing an important part in the wedding.

Will there be Stepsiblings?

As you may have guessed, Carter's mother married a man who did not have children of his own. Carter gained a couple of stepsiblings when his father married so a sand ritual like the one in his mother's wedding would have been more complicated. Gaining new siblings when one is an adult can have both advantages and disadvantages.

One downside is that an adult child can feel like they are losing their special position in the family. For example, if they have been the "only girl," the "eldest son," or the "baby," a remarriage can shake up the order. In addition, adult children, like younger children, may be jealous when they see their own parent relating warmly to a new stepsibling.

They will be sensitive to possible comparisons as to whether the stepsiblings are smarter, more attractive, more athletic, more successful, more attentive. A new stepparent may bend over backward in an effort to bond with a partner's children making their own children feel marginalized and taken for granted. Being aware of these potential dynamics is an important first step in avoiding them.

And there are upsides. When things go well, having new siblings who care about you can feel great. With so many losses, these additions to your "tribe" can be welcome indeed. Chris in Chapter 4 was quite young (19) when she acquired a new a stepbrother and stepsister. They became close over the years to the point that today she barely differentiates them from her biological sibling.

Acquiring stepsiblings much later likely results in less closeness, but it can also bring more resources into a blended family system. Stepsiblings can form an expanded pool of expertise. They may share anything from free professional advice to mechanical know-how and occasional babysitting. An expanded "tribe" can mean greater support and valuable new perspectives.

Have Realistic Expectations for Blending Families

Few blended families fit the stereotype of the Brady Bunch. This is especially true when the children are already adults when the remarriage occurs. The best advice is not to try to force relationships. Some older stepfamilies blend easily. Others function well enough although the stepsiblings hardly remember each other's names, let alone their birthdays.

It is often complicated to gather together siblings from an original marriage once they are adults and live at some distance from each other and their parents. To expect to be able to do this for two sets of adult stepchildren is probably unrealistic on anything other than an occasional basis. Still, it is important and meaningful to encourage this when it can happen. Sometimes when parents are in their later-life stages, it is helpful to have a larger blended family working together to share responsibilities of elder care as we saw with Fran and Gil in Chapter 8.

If the New Person was Part of the Reason for the Divorce

What if you were involved with your new partner prior to the divorce? If this was someone you were having an affair with or someone you started seeing right away, it would be understandable if your adult children have a harder time warming to this person. This is especially the case if it is known or suspected that they may have been the reason for the divorce. Your children may see their other parent as the injured party and your new partner as the homewrecker.

If this is your situation, it's too late to reverse it. Give yourself plenty of time to assess whether your attraction to this person stands the test of time now that circumstances have changed. If it does, then the two of you need to have realistic expectations about if and when your children will come around. They are adults and may eventually have a more sophisticated understanding of relationships, making them more accepting of your new partner. Then again, depending on specifics, they may not.

This is a hard way to begin a new partnership, but if it is a healthy one, allow your children plenty of time to understand your happiness. Chris (in Chapter 4) warmed rather quickly to her father's new wife even though she knew they had been having an affair. Seeing both of her parents happy and moving on made the specifics of their divorce less important over time. It took considerably longer for the adult children of Justin (in Chapter 7) to warm to his new partner even though she was not the object of the affair which had led to his divorce. However, his patience and the positive aspects of his remarriage eventually won them over.

If the New Person is Someone Previously Known to Your Family

Sometimes the partner in the affair was someone known to the family. Dorian's father left his mother for his mother's best friend. Julia's mother left her father for her father's cousin. These are particularly difficult and hurtful situations which can challenge and divide family loyalties to the breaking point. Parents and children in these situations experience both significant loss and deep distrust.

A somewhat less complicated scenario involves one parent's new partner being someone everyone in the family already knew but who was not implicated in the divorce per se. If this person is someone everyone likes, it may be comforting. For example, Jon was about to graduate from college and would be marrying soon when his mother left his father who was a well-respected veterinarian in their community.

Jon's father was devastated and became very depressed. His adult children worried about him living on his own. Absent any reason to suspect an affair, Jon and his brothers were actually relieved when their father got remarried to his devoted long-time office manager, a single woman in her late 50s.

But it is also possible that this could be a person one of the children has negative feelings about. For example, Chris's mother's remarriage was to Chris's high school principal whom she had never liked. This initially made it harder for her to feel comfortable in their home.

When Parents are Elderly or Old

Divorcing parents of Middle-Aged Adult Children are at the end of Erikson's Stage 7 or into Stage 8. The likelihood of remarriage this late in life is less than for the parents of Launchers or Emerging Adults, but it still happens. If you are about to be one of these later-life brides or grooms, how will your children react?

They are probably worried. They may question your decision making if the decision seems hurried or the new partner is significantly older or younger than you. What are the financial implications for you? For your children's inheritance, if there is one? It is important to weigh their concerns carefully.

Having a prenuptial arrangement and other estate planning documents regarding your finances reassures everyone that you and your new spouse have thoughtfully considered your financial obligations to each other and to your children. It ensures that your money will go where you want it to go and lets your children know where they stand. They want to be certain that you have not been swept off your feet by this later-life romance and that you are taking care of your own financial future. If the new marriage does not negatively impact your financial arrangement with your children, it is understandably more likely to result in their approval.

Don't be offended if your adult children seem suspicious that you might be taken advantage of in a later-life marriage. They might be rightfully concerned about your safety, personally and financially. If this new partnership is a healthy relationship, it can withstand a little scrutiny.

SPECIAL CONSIDERATIONS

There are special considerations when the reasons for divorce involve mental illness, substance abuse, or domestic abuse. They are important enough that they merit special treatment here. That they come later in this chapter in no way indicates that they are an afterthought. In fact, it is quite the contrary. Much of the discussion above registers differently if the divorce involved abuse or trauma and you and your children experienced or continue to experience deleterious effects.

If you had divorced when your children were not yet adults, no one would have expected them to take on the responsibility for an impaired parent, and they would likely be legally protected from a potentially abusive parent. However, these safeguards can disappear once they are adults. You may be able to extricate yourself from further negative involvement with an impaired ex-spouse, but that burden could be passed along to your children.

What can you do if you see that they are struggling with this burden of responsibility? First, in your role as parent to your adult children, be aware that this can happen. Be alert to signs that they are sacrificing their own well-being to tend to the needs of their troubled parent.

Second, while still respecting the boundaries your children have established regarding their relationship with their troubled parent's situation, you can check in with them to see if they are okay. They may downplay any concerns out of loyalty, privacy, or reluctance to reveal negative things about their parent. Listen carefully and don't be too easily convinced that "everything is fine." They may well be more burdened than they are willing to admit to you or even to themselves.

Third, without pressing for details, you can let them know they can ask for help either from you or from appropriate familial or professional resources. And fourth, you can encourage them to set healthy boundaries with the other parent when their own well-being is at risk.

It is understandable that your children may be angry with you if they feel you have left them with the difficult situation you moved on from. They may be reluctant to discuss any of this with you. If so, respect the boundary they are setting. You can still gently recommend that they talk with someone else, especially a professional, about the appropriate role to play with their impaired parent. In so doing, you are giving them important permission to put their own well-being front and center.

You can still play an important role in lessening this burden of responsibility your children may be experiencing. Since this is an area requiring special sensitivity to maintaining appropriate parent-child boundaries, let's consider a couple of examples.

In Chapter 3, we met Dana who reluctantly ended a long marriage when her husband Terrance's depression deepened, and he became violent. Her children eventually chose not to have contact with their father out of concerns for their own safety, but they remained his legal heirs. Staying firmly in her role as their mother, Dana comforted and supported them in this painful decision without sharing personal information which would only have hurt them further.

Terrance refused to get help and his situation deteriorated rapidly. His children were both young adults when he died, leaving them to deal with an apartment full of remnants of his disheveled life. At that point they turned to their mother for help. Dana and her new partner labored alongside the children to clean up a host of legal and material messes. They were always careful to do so without judgment about the tragic life Terrance had been living.

We also met Caroline in Chapter 3. She had been deeply in love with her husband Frank until his off and on drug and alcohol abuse worsened and put her life at risk. Up till then, she'd told herself his substance abuse couldn't be that bad because he was experiencing success and getting raises at work. Shortly after their twin boys went off to college, drug dealers started coming to their home.

When Frank refused to get help, Caroline was concerned for the safety of everyone in her family. Reluctantly, she filed for divorce. Frank was devastated and his substance abuse escalated. He begged Caroline to reconcile but this time she held firm.

That was when he began showing up drunk on the campus where their sons were in school, telling them their mother had kicked him out for no reason. They loved their dad, but they were scared and embarrassed. It was clear that he needed some kind of help. Fortunately, they let their mother know what was going on. Caroline was furious at Frank for turning to the twins for support and interfering with their ability to concentrate on their classes, but she was wise enough to know this was a delicate situation.

Caroline was already my client, and we were working on ways she could protect her sons without alienating them from their father or from herself. She needed to give them enough information to know that he was engaging in very risky behaviors, and she wanted to convince them that it was not their responsibility to "save" him. This was hard because at first they didn't want to believe that their dad's situation was as serious as Caroline knew it to be.

Unfortunately, Frank was never able to accept help, but Caroline and her sons were. It took a while, but all three went to Al Anon and the twins got into counseling also. Throughout this process, Caroline made sure to honor her sons' feelings for their father while urging them to set firm limits on their involvement in his deteriorating life.

AND WHAT IF *YOU* ARE OR WERE THE IMPAIRED PARENT?

First and foremost, thank you for your courage in continuing to read this. Please stick around for the next few paragraphs. The recommendations are actually quite simple.

Get help. There are many groups available and ready to welcome you to begin a fresh start with your own life before you attempt a fresh start with your adult children. There is a fuller list of resourcesat the end of the book, but here we will mention AA (Alcoholics Anonymous), NA (Narcotics Anonymous), and NAMI (National Alliance on Mental Illness). Additionally, there are groups available for batterers if you are a perpetrator of domestic abuse. These resources can be a life-line back to a healthy productive life for you even if they do not immediately—or ever—repair an estranged relationship with your adult children. Depending on the depth of trauma your behavior has caused, your children may need to sever their relationship with you in order to live healthy lives, but that doesn't mean you can't improve your own situation.

Do not expect your children to put their lives on hold in order to manage yours. Your children may be actively engaged in getting you into the treatment you need, or they may have already wearied of trying to persuade you to go for help. Whatever the case, it is *your* responsibility to do all you can to do to live a healthier and more productive life as a person and as a parent. Your children have their own healing to do. They have their own personal, school, and work lives to live. These cannot be put on hold waiting to see if they can convince you to make the necessary changes in *your* life so that you can be a healthier force in *theirs*. I sincerely hope you will be able to do this, for your sake as well as your adult children's.

Be patient. Even if you are one of the luckier ones who has already sought the help necessary to make major life changes, you cannot expect your children to recognize this immediately. They may have been disappointed too many times in the past and do not trust that these changes will last. They may still be reeling from the hurt that you caused in the past (by behaviors, absences, broken promises, etc.) and continue to feel safer keeping you at a distance. When you are solidly and reliably in a better place in your life, keep reaching out—gently, respectfully, and persistently. If these efforts fail, find a therapist who understands family systems as well as abuse and keep trying new approaches. Sincere letters of apology which take responsibility for hurtful past behaviors can be healing for you as well as for them.

UNIQUE NEEDS OF YOUR ADULT CHILDREN AT DIFFERENT STAGES OF LAUNCHING

In this final section, we will summarize the main points from Chapters 4, 5, and 6. These chapters were devoted to the needs of adult children at three different, if at times overlapping, developmental stages: The Launchers, the Emerging Adults, and the Middle-Aged Adults. Here we focus on those needs where you as parents play a particularly important, sometimes pivotal, role. When you are able to recognize and address these specific concerns, you will significantly ease the burden of divorce for your adult children at different developmental stages.

A Place to Call "Home"

The youngest adult children are the Launchers. They have much in common with young children of divorce whose needs have received more attention in the literature. An important difference is that Launchers, while young, are legally adults so their legitimate needs may be overlooked even by their parents.

They are still living at home or with one foot only tentatively out the door when their parents divorce. Like adolescent children of divorce, Launchers are still dependent on their families of origin in many ways. They need you to be aware of this and to make arrangements that insure they still have "a place to come home to."

The actual living space may now be different or smaller than you all once knew. Still your youngest adult children want to know that they have a place with you where they are not seen as intruders. If that is not possible, as responsible parents, you need to sit down with them and problem solve where else they could go. Could they live in a grandparent's home? With an uncle or aunt? With a family friend? You should not expect them to resolve this on their own. Without guidance, they are likely to feel abandoned. Out of desperation, they may make choices which are rash or unsafe, or they could end up homeless.

Emerging Adult Children have taken some concrete steps toward establishing a life apart from their families of origin. Although they are likely living on their own by now, they are still reassured by the idea that there is a home base they could return to. They might only think about returning home for the summer or a holiday. Or it might be in the back of their minds that they could go home if they encountered a job loss or a failed relationship. But when their parents divorce, that sense of home changes even if the physical house remains.

Because they may seem to be managing well on their own, you may be unaware of how important having a home base still is for your Emerging Adult Children. Upon hearing of your divorce, they may suddenly feel homeless or displaced. Like the Launchers, they still want to know that they are welcome in the home of each parent. And, because they have been venturing out and focusing on their own busy lives, they may be less aware that one or both of you has started a post-divorce relationship. Hearing of this may take them by surprise and leave them uncertain of where they now belong.

With homes of their own, your Middle-Aged Adult Children are much less likely to experience this sense of displacement. If you and your ex-spouse were still in the family home when you decided to divorce, your children may have felt sadness over a loss of history and tradition. However, often for this oldest cohort the family home of their childhood memories was sold long before the divorce. If so, your home at the time of divorce may have been simply a place your oldest adult children visited with their own families regularly or for holidays and vacations. Your grandchildren may have more sentimental attachment to your home than their middle-aged parents do.

In fact, if you are divorcing very late in life, the tables may be turning. You may even be wondering if it would be possible to move into your adult child's home. For some families, this might work well and be acceptable, but certainly not for all. Many are cramped for space already. Someone might have to give up a bedroom for you to move in, likely creating some resentment as well as stress. This is a time to have an honest and open conversation with your middle-aged children which respects the needs of all three generations.

Financial Assistance

Whether or not divorce is in the picture, parents differ widely in how much financial support they can and want to offer their adult children. Although the legal requirement is lifted at age 18, many who can do so continue to support their children financially for years, paying for school, apartments, cars, etc. But divorce often results in a lowering of financial well-being for one or both parents. While there may be arrangements for spousal maintenance, there is no legal requirement for child support after children are adults.

Just as the youngest adult children of divorce are not likely to be fully launched into their own homes, neither are they prepared to be fully self-supporting. Therefore, as divorcing parents, you need to have frank and conscientious conversations with your youngest adult children about what each parent is able and willing to provide (housing, food, health insurance, etc.) as well as what your children's other options might be. It goes without saying that it is very important to honor whatever commitment you make to your youngest adult children. You may well be their financial lifeline.

Likely less reliant on parents for basic sustenance, your Emerging Adult Children may still be counting on you for major financial help to finish school, co-sign a lease for an apartment, buy a car, or help with a down payment on a house. If your divorce resulted in a large drop in income, all this can change overnight. Your child may need to drop out of college, come home, and get a job when the family income suddenly plummets.

Others of you may feel you can no longer help with smaller expenses like car insurance or a cell phone bill. Help with larger expenses, like a wedding or a down payment on a first house, which may have once looked possible, may now be out of the question. And if you remarry, your new partner may resent money going out to stepchildren even when there is plenty to go around.

As with younger adult children, it is important that you be aware of the economic impact of your divorce on your Emerging Adult Children. You need to have thoughtful conversations with them about what can and cannot be expected from you in terms of continued financial support. If things must change significantly, you can help your children think about their options, apply for student loans, find affordable health insurance, and establish budgets.

Some of you may have Middle-Aged Adult Children who are still counting on you for some level of financial support now or in the future. Maybe you have been helping to send your grandchildren to summer camp or putting aside money for their college years. While that may still be possible for some, for many it won't. Now, with fewer years remaining to accumulate money and fewer opportunities to remain in or reenter the workforce, your joint pre-divorce income must be stretched to pay for two homes or two care facilities. Your children may be seeing the possibility of any inheritance, however small, fading fast.

However, by the time your adult children are in or approaching middle-age, financial assistance could be reversed. Your children may have decent jobs with adequate income. In fact, they may be better off than you are financially. Even so, it is important not to assume that you can ask them for a loan or financial gift. They are at the stage where they need to be saving for their children's education and weddings. They need to be thinking about their own retirement.

Help with Decision-Making Generally

Your youngest adult children still benefit from having involved parents who are willing to help them with many important decisions. Although they are increasingly aiming for independence, they may still want to run ideas by you about jobs, school, relationships, etc. As their parent, you may at times still need to nudge them to address these important issues if they are not doing so.

However, your early Launchers may sense that you are no longer interested in the day-to-day details of their lives. They may feel you are too self-absorbed or too invested in a new relationship to want to hear about what is going on for them. If so, they may not reach out to you and may miss the opportunity for much-needed parental guidance. When *you* reach out to *them*, they are reassured that you are still available to them as their parent.

Emerging Adult Children are in the midst of making important, often life-defining, decisions about future education, occupations, and relationships. Their identities, which are taking shape during this critical time, will greatly influence how the rest of their lives unfold. Ideally, they need the time and space to make these decisions thoughtfully, and divorce threatens to disrupt or cut short the opportunity for a moratorium. More generally, many Emerging Adult Children still benefit from bouncing ideas off parents as people who have their best interests at heart as well as more life experience.

Stretched thin, your Middle-Aged Children are in the peak years of responsibility both at work and in their own families. These are challenging years in their lives as they were in yours at this stage. Perhaps they have been looking to you as an example that they can move through these demanding years with their marriages and finances intact. They may have been using you as a sounding board for managing conflict with adolescent children, investing their money, or dealing with work issues. Your own challenges at this time may render you unable to fulfill those roles, leaving your middle-aged children feeling at loose ends.

In fact, you may even be turning to them for help with your own important decisions. Quite likely, they are willing to listen to your concerns and help you sort through your options, still within appropriate parent-child boundaries. It's important, however, not to expect them to set their own obligations aside in order to get you through the divorce. Your oldest adult children were aware that their parents were getting older. Now they must worry about the two of you growing old separately with double the number of living arrangements and check-in visits to see how you both are managing. No matter how much they care about you, this can, at times, be challenging.

Holidays

Holidays are supposed to be happy occasions, special times for families to come together and celebrate in their own traditional ways. Being realistic, we know they can also be stressful times. That is especially true for divorced families. If you had divorced when your children were young, these arrangements would have been covered in your divorce settlement. Rarely are holidays considered when couples divorce after their children are adults. And, on top of that, you and/or your former spouse may have new partners who have their own ways of celebrating holidays.

It is not fair to expect your youngest adult children, the Launchers, to be able to manage the intricate planning around holidays. As their parents, you need to put aside your negative feelings about each other and agree on a workable holiday plan. If that can't be done, your children will appreciate the parent who is flexible and works around the uncooperative parent. There could be some hard years ahead with perhaps some unfair arrangements, but your adult children will have taken notice. In time, they will likely rectify any inequity. They tend to gravitate toward the parent whose comfortable holiday traditions are not riddled with drama and competition. You might try:

> I'm going to check with your mom to see if we can figure out how to divide up the holidays this year. I know it was tough last year and got a little crazy for all of us. I'll let you know how this goes. I just want it to be enjoyable.

Or:

> Your dad isn't getting back to me about a plan for Thanksgiving. Have you talked to him about it? It's really not your job to do it but I just wondered if he'd mentioned what he and your stepmom want to do. At this point, I'm pretty flexible and can work around

your dad. I don't want you to be caught in the middle.

Organizing holidays remains complicated for Emerging Adult Children as well since it is unlikely that they have established strong holiday traditions of their own. By now, they could be living at a distance and need to travel to come home. Will you have room for them? Will they have to choose whom to visit if you and their other parent now live at a distance from each other? As with the young Launchers, Emerging Adults benefit when their divorced parents are able to agree on a fair and workable holiday plan. They, too, are aware of underlying tensions around transitioning between the two households, tensions which detract from what is supposed to be a festive time.

This is also a time when your Emerging Adult Children could be introducing their own partners into the family. When tensions are palpable between your household and that of your ex-spouse, it will create an awkward, uncomfortable, and perhaps enduring first impression. If you can reduce or eliminate your contribution to this situation, your children will notice and be beyond grateful.

For those of you whose children are Middle-Aged when you divorce, holiday celebrations may have long ago shifted from your home to theirs. While at first glance this might suggest there will be less disruption, your children now have to worry about whether they can invite both you and your ex-spouse to the same occasion. Will your children worry that one of you will cause a scene? Will one of you refuse to come if the other is there? Will your children feel guilty if one of you is left out? What are your grandchildren observing and feeling?

When parents have been in very long marriages and their homes have been the focal point of many holiday celebrations, divorce is synonymous with loss of tradition. Multiple generations will now be grieving this loss, perhaps for years. We saw this with Charla (in Chapter 8) who, thanks to successful fertility treatment, had just found out she was pregnant. After years of observing her older siblings' children bask in elaborate holidays at their grandparents' home, she was saddened that her own child would never have this experience.

Behavior at Other Occasions

Apart from holidays, there are many other occasions where divorce presents a potential complication. These include ordinary occasions like routine birthday celebrations or a grandchild's sporting event as well as milestone events such as graduations, weddings, and births. The significance of a high school or college graduation could be overshadowed by the reality of the parents' recent decision to divorce. Throughout the young adult years, Launchers, and especially Emerging Adults, are moving through a number of rites of passage on their way to full adulthood.

It is important for parents to keep uppermost in mind that these are *your children's* events. *They* are the ones graduating, getting married, and having babies. It is a blessing and a privilege to be included in these events. If your negative feelings about your divorce show up at these occasions and make your children uncomfortable, you may not be on the guest list in the future.

Hopefully, these milestone events signify that your adult children have been able to move on with their lives in positive ways despite the pain and disruption of your divorce. Many have completed school and training programs, earned college and advanced degrees, entered committed relationships, and started their own families. They may have arrived here with or without your financial and emotional support, but if you are invited to celebrate these accomplishments with them, make sure *they*, not *you*, are at the center of the celebrations.

Ideally, these can actually be healing times when you and your former spouse share pride at your children's important achievements. But even if you are not yet to that point, they are times to put aside tensions between you for the sake of your children. We consider these milestone events memorable because, unlike ordinary events, they stand out indelibly in our memories as special. You can be certain that your children will long remember whether and how you participated in these special times in their lives!

Once again, the situation is somewhat different when you are the parents of Middle-Aged Children at the time of your divorce. Your children may have passed these milestone events years ago and now it is your grandchildren who are arriving at this point. Nevertheless, it is your responsibility to see that your behavior does not put a damper on these important moments.

Supporting Relationships Among Siblings

Once your children start leaving home, they may set off in very different directions. No longer living under the same roof, their relationships with each other can undergo drastic change. Before the divorce, they may have been relying on you to keep them informed of the major happenings in each other's lives. Gatherings at the family home, frequent or infrequent, may have been the main way for them to reunite.

With divorce, much of this can change. Siblings may take sides with different parents, and they may react to the divorce in very different ways. Emerging Adult siblings may even move far away to avoid being caught up in the drama of their parents' divorce. Their younger siblings who could still be Launchers may miss the supportive relationship they once had with a brother or sister who moved away. They may also feel trapped and resentful if they feel they have been left with responsibility for their parents and, perhaps, even for younger brothers and sisters still at home. A wise parent notices these things that threaten relationships between siblings.

You may find yourself tempted to compare your children as to which ones have been more supportive of you during the divorce or which ones seem to be leaning more toward your former spouse. While there may be some truth to these observations, remind yourself that they may be temporary. You are all struggling in your own ways. Perhaps your adult children have not experienced *you* as supportive, and there may be truth to that too. No matter what, you are the parent for all of them, and it is important to avoid pitting your children against each other. Neither you nor they need another divorce-related estrangement or loss.

Awareness of the Life Stages Your Children are In

This is a difficult time for your whole family. When you are able to recognize the basic challenges your adult children are facing at each critical developmental stage, you will also recognize how the stress of divorce can add to these and even become overwhelming. You cannot entirely alleviate these inevitable stresses for your children, but you can make an effort not to overburden them by ignoring or downplaying their legitimate concerns.

In short, your youngest adult children, the Launchers, are still quite vulnerable and need you to continue to play an active parental role in their lives. Your Emerging Adult Children are in the throes of making decisions that will largely define the rest of their lives and need the protected time and space to do this. And while the lives of your Middle-Aged Children may appear to be more established, they may be over-taxed. You cannot expect them to abandon their demanding lives in order to play a role in helping you manage the divorce and its aftermath.

In Summary

In this chapter we have looked at a wide range of things you, as divorced and divorcing parents, need to think about as you work to improve or maintain your relationship with your adult children. It is a lot to take in since you are also addressing your own divorce-related and life stage-related challenges. Nevertheless, I hope it has alerted you to the significant concerns and needs of your adult children.

Some of these concerns and needs are unique to the developmental stages they are in at the time of your divorce. Some are common across the different stages. This heightened awareness of how your divorce impacts your adult children has likely instilled greater compassion for their experience. Hopefully it has convinced you to abandon the myth that divorce is "no big deal" once children are adults.

Perhaps as you read this chapter, you became aware of ways you wish you had handled things about your divorce differently with your adult children. Maybe you leaned on them too heavily for support or blurred the parent-child boundaries by sharing personal information they did not want or need to know. Maybe you were blind to the depth and range of your adult children's feelings and needs.

Remember, healing from divorce—for you as well as for them—is a process and not an event. And because it is an on-going process, there is still time to do your part differently. You can't go back and erase how you handled things in the past, but you can take responsibility for your part and make a dedicated effort to be the kind of parent you want to be starting now!

The next chapter will take your adult children's perspective. How can they, from Launchers to Emerging and Middle-Aged Adults, take care of themselves in the midst of your later-life divorce? Chapter 10 underscores the legitimacy of their often-overlooked needs. It encourages your adult children to take care of themselves and to set appropriate boundaries with you. This not only benefits them. It will also increase the likelihood that they will be able to have compassion for you as their parents and the complicated challenges which later-life divorce poses for you. As their parents, I hope you will read Chapter 10 and mark the sections you would like to discuss with your children, just as I hope they will do this with Chapter 9.

Chapter Nine Notes: *What Can Parents Do?*

1. Other books can help with the decision whether to divorce. See, for example, Mira Kirshenbaum, *Too Good to Leave, Too Bad to Stay: a Step-by-Step Guide to Help You Decide Whether to Stay In or Get Out of Your Relationship*, 1996, Plume. In addition, speaking with a mental health professional can be helpful.

-10-
What Can Adult Children Do?

Advice to Adult Children on Taking Care of Yourselves and Your Relationship with Your Divorcing and Divorced Parents.

A Caveat: Like your parents, you may have a negative reaction to the word "advice." You rightly know your situation is unique and that "one size doesn't fit all." So, take the advice that follows in this chapter as recommendations and suggestions. You are the best one to decide if they do or don't fit your particular situation. If they do, consider embracing them with an open heart and open mind.

Chapter 10 also summarizes and reinforces the key points of Chapters 4, 5, and 6. It reviews the challenges for adult children at different developmental stages from Launchers to Emerging and Middle-Aged Adults. Grounded in these ideas, we will recommend concrete ways for you, whatever stage you are in, to take good care of yourself throughout the process and aftermath of your parents' divorce.

As an adult child dealing with your parents' divorcing after 20, 30, 40 or more years, your needs have largely been downplayed or ignored altogether. You are the ones most affected and short-changed by the myth of "no big deal." Professionals have focused their attention on your parents' legal, financial, and emotional needs, and if you were still a younger child, they would have focused on yours as well.

It is precisely your adult status that has led to the harmful misconception that your parents' divorce should now have very little impact on your life. Some of you are only 18 and barely legally adults. Others of you are fully adults in your late 30s, 40s or even beyond. The bulk of you reading this chapter may be somewhere in your 20s and early

30s. This is a wide age span so the impact of your parents' divorce may differ widely as well. But one thing is certain: your lives *will* be impacted.

So, in Chapter 10 we turn to your needs. What can you do for yourself to ease the pain and disruption caused by your parents' divorce? Can you give yourself permission to feel what you are feeling? Allow yourself the time you need to grieve and heal? Set appropriate boundaries with your parents? How can you best deal with your parents during and following their divorce so that you eventually come out with as good a relationship with them as possible?

This chapter also summarizes the key points of Chapters 4, 5, and 6. It reviews the challenges for adult children at different developmental stages from Launchers to Emerging and Middle-Aged Adults. Based on these ideas, we will recommend concrete ways for you to take care of yourself throughout the process of, and after, your parents' divorce.

If you skipped ahead to this chapter, you may run into some concepts and references which are new to you. While this chapter can stand on its own, going back to earlier chapters where these concepts are presented and illustrated with clinical examples will provide a fuller understanding. If you read those chapters already, this one will be a summary and review.

We strongly encourage you to have self-compassion for what a difficult time this is for you. You will benefit from taking your feelings seriously, and it will likely improve your relationship with your parents. Taking care of yourself and staying alert to how you are feeling increases the probability that you will eventually arrive at a more compassionate understanding that this has been a tough time for them too.

Your parents may not have behaved as well as you wished they had. They may have let you down when they were preoccupied with their own lives seeming to come apart. Yet, in most cases, they were doing the best they could at the time.

Chapter 9 was directed to your parents where we outlined ways for them to take care of themselves during and after divorce. We encouraged them to seek out a variety of resources rather than relying on you for their primary emotional and material support. We also emphasized that you, their adult children, have plenty of your own concerns when they divorce after a long marriage. Whether you are just leaving home, have been on your own for a while, or are middle-aged yourself, your lives may be challenging enough before their divorce is thrown into the mix.

Since we encouraged your parents to read this chapter and to make notes on things they would like to discuss with you, we hope you will do the same with Chapter 9. If you haven't read it yet, or when you reread it, underline the parts that particularly fit your circumstances. This could be a first step in initiating a constructive conversation with your parents.

So, where to start?

TAKE CARE OF YOURSELF

Even if you are worried about one or both of your parents, your main responsibility must be to yourself. This is true even when your parents appear distraught over the divorce. They are your parents, and you are their child no matter how far along you are in your adult life. The goal of this chapter is to help you, as much as possible, limit the havoc *their* divorce is wreaking in *your* life!

But first, a caveat: If you think one of your parents is in a life-threatening situation, it may be impossible to think about your own self-care. If you suspect your parent is in one of the following situations, get help immediately:

- You think your parent could be suicidal.

- You think your parent is in a dangerous situation regarding alcohol, drugs, or domestic abuse.

- You think your parent has a serious mental illness and could be making unsafe decisions for themself or others.

- You think one of your parents may have plans to harm the other parent.

Fortunately, these very painful and dangerous scenarios are rare. If you think you are dealing with one of them, you need to enlist help from trusted family members, friends, and professionals and get the assistance you and your parents need. On the other hand, reaching out to others may turn out to allay your worst fears and put this situation into a less dire perspective. Whatever the case, don't try to manage a deeply troubled parent all on your own.

We will have more to say about this later in the chapter. For now, let's assume that there is no immediate danger to either of your parents. While they may be struggling with the divorce, you are too. So, what can you do for yourself?

Allow Yourself to Feel What You are Feeling

One of the aims of this book is to recognize and validate the significant effect of parental divorce on their adult children. In your gut, *you* know your parents' later-life divorce impacts your life. The media have ignored or downplayed the effects of divorce once children are adults, so you need to trust your own experience. You are definitely not alone. Having a range of strong reactions is absolutely normal.

Adult children from late teens to middle-age experience shock, sadness, confusion, anger, fear, and abandonment when they learn that their parents are divorcing. If your family situation involves/involved trauma or abuse, you may be feeling a sense of relief. If the divorce caught you by surprise, you are likely questioning your own judgment and memories about your childhood. You may be wondering whether anything you thought you knew about your parents' marriage was real.

The important message here is this: Do not deny your feelings! Your feelings are just that—feelings. They are real to you. They are not "right" or "wrong." People may tell you that you should not be upset about the divorce because you are an adult. They may tell you how lucky you are that your parents didn't divorce when you were much younger. They may tell you that you should "get over it" or that you should be happy if one or both of your parents has starting seeing someone new.

What outsiders, or even family members, are telling you about how you *should* be reacting or feeling is of no help to you. What is helpful is for people to allow you to feel whatever you are feeling. You need people to simply respect your feelings as legitimate—because they are.

Seek Support from Appropriate Places

It is important for both you and your parents to seek out appropriate support when struggling with divorce-related issues. If you were younger at the time of their divorce, your parents might have arranged for you to see a therapist if they were concerned about you. Your teachers might have noticed you were struggling and arranged for you to see the school counselor or join a divorce support group with other students. Now that you are an adult, no one can insist that you get help, but you can seek it for yourself. What's important is that you know you deserve support.

There is no shame in reaching out for help when you are in a difficult situation. Getting the support you deserve now will likely make you stronger and healthier in the longer run. Perhaps up to this point you relied on your parents for emotional support when you went through difficult times. If so, you might be inclined to turn to them now that you are hurting or confused. For some families, crying together and comforting each other comes naturally when they first hear about divorce. However, sooner or later you and your parents are likely to find yourselves dealing with the divorce from different vantage points and with different needs.

You may be upset that your parents appear self-absorbed and not very attentive to your feelings and reactions. They may be upset that you aren't seeing things from their perspective or validating their feelings about the other parent. They may be oblivious to (or downplay) concerns you have about how their divorce unsettles your world. You may sense that there is simply no room for you to bring up your own issues when they are already so upset.

It's time for you to reach out to other people for the support you need and deserve. If you are in the youngest cohort of Launchers and just starting to move out from your family of origin, you probably don't have a significant other yet. Look around. Who are the trusted adults in your life? Grandparents? Uncles and aunts? An older sibling? An athletic coach? Long-term family friends? A religious leader in your community?

These same relationships can also be supports if you are an older adult child of divorce. In addition, being older, it is more likely that you could be in a committed relationship that can meet many of your needs. However, if it is a relatively new relationship or your partner has a lot going on in their life right now, you don't want to rely on them as your sole support. Adult friendships can be helpful, especially those who have been through their own parents' divorce. Look for support groups for adult children of divorce which you could join in person or online.

As we noted in Chapter 8, while in-person support groups are plentiful for divorced and divorcing *adults* and fairly readily available for *young children*, they are rare or impossible to find for *adult children* whose parents are divorcing. You might consider speaking out about the need and value for such a group. If you are a college student, ask your student health services to start such a group as there are likely many on your campus who would benefit.

When the people or groups you turn to suggest that you might want to talk with a mental health professional, why not consider it? If you choose to go in that direction, look for a counselor or therapist who understands family systems. Ideally, you want someone who primarily supports you but who also keeps in mind the complicated dynamics of your family system.

What matters is to find someone who encourages you to talk about how you are feeling about your parents' divorce. This person should be able to listen to you without judging or downplaying what you are experiencing. They should validate what I am urging you to realize—that you deserve and need support.

Where Possible, Give Yourself the Gift of Time

Don't let anyone tell you that you should "get over it" or "be done with it." There is no formula to tell you how long it takes to deal with and heal from parental divorce. The only answer is: "It takes as long as it takes." That will vary widely for every adult child, even among siblings. The impact of your parents' later-life divorce depends on a myriad of circumstances such as:

- **Where are you in terms of Erikson's Life Stages which we discussed in Chapter 2?**
- **What other challenges are you facing in your life right now?**
- **How much support do you have from important people in your life?**
- **What has been your relationship with each of your parents?**
- **How much contact do you have with them now?**
- **How are your parents dealing with their divorce?**

Although you are busy dealing with the challenges of the life stage you are in, can you step off the path even briefly to face your feelings about your parents' divorce and its impact on your life? In the midst of pressure to downplay or deny your feelings, can you grant yourself permission to simply feel what you are feeling? If at all possible, give yourself the time and space to embrace your legitimate feelings and let the healing process take over.

Ideally, this is the time for a moratorium on making important decisions regarding school, careers, and relationships. A moratorium or "time out" allows you to temporarily suspend or delay a decision until you are in a better position to make it. It allows you to try out different options before you are pressed to make a choice. Making healthy choices in these important areas is always hard. It is considerably harder to make them when you feel your familial world is turning upside down.

Most important, as we saw in Chapter 8, you need time to grieve. Workplaces usually give employees some time off when a close family member dies. Mainly this is time off to attend a funeral, but it can also include leave time to get necessary affairs in order. Sensitive workplaces understand that a person may not immediately be fully effective on the job if the loss involves a parent, a child, or a spouse.

But what if the loss you are grieving is your parents' marriage? The loss of your family as you have known it? What are the expectations here? Quite likely, none! Bosses and co-workers may not even be aware that this significant family event is happening/has happened. The same is likely true of teachers and classmates.

Generally, employees or students take no time off when their parents divorce. They simply put one foot in front of the other and expect themselves to carry on as if nothing has happened, as if the bottom isn't falling out of their world. A death *in* the family is at least fleetingly respected, but not the death *of* the family.

In sum, you need the opportunity to get in touch with your feelings about the divorce. This includes grief. Lean into your grief as we encouraged you to do in Chapter 8. Allow it, respect it, and let it eventually begin to heal you.

Hold Onto Relationships Unless They are Toxic

You are already dealing with more than enough loss. This is not the time to cut off relationships with friends, extended family, or siblings unless there are clear indications that these relationships are toxic for you. With your own emotions running high, it may be hard to judge whether disappointments stemming from relationships are serious enough to justify distancing from or ending them. Before making a rash decision that you could regret, take a step back, table the decision, and buy yourself a little time. The passage of time may yield a different perspective, making it easier to see whether a relationship is healthy or not.

This is especially true for long-standing relationships. We will deal with parents in a separate section below, but here we will consider enduring friendships, extended family, and siblings. Sometimes people in these categories fail to meet your need for support around your parents' divorce. Extended family members or long-time family friends may have taken sides based on their own relationship with your parents or they may simply be unable to provide the support you deserve because of challenges in their own lives. This can be disappointing and even hurtful, but it may not merit drastically altering your relationship with them. You may choose for now to hold onto these relationships (with more modest expectations) for the sake of continuity while you look elsewhere for the support and resources you need at this time.

A repeated theme that ran through Chapters 4, 5, and 6 is that parental divorce can significantly strain relationships among adult siblings, sometimes causing significant rifts. Depending on birth order, life stage demands, and geographic proximity, adult siblings may find themselves disproportionately involved in their parents' divorce. Some may feel they unfairly bear the brunt of experiencing and managing the fallout while their siblings' lives are allowed to go on unaffected. Others may feel a sibling is choosing to be involved in an unhealthy way while their own distance is more appropriate. Anger, resentment, and jealousy may impede siblings' ability to pull together and support one another during this important time in all of their lives.

As with extended family members, you and your siblings may find yourselves taking different sides when your parents divorce. These rifts may follow gender lines, or they may follow affinities between children and parents which predate the divorce. Abuse, trauma, or infidelity as reasons for divorce can increase the likelihood that adult siblings find themselves sympathizing and aligning with different parents. While younger children might experience some of this, they would likely continue to connect with each parent as a sibling group. Adult children of divorce can split off from each other as well as from a parent, creating losses in both generations.

There is no simple answer for how you can keep your relationship with your siblings from becoming estranged during or following your parents' divorce. Much depends on the quality of your earlier relationship. If it has been close up to now, hopefully you will be able to communicate with each other clearly and effectively about your needs and feelings regarding the divorce. You can say something like:

➢I feel like you are pulling back and leaving me to deal with Mom and Dad. Can you help me out? My life is pretty crazy, too, right now.

➢What's going on with Mom and Dad? I know you all live closer and see them more, but I feel completely out of the loop.

➢It seems like everyone is blaming Dad for the divorce, but nothing is totally one-sided. Can we arrange to Zoom and talk about this before we all just end up fighting with each other?

➢Am I the only one who didn't see this coming? What did I miss?

The bottom line is that someday when your parents are no longer alive, your brothers and sisters will be your longest-term relationships. Losing them because of the turmoil of your parents' divorce would be a major—and generally unnecessary—loss.

If resentments or disagreements start to build within your support network, look for people or resources that might help you turn things around. With everything else going on right now you don't need to become estranged from your siblings, extended family, or long-term friendships. However, neither do you need to be putting energy into relationships that invalidate your feelings or create more stress. Processing all this with a mental health professional could definitely help.

DEALING WITH YOUR PARENTS AROUND THE DIVORCE ITSELF

It is important to remember that your parents are whole people. In addition to being parents, they quite likely want to have meaning, purpose, happiness, and love in their lives—just as you do! If you take care of yourself while the shock and aftershocks of divorce rumble throughout your family, you stand the best chance of coming out on the other side with a healthy-as-possible relationship with your parents. This includes compassion for both yourself and them. Don't try to force it. It will come with time, but first things first.

Shore Up Your Boundaries

No matter how old you are in years, you are still your parents' child. Whether you are 18 or 58, you are never their peer before, after, or in the throes of their divorce. Nor should you be part of a role reversal, casting you as their primary emotional caretaker for divorce-related matters. Chapter 7 makes clear how important it is to have firm boundaries for an appropriate parent-child relationship even, and perhaps especially, during the highly emotional times inherent in divorce.

Some of you will be taken by surprise when you learn your parents are divorcing. Others will have seen it coming and may even be relieved. Whatever the case, it is appropriate for you to ask for the information you need in order to have a general understanding so that things make sense to you. You might ask:

➤ What I want to know is *why now*? Have you been thinking about this for a long time?

➤ Is this something you both want?

➤ Can you please tell me *why* you're doing this? It seemed like everything was fine when we were all together at Passover.

➤ What's going to happen now? Are you going to sell the

house?

➤You guys have been together for a long time. Are you sure this makes sense? Have you seen a marriage counselor?

If you begin to feel that you are getting too much information, say so, set a boundary, and expect it to be honored.

It is equally important for you to honor the boundaries your parents may be setting. They may feel some of your questions cross over into highly personal or private areas that they do not wish to share with you. Likely they are staying within an appropriate parental role and are actually doing you a favor—allowing you to be their child instead of their peer or confidant.

Stay out of the middle between your parents. It is not healthy for you to deliver messages for them even if they refuse to communicate with one another. It is not healthy for you to be your parent's confidante even if at first that might seem flattering or make you feel special. It is not healthy for you to hear negative or highly personal information which angry parents may be all too eager share about each other. Quite likely you are hoping to maintain some sort of relationship with both of your parents and do not want to be disloyal to either of them.

In short, set limits around the role you are comfortable with as an adult child of divorcing parents. Even though it can be hard for children of any age to set limits with their parents, doing so bolsters your status as an adult with your own thoughts and feelings. When you begin to experience discomfort, pay attention to what your gut is telling you. Draw a clear line and expect it to be respected. You may need to be assertive when you feel a line being crossed. You may have to repeatedly state that you have heard enough, and you may need to pull back until that message sinks in. For example:

➤Whoa. I don't need to know all that. That's between you two.

➤I'm starting to feel really uncomfortable. Can we just stop for now?

> I care about both of you, so I don't want to hear all those negative things about Mom. It makes me sad. You need to stop.

> I've really asked you to stop telling me this stuff. I'm your kid not your therapist. I'm going to have to leave if you don't stop.

The rewards for setting clear limits and having firm and appropriate boundaries with your parents are worth the effort. You will be taking care of yourself physically and emotionally by protecting yourself from unnecessary conflict and stress. Equally important, you will likely find yourself having more rather than less compassion for your parents and their situation.

Ask Your Parents for What You, Their Adult Child, Still Need from Them

All adult children need to ask their parents to respect their healthy boundaries as well as the legitimacy of their feelings about the divorce. In addition, you have very *specific* needs depending on the particular developmental stage you are in. You may need to remind your parents of these. Their preoccupation with their own needs right now may result in at least temporary neglect of the parental roles they have been playing in your lives. You are not being selfish when you respectfully ask them what you can expect from them in the present and future. You are simply taking good care of yourself.

What follows here is a brief summary of Chapters 4, 5, and 6. There are separate sections for each of the three cohorts of adult children of divorce—Launchers, Emerging Adults, and Middle-Aged Adults. While you may want to focus more on the section corresponding to your own developmental stage, I hope you will read them all. You may have older or younger siblings whose concerns are different from yours. Furthermore, you may be in a different stage now than when your parents divorced so you may relate to more than one stage.[1]

IF YOU ARE A LAUNCHER

As one of the youngest adult children, you are likely still dependent on your parents for many of your basic needs. Still living at home or with one foot barely out the door, you are likely quite worried about how your parents' decision to divorce will impact your life. Your world seems to have turned upside down just as you were getting ready to strike out on your own. You have many fundamental and legitimate needs which may now not be fully addressed. You may feel abandoned and thrust out on your own long before you are ready.

A Place to Call "Home"

One immediate need is to know if there will be a place for you in your parents' homes. This was a primary concern for Jaden, Talia, and Chris in Chapter 4. All three wondered if there would be a place to go home to when their parents divorced. Unfortunately, this fundamental concern was not addressed by any of their parents when they told their children they would be divorcing.

Jaden, a new college freshman, sensed his distraught mother would need to sell the family home, and his father had immediately moved onto a new relationship with someone Jaden had never met. Where would he go for holidays? For the summer when school ended?

The home Talia had grown up in had been sold when she needed to return there after losing her entry level job in another city. Both of her parents had moved to smaller places and neither had given thought to whether they would have space for her. She, too, was feeling adrift, unanchored, and basically homeless.

In large part to avoid facing whether she *had* a home, Chris dropped out of college and escaped to Europe with a friend. Chris's father had moved to another city and was living with his new partner and her children. Chris saw this as a whole new household. Her mother hastily married Chris's high school principal and moved into his house. Since Chris had never liked this man, this also wasn't an appealing option.

Looking back now after many decades, Chris thinks this early sense of "homelessness" affected many of her adult decisions. Now an empty nester, she is an inveterate and gracious hostess. Whenever she has moved, she is drawn to large houses with many bedrooms "so no one has to stay in a cold basement."

In all three of these cases, it was not that the parents didn't care about their children. It was more that the parents' own lives were in such upheaval that they had lost sight of how their housing changes impacted their young adult children. Had Jaden, Talia, and Chris not been young adults when their parents divorced, their housing arrangements would have been spelled out in their parents' divorce settlement. As it was, all three had to muddle through and piece together an informal sense of "home."

If your circumstances are anything like these three faced, you are not alone *and* you are in a very uncomfortable situation. You have every right to ask your parents if there will be a place for you in their new homes. Ask them, "Will I still have a place to live with you?" "Will I have a place to keep my belongings for a few years until I get more settled on my own?"

If your parents' new circumstances do not allow for you to live with them, ask them to help you figure out what your other options are. If they are not able to help you with this, reach out to other family members or family friends. You deserve to know where you can land and feel welcome. In short, you deserve to feel like you have a home when you still need one.

Financial Assistance

You may have relied on your parents for help with some or all financial obligations prior to their divorce. It is reasonable to wonder whether their changing circumstances will result in changes to your own financial situation. It is stressful not to have an answer. Can you count on your parents for help with your cell phone bill? With your car payments or insurance? Will they still be willing to co-sign on an apartment lease? What about health care expenses? If you are in college, will you be able to stay? Will you need to come home or transfer to a less expensive school?

Again, as with the question of home, you may need to ask for clarification. Perhaps your parents are struggling to meet their own financial obligations now that they are not combining their resources. Maybe one (or both) is in a new relationship with a partner who may disapprove of your parent's financial arrangement with you.

Whatever the circumstances, it is your right to ask your parents if they are still able and willing to help you. If there will be a drastic reduction in resources from what you had been accustomed to, ask them to help you figure out other options or work with you on setting up a budget. Without some parental input at this stage of your life, you could easily flounder or incur debt that will compromise your future financial independence and solvency.

Help with Decision-Making Generally

Financial assistance is not the only area where you may have been relying heavily on your parents. At your life stage, you are making many important decisions which might benefit from discussions with your parents or other older adults with more life experience than you have yet accumulated. Of course, while you might be pushing for more independence from parental advice around jobs, school, and relationships, you might still benefit from their input where you think it could be of value, that is, on your terms.

If you sense that your parents are too focused on their own challenges or new relationships to be interested in the details of your life, you may decide not to reach out to them. You may be angry at them and choose to distance from them. You may be protecting yourself from possible rejection. However, if you think their input could be useful, at least give it a try. They may still be available to be in your life as interested and concerned parents. In fact, they might welcome the opportunity.

Holidays

Whatever holidays were like in your family prior to the divorce, they have now become more complicated. As with living arrangements, if you were younger, the divorce agreement would have spelled out how and where you and your siblings would spend the various holidays. If you have younger siblings, such an arrangement is likely in place and perhaps you can follow it too.

However, once you are all adults, there is no guarantee that your parents will be able to reach an agreement about holiday plans on their own. Hopefully, they will be able to put any animosity aside and propose a fair arrangement that works for all of you so that holidays can be positive occasions. It shouldn't be your (or a sibling's) responsibility to go back and forth between your parents trying to make all this work. Sometimes that happens for the first several years.

You may feel that one of your parents is willing to be more flexible than the other, and thus, that the arrangements are not entirely fair. You can let your more flexible parent know your appreciation for their de-escalation of tension. You can let your less flexible parent know that you are uncomfortable with the stress this causes and hope it can be different in the future.

Once again, good boundaries are essential. Be prepared to tell your parents that you do not want to hear details of their difficulties dealing with each other around holidays (or anything else for that matter). Then, as best you can, enjoy the family (including siblings), you are with at the moment.

If you are an only child, holidays may be particularly hard and awkward, especially in the early years after the divorce. It's just you and your mom or you and your dad. The traditions the three of you shared probably no longer exist, and when you are with one parent you may worry that the other is all alone.

Sometimes parents of an only child continue to celebrate holidays as a family and feel they can do so without animosity. This may be comforting for you and relieve some sadness at least temporarily. Or it may seem stilted and unreal and even make you feel worse. Whatever you are feeling is okay and normal for you. Over time, or if one parent has a new partner, this all may change, so be ready to adapt.

Relationship with Siblings

It's not just at holidays that only children have a hard time when their parents divorce. Like Victoria in Chapter 8, they have no siblings with whom to share childhood memories or compare notes on whether they saw signs that their parent's marriage was in trouble. And as their parents grow older, and each needs more attention, there is no sibling to help shoulder that responsibility.

For those of you who have brothers and sisters, they can sometimes be a buffer lessening the negative impact of parental divorce. Yet it can be harder for you and your siblings to stay in touch following your parents' divorce if some of you are living at a distance. Your parents' home may have been the magnet that pulled you back together. Now there may no longer be a home with enough room for everyone to stay or even visit at the same time.

A parent who once served as the hub keeping you informed of each other's lives may have dropped the ball in the throes of divorce. As noted earlier, some of you may have sided with different parents about the divorce, and you may find yourselves estranged and distant from each other. Furthermore, if the only times you are together now are holidays, and if they are stressful occasions, times together may be strained.

Nevertheless, while much about your family changes when your parents divorce, your relationship with your siblings can be a thread of continuity. You have a history and traditions which you share with no one else. Cherish the opportunities you have as young adults to stay connected to each other as much as possible, at least with those siblings who have played positive roles in your life. Be sensitive to the possibility that you and they could have different feelings and perspectives about the divorce itself. Respect these differences as legitimate based on each person's unique experience and try not to allow them to divide you.

IF YOU ARE AN EMERGING ADULT

Further along than the Launchers, you are well into your 20s and even 30s. You have likely established more of a life apart from your family of origin. Even though today it is taking longer to achieve full adulthood, your life clearly shows some of the trappings. You may have finished school and gotten a job. You likely are living on your own and you may be in a committed relationship. Some of you will have married and started your own families. While you share some concerns with the youngest adult children of divorce, your concerns are less immediate since you are further along in the transition to adulthood and are living a life more independent from your parents.

However, you still have legitimate needs regarding your parents' involvement in your life. You still may be relying on them for some sources of financial and emotional support. And since you are at the stage of life when many milestone events are occurring, these may involve family celebrations that are particularly challenging when your parents have recently divorced or re-partnered. As with your younger counterparts, it is important for you to know that you have a right to voice your concerns to your parents and ask for what you need from them.

Base Camp Reassurance

As poet Robert Frost wrote in "The Death of the Hired Man," "Home is the place where, when you have to go there, they have to take you in." Has the divorce changed all that? Despite living on your own when you learned of your parents' divorce, you may have felt like your home base just disappeared. Even if you were not expecting to return to their home to live, learning that their living situation is changing can still be very unsettling. One or both parents may be moving out of the family home. One or both may be moving to smaller residences or to different cities.

With your sense of their home changing, Emerging Adults often feel displaced and homeless even though they had been doing fine out on their own. Perhaps you had it in the back of your mind that you could go home for the summer, or if you lost your job, got sick, or had a falling out with your partner. That may no longer be an option. Knowing there was a base camp to return to may have given you the confidence to try something risky and venture out a little further on your own.

Again, if your parents don't specify that there is a place for you in their new homes, ask them. Will you be welcome there for holidays? Is their home a back-up plan if things get rough for you down the road? It would be reassuring to know that they have thought about this even if it never comes to pass. And you have a right to ask!

Financial Assistance

You may not be relying on your parents for basic sustenance like the Launchers, but you may still be counting on them for major financial contributions. They may be paying for college. They may be helping with health insurance, car insurance, and car payments. You may be on their cell phone plan and AAA plan. Up to now they may have been paying all or part of your rent.

Has the divorce impacted their ability to continue to support you in this way? Sometimes divorce results in a drop in income for one or both parents to the point that they are worried about their own economic viability. They may need to make drastic lifestyle changes, sell their home, enter or return to the workforce, or get a second or third job. If so, they may no longer be able to help you with larger or even smaller bills, and their preoccupation with their own financial worries may render them unaware of the impact on you. If you are unsure about their continued support, ask for clarification so you can plan accordingly. This could be a hard time that all of you can face together and one that stimulates thoughtful conversations.

Even when the situation is far from dire, some of the ways your parents might have once hoped to help you financially may now be out of the question. Helping with major expenses like a wedding or a down payment on a first house may no longer be possible. If one of your parents remarries and is part of a new family, their new partner may resent money going to stepchildren even if there is plenty to go around.

Decision Making

Even though you are approaching full adulthood, you are likely still dealing with some issues of Identity and Intimacy: Erikson's Stages 5 and 6. You may still be making important decisions about school, jobs, relationships, starting a family, or buying a house. Your sense of identity, who you are and want to be, is still taking shape. These important decisions require the time and space which a moratorium provides—a protected period where you can still experiment with roles before making life-defining choices. This moratorium may be harder to hold onto when your family is facing major changes brought on by divorce. You are still at a stage where you could benefit from running important decisions by a parent who knows you well, has your best interests at heart, and has accumulated more life experience.

Holidays

Family holidays are still a source of stress for Emerging Adults. You may not yet have established holiday traditions of your own. Until the divorce, you were going "home" to celebrate. Now, at best, you have two homes to go to or between, and these may involve stepparents or stepsiblings when you get there. As with the Launchers, you should not have to make these arrangements yourself.

To add a further complication, you may be in a committed relationship. This could mean having to coordinate plans with a third (and possibly even a fourth) family. You can let your parents know that this is hard on you and that you appreciate all they can do to reduce any underlying tension.

Behavior at Milestone Events

Unique to you as an Emerging Adult are the many important events which occur during these young adult years. Significant accomplishments such as graduation from trade school, college, or obtaining an advanced degree often merit celebrations involving your extended family. Certainly, this is true as well for weddings where family members generally expect to be involved. The arrival of children of your own adds the role of grandparent to your parents' lives.

Your parents' divorce during these years can complicate these important milestone events. In Chapter 5, we saw how much harder these events are when parents refuse to speak to each other, don't want to be in the same room with each other, or generally exude almost palpable dislike for one another. Their adult child is left to manage them carefully so that a supposedly positive event does not erupt into something unpleasant. The presence of a new partner for one or both parents can make these situations even trickier although new partners can sometimes defuse or even greatly improve a situation.

In any case, these are *your* milestone events. You and your partner or child should be the center of attention at such times. You should not have to be concerned about how your parents might behave. If you find yourself worrying about how they might act, it is time to take a deep breath, square your shoulders, and put those firm boundaries into play. Tell your parents how important this event is to you. Stress how much it means to you to have them be part of it and emphasize that you expect them to be a positive presence. Sadly, if they cannot reassure you that they will behave appropriately, you may need to ask them not to attend. Your job is to protect yourself and your own family.

Meeting a Parent's New Partner

You may not be the only one entering into a committed relationship during these years of Emerging Adulthood. Your divorcing and divorced parents may be forming new partnerships. If they were unhappy together for a long time, they could be eager to see if there is a chance to find a loving relationship. How will you feel about one or both of your parents starting to see new people? How *do* you feel if that has already happened?

Give yourself a chance to get in touch with whatever it is that you are feeling. You may never be ready to hear that a parent is moving on. "Moving on" is synonymous with realizing that their divorce is real, that it is final. This acknowledgement disrupts any denial you may have been holding onto, so you could notice new waves of grief coming up. Once again, lean into your grief knowing it gives you the opportunity for deeper healing.

How much do you want to know when one of your parents starts to date? When they enter into a serious relationship? Much depends on how much time has passed since you first knew about the divorce. It also depends on how your other parent is doing. One may be ready to venture out while the other is still sad and distraught.

At first it could seem like your parent is acting like a giddy teenager when they begin to date. They may dress and act differently from the mom and dad you were used to. If not taken to extremes, this makes sense since they are feeling hopeful and wanting a fresh start. Whether or not you are happy for them when they begin to date, it is not appropriate for you to hear the details of their dating experiences just as it is generally inappropriate for you to share intimate aspects of your own relationships.

Once again, good boundaries are vital here. If you feel uncomfortable with what a parent is sharing, if you don't want to help them fill out an online dating profile, draw a line. Tell them that, as their child, this feels too personal and suggest they share it with someone other than you. You certainly don't need to hear how a new person measures up to your other parent.

Good boundaries work both ways. Sometimes adult children are curious about a parent's dating life and ask for more information than their parent wants to share. You need to respect the limits they set. These are a sign that your parent wants to maintain a healthy parent-child relationship with you. They don't want you in their lives as a confidante or peer. They haven't forgotten that you are still their child.

You don't need to meet or hear about people your parents may be dating casually. That changes when they feel they have found someone special. Again, stay in touch with the feelings this brings up for you. It may be especially hard if your other parent is still grieving the divorce or seems lonely and hopeless about ever finding love again. You may experience loyalty tugs and not feel ready to like someone new.

Take your time. You don't need to meet this new person right away or spend a lot of time with them. Tell your parent what pacing seems comfortable for you. This new person may seem too eager to win you over or they could be standing back not knowing how best to position themselves. Rest assured that if they really care about your parent, and know that your parent cares about you, they could be more nervous than you are.

Once again, grief may resurface. You might think, "If Mom (Dad) acted in such an appealing way when she (he) was still married, maybe they wouldn't have divorced." Give yourself time to decide how you feel about this new person. If they treat your parent well and your parent seems to be happy, it could be that your parent has found a better match. The fact that this new person may seem quite different from your other parent may be precisely why this relationship could work better.

Whether or not you warm to this new person quickly, let your parent know that you still value time with just the two of you. It may be easier to talk about family history, in-jokes, or highly personal matters without the outsider. That may change over time, but if this is how you feel, be clear with your parent. And let your parent know that your preference should not be taken as disapproval of the new partner.

If there is a wedding, will you be involved? Hopefully, it will not be sprung on you after the fact. Ideally, your parent will let you know of plans to remarry far enough in advance for you to sort through the thoughts and feelings this brings up. It is best if your parent presents this to you and your siblings without their new partner present in case it triggers complicated or hurtful feelings.

This is also a time when loyalty conflicts can arise. If you like a parent's new partner, you may feel you are being disloyal to your other parent. In reality, adding new people to your sense of family will not diminish your feelings for other family members. And it is not appropriate for a parent to press you for information about your other parent's partner or wedding plans.

You need to know you have a choice about whether and how to be involved in your parent's wedding. Do you want to attend? Will you be asked to play a role? Take the time you need to think it over on your own. Talk with your parent and siblings and let them know what you are comfortable with. Then give yourself a chance to warm to the idea that the changes happening in your family could actually be positive ones.

Another complicating factor when a parent remarries is the possibility of stepsiblings. If so, this can bring up strong feelings too. Will your position in the family be altered? Were you always the "only girl," the "oldest son," or the "baby"? Do you sense that you and your siblings are being compared favorably or unfavorably to the new partner's children? You may feel jealous simply seeing your own parent reaching out warmly to them.

IF YOU ARE A MIDDLE-AGED ADULT

As the oldest group of "children" of later-life divorce, your concerns are especially likely to be overlooked. From late 30s into your 50s and 60s, you are beyond launching and emerging into adulthood. You have been out of your parents' home for some time now and are likely in the peak years of responsibility at work as well as at home with your own family. You are aware that your parents are growing older, but your day-to-day attention is primarily focused on your work, your children, and your spouse or partner if you have one.

As a Middle-Aged Adult, you are concerned with Generativity and Legacy, the challenges of Erikson's 7th Stage. You are hoping to be creative and productive at home and at work in ways that contribute to the larger society and future generations. You are hoping to avoid a mid-life crisis or a sense of stagnation. Your parents are probably in Erikson's 8th and final stage of Ego Integrity vs. Despair. This is a time of reflection. They are looking back on their lives with a sense of satisfaction that they took care of important things, or they may be riddled with a sense of regret and failure.

Whatever the quality of your parents' long marriage, you likely thought it would continue "as is" until one or both of them became ill, incapacitated, or died. You were likely relieved that they had each other as they aged. That allowed you to worry less about them and put your energy into your own life which may have already felt beyond full. And then came news that they were planning to divorce. No longer could you hold them up as an example that if you weather these tough years your marriage will remain intact.

As with younger cohorts of adult children of divorce, you have legitimate concerns and feelings. Some are the same concerns but many are unique to both your middle-aged status and the advanced age of your divorcing parents. You may be surprised at the strong feelings that your parents' divorce brings up even at this stage of your life, but these feelings need to be honored and acknowledged as much as if you were younger. Your mature age does not protect you from feeling anger, sadness, and confusion. You still need to give yourself time and space to grieve.

And precisely because of your greater maturity there is an even stronger risk that your parents will see you as a peer. You may have been married for years yourself and you may even have been through a divorce of your own. It is still important to maintain boundaries about what it is appropriate to know about your parents' marital problems. Be prepared to set firm limits if they try to share highly personal, including sexual, matters which make you uncomfortable.

Financial Concerns

Likely your parents are at or beyond retirement age and won't be increasing their financial cushion. You may be worried about how they will make out financially now with the additional expenses of two households. You may be worried that they might turn to you for help when you are already concerned about paying your mortgage, putting your children through school, and saving for your own retirement. You may be wondering if ways they have helped you in the past (e.g., with down payments on a house) or promises to help in the future (e.g., contributing to their grandchildren's education) will continue.

Many families have difficulty talking about money. For some it is even a taboo topic. Family members—adult children but perhaps parents even moreso—may feel shame admitting to financial troubles and needing to ask for help. Adult children may fear that they'll look greedy or opportunistic if they ask their parents how much money they have even if all they want to know is whether Mom and Dad can make it with their current assets. Siblings may be jealous or resentful if some feel they are giving more to, or getting less from, their parents monetarily.

So, if you are concerned about your parents' financial viability following divorce, you may need to have some difficult conversations. The key is to talk frankly and constructively with your parents about your financial concerns for them and for yourself. Younger adult children are often reluctant to initiate such conversations, but hopefully your greater life experience will make it easier:

> Mom (Dad), I don't want to intrude, but I'm just wondering if you feel you're going to be okay financially after the divorce?

If they tell you they don't want to talk about money, respect this boundary and drop the subject. But if Mom or Dad shares significant concerns, you don't need to be their financial advisor, but you might direct them to one. And that would be the time you let them know whether or not they can expect any financial help from you.

If they say they're *not* concerned about finances, you may still need to ask about how their divorce will impact you. Depending on how comfortable the conversation is feeling, you could bring up your own concerns then or at a later time.

> I'm really glad to hear that you're feeling okay about money. I know you've got more expenses now with each of you needing your own place to live and everything. I could imagine that money could be tighter now, so I'm relieved that you're feeling okay about it.
>
> I feel awkward bringing this up when you have so much going on, but I've wondered if you think you'll be able to continue to pay your grandson's college tuition. I would understand if that's not possible now. I just need to know because it's due in a month or so and I'd need time to figure out something else if you can't do it.

The goal of such conversations is to clarify any financial obligations between you and your parents. Awkward though these conversations are, when they are done respectfully, everyone knows where things stand and if they need to look elsewhere for help.

Non-monetary Ways You Contribute to Each Other's Lives

The same is true of services you've been providing for each other. Will they continue after the divorce? Perhaps your parents have been providing childcare for your children or picking them up from school. It is okay to ask whether you can continue to count on them post-divorce using the same sort of frank and respectful conversations as you would with finances.

There may be reason to think that one or both of your parents will be needing more help from you after the divorce. Some of this you will have foreseen when thinking about them growing older or becoming widowed, but now there are two of them who will be living apart. This could mean double duty in worrying about them and whether they are able to live on their own.

These are concerns and responsibilities not generally faced by Launchers and Emerging Adults whose parents tend to be considerably younger when they divorce. Furthermore, parents probably expect less material and logistical support from younger versus Middle-Aged Adult Children. So, what should you do?

With your own lives as full as they have ever been, how can you take on this additional load? How can you *not*? It is important for you to sit down with your own family—your partner and children—to discuss what you can and cannot do for your parents while maintaining your commitment to your own family and work situation. Then you need to communicate with your parents the limits of your involvement.

Some Middle-Aged Adult Children have little or no problem helping a parent or parents with finances. Some have no problem having a parent live with them. Their homes are large enough or may be emptying out as their own children move on. If there are two working parents with young children still at home, a grandparent's presence might be an asset. In some families it is simply the expected custom to help elderly parents in these ways. However, for many there is not sufficient money or space to go around as it is, so that may not be an option.

Addressing these logistical issues is stressful even when considering the needs of one widowed parent or even an elderly couple. But now you are dealing with two individuals. Can you help one out and not the other? Certainly you can't move them both into your home since they have chosen not to be together. With all these considerations it becomes clear that parents divorcing later in life can pose a unique and significant challenge for their middle-aged children.

Siblings

This is the time to connect with your siblings who are probably also middle-aged with very busy lives. Perhaps you have grown apart over the years, but your parents' later-life divorce can pull you back together as much as if one had died. What are your concerns? What needs to happen now? Who is able to step in where needed?

When possible, sharing responsibility for your parents' well-being increases the likelihood that none of you will feel unfairly burdened. Siblings can contribute in the ways that work for them. One of you may live closer and be able to handle the more hands-on concerns. Another may be better at locating resources or have expertise with financial matters. Working together can reduce resentment between you as well as toward your parents.

This is a critical time in your relationship with your siblings. How well you pull together around your parents' divorce will impact your relationship from here on out. Hopefully it won't result in acrimony and estrangement. Once your parents are gone, your siblings will still be the people who share your childhood memories, and you will be each other's longest relationship.

Grandchildren

In Chapter 6 we saw examples of how later-life divorce affects not only adult children but also grandchildren. For a while, your divorcing parents may be preoccupied with feelings and activities related to the divorce. They may appear to have little interest in your and your children's lives. As a mature adult, you may understand this self-focus and not take it personally.

But what about your children? How much they need to know about their grandparents' divorce depends on their ages and the closeness of their relationship. They are probably picking up that something is going on. Likely they are aware that you are upset, sad, or preoccupied. If they have regular contact with their grandparents, they will notice differences in their behavior and might worry that their grandparents don't care about them anymore.

A simple explanation may be all that younger grandchildren need. For example:

➢Grammy and Poppy decided they don't want to live together anymore but they both still love you very much.

➢Grandpa wants to move to California and be by himself but Grandma still wants to live here so they don't want to be married anymore. We won't see Grandpa as much, but we'll go out to visit him. And Grandma will still get to come to your basketball games.

Watch for signs that even very young grandchildren may be worrying about what this all means. Let them know they can ask you any questions or tell you about their feelings. It would not be surprising for them to wonder if you are going to get divorced, too, whether or not they put it into words. If appropriate, you can reassure them that you and your spouse are happy together.

Older grandchildren need to know enough to make sense of what is going on. One high school senior, Tyler, was satisfied to simply know that his grandparents had grown apart and had separate interests. He made it clear to his parents that he didn't want any further details. This seemed to allow him to hold onto the image of both of his grandparents as "super people … amazing people … I have them on a pedestal." Later he might want to know more but his parents were wise to respect the limits he set on what he wanted to know.

Other older grandchildren might want to know more. If they are thinking about what they are looking for in their own partners, or what makes marriages last, they may be curious and ask for specifics. Whether they ask their grandparents directly or have this conversation with you, their parents, it is important to respect their feelings. How close a relationship has this been? What are the advantages and disadvantages of going beyond a general explanation? They don't need to hear unnecessarily personal or negative things that make them feel uncomfortable.

It is a good idea to be proactive with your parents, the grandparents, about your concerns for your children. Let them know that you are going to maintain good boundaries in what you tell your children about their divorce, and you expect the same from them. You can ask them to reassure your children—with both words and actions—that the divorce doesn't change their love for them, assuming that is honestly the case, of course.

Remarriage/New Partner Concerns

Parents divorcing in the final stage of life (Erikson's Stage 8) are less likely to remarry or re-partner than if they had divorced earlier. This is true because of issues unique to their advanced age (such as their own health concerns or not wanting to take on a caretaker role) as well as the reduced pool of eligible partners. This is part of why adult children worry about their older divorcing parents who will mostly be living on their own.

However, remarriage and re-partnering do happen, and this can be a source of worry as well. As we saw in Chapter 6, adult children often have concerns about their elderly parents' finances when this happens especially if it appears sudden or if they do not know (or do not like) their parent's new partner. You may be concerned that your parent is being taken advantage of in ways that might risk their future financial viability. In addition, you may have concerns about any inheritance there might be. Your understanding about what your parent planned to leave for you and your children may be affected.

It is perfectly appropriate for you to respectfully bring up these concerns with your elderly parent. It is especially important for you to do so if you have reason to question your parent's ability to make an informed decision. In all cases, it is wise to encourage your parent to seek an attorney specializing in prenuptial arrangements. Having a prenuptial agreement increases the likelihood that your parent and new partner will have carefully considered their wishes and financial obligations to each other and to their children and grandchildren.

If your parent initially resists this recommendation, hopefully you can talk it through further. You can present this as a standard step to ensure they are fully aware of the financial consequences of the decision to marry at this stage of life. If the new marriage does not negatively impact you and your children financially, it may more readily be met with your approval and support. But what is more important is that your elderly parent is not adversely affected by this decision.

Concerns About Their Welfare

Concern about an older parent's well-being goes far beyond finances and new relationships. How easily you are able to have hard conversations with your parent largely depends on the quality of your pre-divorce relationship. Do you trust one another? Does your parent feel you have their best interests in mind when you bring up concerns about their safety in general, their physical and mental health, or their living arrangements?

You may be anxious about how your parents will manage on their own following a later-life divorce. You may be eager to get things resolved so you can return to pressing concerns in your own life. Be aware that your parent may experience you as coming on too strong or trying to take control of decisions that they want to make for themselves. Instead of telling them what they should be doing, ask them questions and listen with respect to what they say. This is the time to take a deep breath and realize that you have an opportunity to connect with your parent in a respectful way and at a deeper level.

SPECIAL CONSIDERATIONS AT ALL STAGES: YOURS AND THEIRS

So far, we have been looking at the challenges adult children of divorce face from three different vantage points—from Launching to Emerging and Middle-Aged Adulthood. These are general concerns (housing, finances, decision making, holidays, meeting a parent's new partner) which take on unique twists depending on which of the three cohorts you are in. We will now turn to special considerations which pose particularly difficult challenges at all stages of your and your parents' lives.

When You Have an Impaired Parent

When one or both of your parents is struggling with substance abuse or mental illness, you, their adult child at whatever age, has special challenges. Perhaps your mom decided to end her marriage because of your dad's drinking or your dad grew tired of dealing with your mother's mental illness. When one parent chooses to leave their impaired spouse in the hopes of a better life, they may have relieved themselves of a heavy burden.

But has it been passed along to you? If you were still legally a child when this happened, no one would have expected you to take responsibility for your impaired parent. But, as an adult, you may feel obliged to step in. You may do this willingly out of love and loyalty to your parent, or mostly out of a sense of duty. You may feel anger that your non-impaired parent was able to walk away, leaving you with a difficult situation on top of everything else going on at the stage of life you are in.

Probably, if they were thinking clearly, neither of your parents would want you to sacrifice your own life in order to deal with a troubled parent. This problem was beyond what your non-impaired parent could fix, and it is likely out of your reach as well. You should not try to deal with this all on your own. So, what role can you play in getting your parent the help they need while still taking care of yourself?

You need to reach out for help and you need to set firm boundaries. Reach out to adult members of your extended family, especially those in your impaired parent's family—your uncles and aunts, grandparents. Reach out to family friends as well. Tell them you are worried about your parent and need their assistance. Reach out to your siblings and support each other in setting limits on your involvement while taking steps to get help for your parent. Go to Al Anon or NAMI (See Resources), by yourself or with family members, and learn whether you can have a healthy relationship with your parent if they don't get help.

It is not your job to put your own life on hold while you wait and hope for your parent to seek help, get healthy, or go into recovery. Finding a good therapist and/or committing to regularly attend a 12-step program will help you learn to set and maintain firm boundaries with your impaired parent. They will also help you understand and accept the limits of your ability to control your parent's situation no matter how hard you may want to try.

Sometimes your other parent can help you figure out a healthy role to play. They may be the person you turn to when you are worried about things in general. Now, however, you may be reluctant to share with them negative things about your impaired parent.

If you are lucky, you might have a mother like Dana (in Chapters 3 and 9) who recognized the burden her children were carrying. She wisely refrained from disparaging their dad but let her children know they could count on her to help them deal with him. You will be more likely to reach out to your healthier parent for the support you need if you don't have to sacrifice loyalty to your impaired parent. In time, you may gain a better understanding of why your healthier parent had to put their own needs first and leave the relationship. This may give you permission to know if and when it is time for you to do the same.

When You Have an Abusive Parent

And what if one of your parents has been abusive or violent? This is also a painful and complicated situation. When one of your parents has been violent or abusive to the other, you may side against the perpetrator and want to be sure that your other parent is safe. Quite likely, you would benefit from finding a therapist to help you figure out what you want to do. Resources are available to you and your abused parent in most communities. (See Resources.)

Was the violence or abuse directed toward you? If so, the most important thing is to be safe and to protect yourself from further abuse. You do not have to have contact with anyone who abuses you emotionally, physically, or sexually. You will need to be assertive and erect strong, protective boundaries—perhaps even barriers. Even if your abusive parent owns their behavior and seeks help, you need to be cautious until you are absolutely certain that this behavior will not be repeated.

When a Parent has had an Affair

If you find out that a parent has had an affair, you are likely to be both disgusted and angry. You may feel protective of the parent you feel has been wronged. What you don't need are details about the affair from *either* of your parents. Details offered are often exaggerated or even false and are nearly always inappropriate for you to hear.

Extramarital affairs occur for many reasons and do not always result in divorce.[2] Sometimes they are a symptom that a marriage is in trouble which the couple recognizes, deals with, and puts to rest. When an affair leads to divorce, it may well be that other more serious incompatibilities or problems pre-dated the affair. Finding out details will probably not help you sort out your own feelings about your parents' divorce and can leave you feeling confused and perhaps distrustful of both of your parents.

In Summary

Throughout this chapter, I have encouraged you to take good care of yourself when your parents divorce after a long marriage. You need to recognize, validate, and respect the whole range of feelings this important event brings up for you even if other people ignore or question their legitimacy. You need to look for support in appropriate places and give yourself the time and space to grieve the losses triggered by divorce. You also need to ask your parents for what you still need from them depending on where you are in your own life's journey. Throughout all of this, it is important to set and maintain clear boundaries with them in order to preserve a healthy parent-child relationship.

With so much going on for everyone in your family when there is a later-life divorce, focusing on taking care of yourself may seem to be selfish and even a luxury. In fact, it is far from that. You need to take control of the pieces of the family picture that actually are in your control.

Practicing self-care, hard as it may be, is at the top of the list. What we know is that people tend to treat us about as well as we treat ourselves or as we expect to be treated. Somehow, we send out an unspoken message of what we will and won't tolerate from other people. So, if you aren't good to yourself, how can you expect anyone else to treat you well?

If indeed you are able to take care of yourself in these important ways, you will be able to move past the pain of your parents' divorce. You will be able to get back on track to focus on the challenges of the life stages you are in—Identity and Intimacy for Launchers and Emergers, and Generativity for those already Middle-Aged.

Eventually, you will be able to think of your parents and their divorce with greater compassion and acceptance. It affected you deeply in ways your parents may have been unable to recognize at the time. By taking care of yourself when they may not have been able to see or meet your needs, you will harbor less resentment toward them in the long run.

Probably most of you have parents who sincerely hoped their divorce would not greatly impact you. They may have bought into, and been falsely comforted by, the widely-accepted myth that divorce is "no big deal" for children once they are adults. Paired with this hope could be the fear that they might lose you as a result of initiating the divorce or because they behaved poorly at some points in the divorce process. Like you, they are hoping not to experience another loss or severed relationship.

Your parents are whole people with assets and liabilities, positive qualities as well as human frailties. But they are *your* parents, and they are still *your* family. If they access the help and resources they need during and after the divorce, there is a chance that they will emerge from this process happier and healthier than they were before. They may be able to be a better parent to *you* as a result. You play an important part in this outcome when you ask for what you need from them and hold them accountable in their role as parent.

Whether or not your parents remain single or re-partner, if they are healthier and happier post-divorce, the new family formations you build together will likely be healthier and happier too. We will see examples of this in the next and final chapter. All of this underscores what we have said throughout this book:

Divorce is a process and not an event.

You don't have to be unusually strong or brave to eventually feel like you have survived your parents' divorce. But you do need to be able to accept and manage change. Don't get stuck hanging from the monkey bars. When you are ready, let go with one hand so you can move ahead. Gather the courage to ask for what you need and seek out the support and resources necessary to grieve and heal. You deserve it. It is worth it. And you can do it!

Chapter Ten Notes—*What Can Adult Children Do?*

1. In a comparable section of Chapter 9, we combined the three cohorts when giving advice to parents regarding their adult children's concerns re housing, finances, etc. Parents may have children in two (or even three) different developmental stages.

2. See Chapter 3, Note 4 which gives references regarding affairs.

-11-
A New Sense of Family Post-Divorce

Continuity gives us a sense of stability and rootedness, but change is inevitable. When divorce occurs it often feels like a sea change that shatters your family's very foundation. Perhaps it feels like you have hit rock bottom. Fortunately, your new family, now a binuclear family, can be built from the bottom up. Whatever you call it—your family, your tribe, your crew, your people, your family of choice—this is your new family, and you will likely benefit from being a member of it.

Almost everyone wants to feel like they belong somewhere. With familiar people who care about them. In a place where they feel welcome and respected for who they are. In a situation that feels safe.

Most families want to provide this for their members, but few are able to consistently match this ideal on a daily basis. Quite apart from whether divorce becomes part of the story, all families face challenges day-to-day as they strive to meet their members' needs. We need to be realistic about what is a "functional" family, divorced or not.

Functional families are not perfect. They can't be because they are comprised of human beings who are going to be flawed at times. But functional families have healthy boundaries as well as clear rules and roles. Members demonstrate mutual respect for each other, including their differences. They create an environment where feelings and opinions can be shared without fear of harsh criticism or shaming. Communication is open among all, and both conflict and strong emotions are allowed within safe limits. Family members have a sense of belonging together and being a welcome part of each other's lives. Hopefully, there is also humor, enjoyment and love. Clearly, there must be the absence of abuse and neglect.

This is a Tall Order but One Worth Aspiring To

Perhaps you noticed that we did not say that functional families have to be two-parent families. They can be headed by only one parent. If there *are* two parents, they can be a mom and a dad, two moms, or two dads. And they can be stepfamilies. What matters is that you and your family members embrace love, respect, acceptance, and boundaries. You provide each other with the sense of belonging and safety.

Why This Book? A Summary and a Look Ahead

Before we look more closely at post-divorce family formations, let's review what we set out to accomplish. In Chapter 1 we stated that our goal was to put to rest the myth that parental divorce when children are adults is "no big deal." Whether adult children are Launchers, Emerging, or Middle-Aged Adults, they are still significantly impacted when their parents end long marriages. To ignore, downplay, or deny this prevents family members from grieving and healing individually and together.

We took a family systems perspective throughout this book in order to consider what is happening for both parents and adult children when there is later-life divorce. We focused with empathy and compassion on the challenges divorce poses for both generations. As essential parts of the family system, parents and adult children significantly affect—and are affected by—each other's divorce-related experiences and reactions.

We found it useful to roughly view both adult children and parents in terms of Erik Erikson's Eight Life Stages. It makes a difference whether divorcing parents are still young enough to have time to begin new chapters in their lives. There are special concerns both for them and their children if they are already facing old age. Younger adult children are still in the midst of forging solid identities and lasting relationships. Older ones may be facing their own mid-life crises.

Chapter 3 looked at trends for parents ending long marriages after 20, 30, 40 or more years. We considered a variety of explanations and reasons, differentiating between those involving abuse and trauma and those which were more benign such as growing apart. In Chapters 4, 5, and 6 we looked closely at the unique needs and experiences of adult children at three different developmental stages. We encouraged both parents and children to read the chapters devoted to their own as well as to each other's developmental challenges in the hopes of fostering greater understanding and empathy across the generations.

In Chapter 7 we saw that throughout the divorce process, maintaining healthy parent-child boundaries is as essential as it is challenging. Lapses may occur, especially when emotions are running high, but parents and adult children share responsibility for re-establishing and maintaining boundaries. Both generations need permission and time to grieve the divorce-related losses they encounter as we saw in Chapter 8. They need their grief to be validated and witnessed so they can heal and move forward as individuals and as a family.

In Chapters 9 and 10 we focused on ways parents and their adult children can take care of themselves as well as their relationships with each other during and following a later-life parental divorce. Doing so greatly increases their chances of emerging or becoming a functional—or *functional enough*—family despite the experience of divorce. We have seen that while divorce entails many losses, including the loss of the original family, it does not mean that you no longer have a family.

Woven into these chapters are vignettes or stories that illustrate the issues and challenges of later-life parental divorce for both parents and adult children. Most are composites drawn from over forty years of my psychotherapy practice with individuals, couples, and families, at times supplemented by other interviews and sources. True to my early training as a social psychologist, I tried to choose vignettes highlighting that a person's experience with divorce always occurs in a context. Parents and adult children experience later-life divorce both in the context of the life stage they are in and in the context of how their family members respond to, and cope with, divorce from the perspective of their own life stages.

We have respectfully put to rest the myth that later life parental divorce is "no big deal." Acknowledging that later-life divorce profoundly impacts the divorcing couple and their adult children, and that divorce is a process and not an event, we can now look ahead with hope to the possibility of forming healthy new families.

HOPE FOR POST-DIVORCE FAMILIES

For Parents

As the divorcing/divorced parent, your marriage may have worked for a while. Then after 20, 30, 40 or more years, one or both of you chose to end it. Whether you grew apart and had hopes of finding greater meaning on your own or with a new partner or whether you felt the need to leave an abusive or impaired partner, you paid a price for this decision—economically, socially, and emotionally. Your children may have trouble understanding your experience because marriage is a complicated and largely private relationship and because they have not yet reached the life stage you are in. You worry: Will you and they still feel like you are a family?

For Adult Children

As an adult child, your parents' decision to divorce may have been a surprise or you may have seen it coming. Either way, it unsettled your world and threatened to detract from your ability to grapple with the developmental challenges of the life stage you are in. Your parents may have been blind or insensitive to the ways their divorce has affected you, but they may well have been doing the best they could at the time. You worry: Will you continue to feel like you have a family?

> **Just as divorce itself is a process and not an event, forming a new sense of being a family after divorce is also a process.**

At first things likely feel strange, even fractured. That is the time to lean into your grief and remind yourself that "it takes as long as it takes." Eventually, things are likely to get easier. With sufficient time and resources, you will begin to focus less on what is lost and more on what remains. You will identify the ways your sense of family still exists although it is now a binuclear family. Adult children are now members of two families, each headed by one of their now-divorced parents.

To honor and illustrate that divorce (and successful healing after divorce) is a process, let's check back in on three families whom we met in earlier chapters. These stories remind us to take a longer time perspective when we are assessing how much healing and growth there has been so far. They also demonstrate some of the challenges and pathways to forming a healthy family post-divorce. As you read them, pay attention to these families as systems. Different family members' behaviors can have profound effects on one another. When one member makes a healthy change (such as taking better care of themselves or starting therapy) or makes a healthy request (such as setting a clear boundary or asking for their feelings to be respected) there can be a ripple effect throughout the family.[1]

Fran's Family

After her divorce from her critical, judgmental husband, Fran was single for eight years. Although she was a very competent and attractive woman, her self-esteem had plummeted when her husband filed for divorce. Fran dated a number of men, but she wisely kept these relationships separate from parenting her young adult daughters, Hazel, Phoebe, and Rachel. That changed after she met Gil and realized that this was a serious relationship even though he had been married multiple times, as we saw in Chapter 8.

Fran and her daughters were a single-parent family for many years before they eventually became part of a blended family. Both families were healthy and functional in their own ways, but initially it felt hard. Fran vividly recalled when her daughters came home the first Christmas after the divorce (two from college, one from working out of state). She still lived in the family home and had forced herself to decorate as she had always done for the holidays even though her heart wasn't into it. Nevertheless, things were anything but festive. Her daughters seemed tense and unhappy. Clearly all four of them were feeling like something/someone was missing.

By now, Fran was in therapy and had put together a strong support system for herself. She recognized that she and her daughters were reacting to the divorce in their own unspoken ways. She also knew that she was still the parent, and her daughters needed her to stay in that role. So, she got them all to sit down and talk about what was really going on. Rachel remained silent, but Phoebe and Hazel snapped that everything was "FINE!" Fran cautiously shared that she was thinking about how different things were without their dad there. This was all it took to open the flood gates, and all four cried together.

Fran was able to validate and witness her daughters' grief. They then shared concerns that their dad would be alone even though he chose not to celebrate the holidays. Fran understood this and made it easy for them to spend time with him even at the expense of her own preferred schedule. She made sure to keep her negative feelings about him to herself knowing that her daughters still cared deeply for their dad.

Once they had acknowledged there was no point pretending this would be Christmas as usual, they started making alternative plans. Hazel and Phoebe decided they just wanted to have fancy salads and desserts for their holiday meal. This was something their meat-and-potatoes Dad would never have agreed to. Rachel suggested they spend Christmas day playing board games and doing jigsaw puzzles which their dad considered a waste of time. This felt surprisingly liberating. Letting go of past holiday expectations had opened up possibilities which eventually became beloved new traditions for Fran and her daughters—traditions the three young women later shared with partners they brought into the family.

When Fran met and married Gil, these traditions were renegotiated since he came with his own holiday routines. Earlier we detailed how Fran and her daughters blended surprisingly quickly with Gil and his adult children over the course of Gil's serious illness and recovery. Over the years, Phoebe, Hazel, and Rachel happily incorporated a virtual smorgasbord of holiday foods and observances from this new "tribe." Fran and Gil always made it easy for them to slip away to spend time with their dad who had remarried and lived a quiet, reclusive life.

Fran's story illustrates that healthy-enough new families can be headed by a single parent, as hers was for eight years, or a re-partnered parent after she married Gil. During those intervening years Fran did not involve her daughters in her dating experiences until she met Gil. Whether single or re-partnered, Fran respected her daughters' loyalty to their father and refrained from speaking negatively about him even though he was never willing to cooperate with her around holidays or other issues. Although no one talked about it, Fran knew her daughters noticed and were grateful to her for making their lives less stressful. Her early willingness to witness her daughters' grief opened up honest communication between them. Together they acknowledged how divorce had changed their family. They honored the losses, but they also recognized ways they were freed up to experience new possibilities.

Chad's Family

It took time for Chad (from Chapters 3 and 8) to position himself in a healthier place with his parents after their divorce when he was in college. He'd been aware that his mother's serious drinking problem was an embarrassment to his father's professional career, but he was relieved that his father seemed committed to their marriage. This seemed to allow Chad to prioritize his own life when he was off at school. All that changed when his mother had had enough of his father's comments about her drinking and filed for divorce.

Chad felt caught in the middle between two miserable parents. He was concerned about them both and felt a heavy load of responsibility. When he graduated from college he leapt at the offer of a job overseas, but he also felt guilty for running away and abandoning his younger sister Lily who "escaped" the stress of her parents' divorce by smoking marijuana on a daily basis.

After a few years, Chad returned to his hometown and started a demanding new job. By then his father was in a new marriage to Louise, a woman who seemed to control his every move. She took up much of his time and showed no interest in getting to know Chad and Lily. Chad's contact with his father was sporadic and superficial.

His mother's drinking problem had worsened. Instead of going out with peers, Chad spent time on weekends trying to convince her to get help. He would plan social activities for them that didn't involve alcohol and would be distraught when he arrived at her home to find her intoxicated. His young adult life had been mainly reduced to going to work and checking on his mom.

By this time, Lily had found a psychotherapist she really liked and who was helping her deal with her unhealthy reliance on marijuana. Seeing the benefits of therapy for herself, Lily convinced Chad to talk with a mental health professional about what she saw as his over-involvement with their mother's problems as well as his gravitating toward relationships where he was treated poorly.

Next time he met his father for breakfast, they had a more honest connection. His father was appalled to hear how involved Chad had become with his mother's drinking problem. The two began to meet regularly to discuss this situation. Chad's dad shared how he had gone to Al Anon to understand the limits of what he could do about his ex-wife's drinking and encouraged Chad to do the same.

Chad was touched by his father's concern for his well-being. He and Lily started going to Al Anon, sometimes together, and they shared their sadness that their mother was unwilling to get help. Chad was increasingly able to set limits with his mother and began to spend more time with other young adults. He was determined he wouldn't marry anyone who made him feel badly about himself.

These father-son meetings benefitted Chad's father as well. He realized he was allowing Louise's possessiveness to run his life almost like his ex-wife's alcohol had done. He became more assertive with her, telling her he was committed to spending more time with Chad and Lily and letting her know he was disappointed that she had little interest in his children. She heard in his voice a new-found strength and confidence and she made sincere efforts to change. As things began to lighten up, Louise felt less threatened by her husband's involvement with his children and rarely felt resentful.

It still took a while for Chad and Lily to warm to Louise. Gradually, she was included more and more when they got together, but Chad and Lily still valued time with just their dad (especially when they wanted to discuss concerns for their mother). As things became easier between them, the four cautiously began to feel like a family. The young adults started to consider their dad's wife as their stepmother although they always called her Louise and appreciated that she never spoke negatively of their mother. They even appreciated some new traditions she introduced them to from her own background and history. Further down the road, both siblings were comfortable introducing their own partners into this new family. What once felt impossibly awkward and unconnected had become a functional-enough new "tribe."

Sadly, Chad and Lily's mother continued in a downward spiral with alcohol. They remained in contact with her but encouraged each other to maintain firm boundaries. Their father and Louise would be the grandparents their own children would spend time with.

Chad's story speaks to the importance of having good boundaries. When his parents first divorced, Chad felt sucked into both parents' concerns. His mother had a serious drinking problem, and his father was crushed by the divorce. When he couldn't set limits on his involvement in their lives, he created a barrier by leaving the country for several years.

When he came back home his father had remarried Louise, but the problems were still there until Chad and his dad both set healthy boundaries—Chad with his mother and his father with his new wife. These brave steps eventually paved the way for Chad and his sister to be part of a functional-enough stepfamily with their dad and Louise.

Martin and Jillian's Family

Martin and Jillian, the academic couple we encountered in Chapter 1, eventually felt that even the campus of a large state university was too small to house the two of them after their divorce. Martin fairly quickly remarried Esther, a bright younger colleague from another department, and they took jobs at neighboring colleges in New England. They soon started their own family so Martin's three adult children found themselves part of a stepfamily with two young half-siblings.

Jillian had returned from her sabbatical with the woman she met in France. When this relationship ended after a few years, Jillian moved to the West Coast in part for the climate, in part for a fresh start. Although she remained single, she was quite happy with her wide social circle of fellow academics, and she became a prolific writer of best-selling fiction.

Bitterness flourished between Jillian and Martin in the early years following their divorce. Their three adult children were reeling from this acrimony and floundering as they tried to launch their own lives. With neither parent providing a consistent home base where they could gather, they were losing their connection with each other as siblings as well. They felt caught in the middle between their parents when trying to negotiate holidays, not sure they were really welcome anywhere.

Lucky for them, both of their parents noticed their struggles and realized they were contributing to their children's distress. It helped that their older daughter had married a man who encouraged her to confront her parents about the impact of their behavior. She let them know that the pressure she felt to fill in for them with her younger siblings was straining her marriage.

Now with physical distance between them as well as having moved on to happier new lives, Martin and Jillian called a truce and began to work together to make things easier for their children. First of all, they agreed not to speak negatively about each other's choices and lifestyles. They recognized that they were putting their children in an uncomfortable place by not cooperating around vacation and holiday plans. They compromised on a plan for their adult children, when possible, to spend winter holiday times with Jillian in California and summer holiday times with Martin, Esther, and their young children at their cottage on a lake in New England.

They knew there would be a number of milestone events coming up in their adult children's lives. Jillian and Martin agreed to share expenses and to be on their best behavior at these events. Almost immediately they observed a palpable sense of gratitude and relief from their children as well as in themselves.

Jillian respected Martin's wife as a fellow academic. She was grateful that Esther had a good relationship with the three adult children but never attempted to replace Jillian as their mother. With so much contact around the adult children's milestone events, the two women actually became friendly, and Jillian took on a role as "distant aunt" for Esther and Martin's children. A pleasant surprise for all: they had become a "tribe."

Jillian and Martin's story highlights the negative effects of continued acrimony on adult children. Martin had happily remarried and started a new family, and Jillian, while single, was living a good life with many friends and professional success. Things were going less well for their three adult children who had lost their sense of "home" when their parents moved to different coasts with no reassurance they would be welcome in these new homes. The siblings were drifting off in different directions, but they shared a sense that their parents had lost interest in their lives. Perhaps their parents had just assumed that their children, because they were all adults, were not particularly impacted by the divorce. Fortunately, when their married daughter confronted them about the negative effects of their behavior, both Martin and Jillian listened and stepped back into the parental roles they had once performed thoughtfully. It was amazing how quickly things turned into a win-win situation for the whole "tribe."

These three stories illustrate different paths to successfully forming a functional and healthy post-divorce family as well different issues that arise along the way. Honest communication has improved among these family members. Conflict and strong emotions are generally tolerated, and individual differences are respected. These families appear to have healthy boundaries as well as clear expectations for the roles of parents and adult children which promotes a sense of safety and comfort for both generations. Most importantly, all three families are emerging from later-life divorce with a new sense of belonging.

What are the lessons we can learn from these families about the process of forming healthy families post-divorce?

➢ Give It Time

Becoming a new family is a process without a time schedule. Nothing happens overnight. First there must be plenty of time to acknowledge losses and grieve.

➢ Be Open to Change

Things are going to be different and that may even be a good thing. What old traditions can be maintained? Which ones might you happily replace? New ways of doing things might be a better fit for your new family formation. They might also be more appropriate for the evolving developmental stages you are all in.

➢ Don't Try to Force It

Family members, whether parents or adult children, are healing and evolving at different rates. It's okay if some are more ready than others to accept and embrace a new sense of family. Respect each person's situation without judgment.

➢ Be Realistic

No families are perfect whether or not they experience divorce. Your new family formation will be less than perfect also, but if it is healthy enough and functional enough, celebrate it. It is your family. They are your people.

➢ Respect Adult Children's Loyalties to Both Families

Like it or not, adult children are now in a binuclear family. No matter how happy they may be in one parent's post-divorce family, they are likely to still value their involvement in their other parent's family too.

➢ Respect a Parent's Growing Involvement in a New Partner's Family

When a parent's new partner has children (or if a parent and new partner have their own children) it is healthy for that parent to bond with these new children. It needn't mean they love their own adult children less. That is not how love works. It is not a fixed pie.

➢Don't Compare or Compete

For both children and parents, comparisons and competition can be destructive. Differences between adult children, between parents, between parts of the binuclear family are just that—differences. They don't need to be evaluated as better or worse. There is room for everyone in healthy families.

➢Play to Your Own Strengths and Be Your Best Self

In your new family formation, focus on who *you* are and what *you* do best. It doesn't matter what the other part of the binuclear family looks like. They may do things differently, have more money, seem to spend more time together, and even seem happier. Be true to yourself. You need to value who you are and what you have to offer. That is your strength.

➢Be Open to Being a "Tribe"

Cherish a wide variety of new relationships between and among parents and children in the newly formed and forming binuclear family. There is strength in numbers and strength in diversity. Embrace the new possibilities. Observe and learn from these new people and new relationships.

➢Embrace a New Sense of Belonging

Much has changed. The family you knew for decades no longer exists, but with time, your new family formation will be taking shape. If it feels healthy and welcoming, embrace it and allow yourself to feel like you belong.

In Summary

I hope this book will increase the chances that you and your family will be among the ones who are able to grieve, heal, and move on to healthy new family formations no longer defined by divorce. Hopefully, reading it on your own, and perhaps sharing it with family members, gives you things to think about and examples to follow that will keep your hopes alive and your healing process open to positive input. Throughout the process of healing from later-life divorce, however long that may take, remember that no matter how difficult things may seem at the moment, they may very well usher in healthy new possibilities.

Whether you are a parent or an adult child, keep taking good care of yourself. Remind yourself that reaching out for support from appropriate places is a strength not a weakness. With self-care and plenty of support you will be able to grieve and heal from divorce-related losses and challenges. And you will be more likely to have tolerance and compassion for other members of your family as they deal with divorce in their own ways. Set your sights on creating and embracing a healthy new sense of family wherever you can. It is possible and you deserve it.

Chapter Eleven Notes—*A New Sense of Family Post-Divorce*

1. We have seen other examples of healthy post-divorce families in earlier chapters. Some are longer stories and some are only snapshots, They, too, illustrate that healing takes time; issues need to be identified, respected and dealt with; and both parents and adult children need to be able to adapt to changes in their own and each other's lives. For example, see the "stories" of:

Caroline:	Chapters 3 and 9
Charles:	Chapters 3, 8, and 9
Chris:	Chapters 4 and 9
Dana:	Chapters 3, 9, and 10
Emma and Enrico:	Chapter 3
Justin:	Chapters 3, 7, and 9
Kelsey and Meg:	Chapters 4 and 8
Lynette:	Chapter 5
Molly:	Chapters 5 and 7
Sophia:	Chapters 1, 3, and 7
Zeke:	Chapter 3

Epilogue

I am a firm believer that once we become aware of important problems or issues we can begin to address them in constructive ways. Ignoring them—sweeping them under the rug or wishing them away—only further complicates a situation in the long run. We need to name and confront problems, or they can adversely affect our relationships.

What differentiates healthy and dysfunctional families is not whether they "have problems." Problems are inherent in the human condition. What matters is how we handle the problems that inevitably arise in our lives and in our families. The hallmark of a healthy family is the willingness to acknowledge and confront problems and to reach out for whatever resources are available. This definitely holds true for problems related to divorce.

I was drawn to write this book about the impact of later-life divorce primarily because of my experiences as a psychotherapist. However, it has also significantly affected my own life. This is true despite the fact that I have been happily married for 58 years, my parents did not divorce, nor have my children, now 50 and 54. Let me explain through a final vignette about a young couple—David and Ferne.

When David was in law school and engaged to marry Ferne, his parents divorced. He was from a prominent Kansas family, all of whom had followed the family tradition of going to the University of Kansas and moving on to successful careers in the sunflower state. David's father was a judge in Topeka and his mother, while officially a "housewife," had master's degrees in Latin and music. She traveled frequently to spas in Canada to treat her arthritis. When at home, she played golf, played the piano, and (when she had to) entertained with her husband.

David's cousin Virginia described him as "cocky" growing up. He would brag about his achievements, his family's social position, and his girlfriends. Virginia had introduced him to her sorority sister, Ferne, and both saw through this bravado to a sense of inferiority and vulnerability.

When Virginia was newly married, she invited David and Ferne to Easter dinner in her tiny apartment. When they arrived, David had clearly been drinking. Ferne took Virginia aside and told her he had just gotten word that his parents were divorcing. By the end of the evening, David was less in shock and more in tears—something neither his cousin or fiancée had seen before.

David admired his father and couldn't believe he would file for divorce. Neither could his three brothers. They remained loyal to their mother, but they were also aware of her self-centeredness and knew she had not been a real companion to their father for years.

Nevertheless, the divorce ruptured their sibling bonds. The oldest and youngest fiercely sided with their mother. The two middle brothers (including David) were more sympathetic to their father. Although members of this extended family had a long history of settling in Kansas, only David remained while others took off for New Mexico and California. The brothers rarely got together and never visited Topeka after their mother died. Their own children barely knew the names of their cousins, which was a stark contrast from the close relationships among David's and Virginia's siblings.

David, his parents, and his siblings had no resources to guide them through this process. The year was 1936 when divorce, especially later-life divorce, was rare indeed. He and his brothers simply buried their hurt, confusion, and shame and soldiered on in their busy, young adult lives.

But the effects seeped out in unexpected ways for generations to come. How do I know? David was my father. And my first exposure to the reality of later-life divorce was at its core a carefully guarded family secret.

Before I was born, my grandfather had remarried but died six months later. This was convenient for keeping the divorce a secret. My brother and I were not yet born so we grew up thinking our grandmother was a widow. We thought our "Aunt Mildred," to whom we dropped off Christmas gifts once a year, was some kind of distant relative.

Quite by accident, when I was in college, I discovered that Mildred was my step-grandmother. When I confronted my parents with this revelation, they confirmed it but offered nothing further. My grandparents' divorce was never discussed again as if it were "no big deal."

It was years later that my father's cousin Virginia decided to write to me. She was facing her advancing years and felt I should know how the divorce had affected my father and his brothers. That is when she shared the story of the Easter dinner.

In addition, I had somehow ended up with a 20-year set of my great grandmother's diaries. I gleaned her sparse daily entries to see what she might have written about her daughter's shocking divorce. A week before any mention of marital difficulties (let alone impending divorce) she wrote that my grandparents had hosted a luncheon for the governor and his wife. A week later, she tersely wrote that their divorce was final. There were less than a handful of mentions of divorce after that entry. Talk about sweeping things under the rug!

So, this is the book I wish my father and his family had access to. It might have helped them stay connected in a healthy way both to their own feelings and to each other. It might have encouraged them to grieve their losses and heal. Perhaps it would have helped my father be more open, and less rigid and fearful of conflict. While it is too late for that, I hope it can still be helpful for you and your family.

Resources

Books on the Impact of Later-Life Divorce on Family Members:

Noelle Fintushel and Nancy Hillard, *A Grief Out Of Season: When Your Parents Divorce in Your Adult Years,* 1991, Little Brown & Co.

Brooke Lea Foster, *The Way They Were: Dealing with Your Parents' Divorce After a Lifetime of Marriage,* 2006, Three Rivers Press.

Carol R. Hughes and Bruce R Fredenberg, *Home Will Never Be the Same Again: A Guide for Adult Children of Gray Divorce,* 2020, Rowman & Littlefield Publishers.

Divorce Support Groups:

For parents, search online for "divorce support groups near me" and find in person and online groups for women and for men.

For adult children, search online for "ACOD" (Adult Children of Divorce" and find a Reddit community of adult children experiencing parental divorce.

Substance Abuse:

Alcoholics Anonymous is a global peer-led mutual-aid fellowship focused on an abstinence-based 12-step recovery model. Founded in 1935. Help line: 866-338-1591. Go online to find local and online meetings.

Al-Anon/Alateen offers groups for people who have been impacted by another person's alcoholism. Founded in 1951. Help line: 888-425-2666. Go online to find local and online meetings.

Adult Children of Alcoholics and Dysfunctional Families is a 12-step recovery program. Help line: 310-534-1815. Go online to find local and online meetings.

Mental Illness:

National Alliance on Mental Illness (NAMI) is a grassroots organization dedicated to building better lives for the millions of Americans affected by mental illness with 600 local affiliates. Help line: 800-950-6264.

Dysfunctional families:

Lindsay Gibson, *Adult Children of Emotionally Immature Parents: How to Heal from Distant, Rejecting, or Self-Involved Parents,* 2015, New Harbinger Publications.

See also Adult Children of Alcoholics and Dysfunctional Families (above).

Andra Medea, *Going Home Without Going Crazy: How to Get Along with Your Parents & Family (Even When they Push Your Buttons),* 2006, New Harbinger Publications.

Domestic Abuse:

National Domestic Violence hotline: 800-799-7233.

National Network to End Domestic Violence: www.nnedv.org

Financial and Legal Issues in Later-Life Divorce:

Jocelyn Elise Crowley, *Gray Divorce: What We Lose and Gain From Mid-Life Splits,* 2018, University of California Press.

Janice Green, *Divorce After 50: A Guide to the Unique Legal and Financial Challenges of Your Divorce,* 2025, NOLO.

Additionally, you can search online for recent articles about legal and financial concerns in "gray divorces."

Boundaries:

Brene Brown, *Atlas of the Heart: Mapping Meaningful Connection and the Language of Human Experience*, 2021, Random House.

Nedra Glover Tawwab, *Set Boundaries, Find Peace: A Guide to Reclaiming Yourself,* 2021, Tarcher.

Grief and Loss:

Elisabeth Kübler-Ross and David Kessler, *On Grief and Grieving: Finding the Meaning of Grief Through the Five Stages of Loss,* 2014, Scribner.

David Kessler, *Finding Meaning: The Sixth Stage of Grief,* 2020, Scribner.

Acknowledgments

There are a great many people to thank with a book as long in the making as this one. It is the culmination of my more than 40-year career as a psychologist. I am indebted to writers, mentors, and ideas I encountered in my training in social and clinical psychology which gifted me with a dual lens (both panoramic and zoom) for understanding human behavior.

I am especially indebted to the courageous people who shared their stories of later-life parental divorce with me—both divorcing parents and adult children. Early on, they alerted me to the significance and ramifications of this often overlooked and discounted experience. Later, as I gained clarity as to its importance, they reinforced my conviction that this *is* a "big deal" and provided additional poignant examples of its impact. To protect confidentiality, their stories in this book have become composite cases which capture the essence of a situation but disguise actual identities. If you feel you recognize a specific person, it is likely because many people fit within the composite case.

It has been a joy to work with Thea Rademacher, president of Flint Hills Publishing (FHP). I have benefitted from her sharp mind as well as her enthusiasm and integrity. Thanks also to Nicole Lopez of FHP for her careful reading and editing and her encouraging me to expand on case examples. I would never have found my way to FHP if not for my life-long friendship with FHP author Elizabeth Farnsworth who put me in touch with Thea. I am grateful for this connection.

I want to acknowledge people who encouraged me to turn my early concerns about this topic into a book. My dear friend, Rhea Kish, kept nagging me to start writing so that she could start editing, but she died at age 100 having only read and edited the very first introductory pages. I'm sure she would have had lots of reactions to its final form, and I expect her insights and input would have made it a better book.

Many readers along the way have made important contributions.

While I followed many of their suggestions, the final product and whatever shortcomings it may have are my own. Karen Mikus, a competent and sensitive clinician, graciously read many drafts and, in addition to recommendations, shared composite examples from her own psychotherapy practice. Fellow social psychologist Mark Chesler provided both steady encouragement and an eye for where context and continuity were needed.

Two readers were especially tenacious in their willingness to read entire drafts. Barbara Cain, a pioneer in alerting us to the impact of divorce on adult children, soldiered through the first full draft making voluminous recommendations of both style and content. I am forever grateful for her generosity of time and professional perspective. I'm certain she did this out of her own commitment to debunking the myth that later life divorce is "no big deal" for adult children.

Teri Levitin, a fellow graduate student in social psychology at Michigan, has been a life-long friend. Our friendship was rekindled by Zoom sessions during and following the COVID pandemic. Since then, she has been the most steadfast reader and supporter of this project, tirelessly reading every version I shared with her. My book has greatly benefitted from her careful and competent perusal. I credit her with the inclusion of Chapter 11, bringing the book full circle back to focusing with empathy and hope for new family formations. Teri provided unrelenting encouragement as well as a sense of humor. She also put me in touch with Carol Tavris, another fellow Michigan grad student, who further encouraged getting this book into print.

Thanks to other people who helped to move this book along: To Connie Cook and Abby Adams for sending me countless articles they came across showing the lack of appreciation for the needs of families experiencing later-life divorce. To my brother, Dave Fisher, as well as friends Nancy Brown, Barbara Eagle, Jo Reuss, and Ron and Susie Friedman for regularly nudging me to stay on task.

I owe thanks to my original family where later-life divorce was the elephant in the living room until my brother Dave and I discovered that our "Aunt Mildred" was really our step-grandmother. Later, aware of her own advancing years, my father's cousin Virginia spontaneously chose to write to me giving the missing details of how my father and his siblings were rocked by their parents' later-life divorce. I only wish my father and his brothers had a book like this in their hands which might have helped them stay connected in a healthy way. Fortunately, my mother was always in the picture and instilled in me a deep appreciation for honesty and compassion in dealing with all people.

I am especially grateful to my current family. Jim, my husband and love of my life for nearly 60 years, is always the first person I run ideas by. We met as social psychology graduate students and have had the good fortune to share a great many interests both professional and personal. He has supported me in writing this book in every way possible—from careful reading and constructive criticism to celebrating every milestone along the way to the book's completion. He is a blessing in my life.

Our incredible children and their partners have been along for the ride as well. Jeff and his partner Laura made time despite significant work and parenting demands to read and discuss numerous early versions. Erin and her partner Allen, among other roles, were my unflinching tech support, routinely and at times when it looked like whole chapters had disappeared. They, too, were unselfishly willing to spend hours discussing the issues in the book. As I say throughout these pages, family—whatever form it takes—is not only important, it is everything!

About the Author

Wendy Fisher House, Ph.D. is a psychologist with training in both clinical and social psychology. For over forty years she met with individuals, couples, and families, first at Community Mental Health and then in her full-time private practice in Ann Arbor, Michigan. Most of the clients she had the privilege of meeting with were seeking help to deal with problems or changes in their lives. Over the years, she began to notice stories accumulating in her office alerting her to the profound effect which one particular change—parents divorcing after 20 or more years—had on the entire family system, including grown children.

She observed this from the vantage points of parents' accounts, adult children's accounts, and even from adults recollecting the turmoil their parents' later life divorces had caused them, now many years ago. Few resources were available for this population then and even now. So, after she retired, she decided to write a book for families experiencing later life divorce as well as for mental health professionals working with them. This is that book and, hopefully, it puts to rest the harmful myth that this increasingly common experience is "no big deal."

During her career, House conducted court-ordered family evaluations for Child Protective Services, provided clinical supervision for the Visiting Nurses Association and the Assault Crisis Center, and initiated and supervised a readjustment treatment program for Vietnam veterans. She also led groups for adults who experienced parental loss in childhood and co-led groups for survivors of childhood sexual abuse, including groups for therapist survivors.

Dr. House was born in Topeka, Kansas. She graduated from the University of Kansas in 1965 with a double major in psychology and sociology. From there she went to the University of Michigan where she met her future husband and life-long partner, Jim House, a fellow student in the same social psychology doctoral program. They lived in North Carolina for 8 years, teaching at Duke and UNC, before returning to Ann Arbor where they raised their two children. Until they recently moved downtown, they lived in a house on the river with two rescue cats, Daisy and Lily.

www.wendyfisherhouse.com